THE BARRETTS AT HOPE END

The Early Diary of

Elizabeth Barrett Browning

CONTENTS

ILLUSTRATIONS

*Reproduced by courtesy of Mrs Violet M. Altham
†Reproduced by courtesy of Stephen Ballard Esq

PREFACE

The discovery of this Diary of Elizabeth Barrett Browning was made in 1961 by Philip Kelley in a solicitor's office in St James's, London. He had been seeking for some time the missing letters that she had written to her father after her marriage to Robert Browning, explaining her position and asking his forgiveness. Mr Kelley hoped to find them among the Moulton-Barrett family papers that had come into the possession of Mr Kenneth A. Moulton-Barrett from his father, Lt.-Col. Harry Peyton Moulton-Barrett (a nephew of Elizabeth Barrett Browning).

The letters were not there. They are still missing, believed to be in a concealed drawer of a desk sold by public auction in 1945. They had been summarily returned by Mr Moulton-Barrett to Robert Browning, when, in 1851, Browning had written in the hope of a reconciliation as he and his wife and child were coming to England. Browning left them to his son, Pen, and after Pen's death, his wife Fannie held on to them illegally. In 1913 she showed them to Thomas Wise, who naturally wanted to buy them: 'eight tiny letters, all but one unopened. The one I saw painful in the extreme'. The Moulton-Barretts requested their return and entrusted them to a London solicitor until 1924, when Lt.-Col. Moulton-Barrett took charge of them, issuing a statement to the effect that he had burned the letters in the presence of a witness. Philip Kelley tells an interesting story concerning *The Barretts of Wimpole Street* in this connection.

While researching for the Ohio University Press edition of the *Diary by E.B.B.*, Mr Kelley interviewed the Colonel's parlourmaid, who told him that one day, while she was serving him his soup, a registered letter had arrived which made him very angry. 'He cannot use them for his play!' he exclaimed. 'I shall tell him they are burnt!'

This remark is, to say the least, ambiguous. If one repeats it aloud with varying intonations, the emphasis falling perhaps on *cannot* and *tell*, the implication is that the letters have indeed been destroyed. If, however, the emphasis is on *use* and *burnt*, a very different meaning can be elicited. As we shall never know exactly how the Colonel spoke that day over his soup, the opened letter in his hand, his parlourmaid's astonished face as she turned from the table smothering any further indignant remarks, speculation would appear to be fruitless. He did, however, loathe Rudolph Besier's play, and maintained until the end of his life that he *had* destroyed the letters. And yet . . . a further teasing situation arises when, in the inventory discovered in the sealed black coach-box with the family papers, there is the cryptic entry: '2. Desk containing (destroyed) letters together with several sketches and obituary notice of EBB'.

Instead of the letters, which, in view of their painful content, might well be left in decent oblivion, Mr Kelley and Mr and Mrs Moulton-Barrett found a manuscript, wrapped in manilla paper, and annotated in Robert Browning's hand 'Diary by EBB'. It was enclosed in a black silk slip-case of the period.

This was the first half of the Diary, and covered the year 1831, from June to December. The entries were written on 85 sheets of folded quality paper and sewn together with silk, decayed and discoloured.

The second part of the Diary, containing the entries for 1832, January to April, was in a volume bound in Russian leather, stamped with a diamond sign, and fastened with a brass clasp. They were written in the central part of a book EBB used for making notes on her reading. Of the 144 pages used, 56 had been completely excised and 18 cut in half.

These two halves had separate histories. The first part

had passed into Pen's possession upon his father's death, and remained untouched. It was withheld with other items by his heirs when the estate was sold by auction in May, 1913, until Lt.-Col. H. P. Moulton-Barrett took charge.

The second half of the Diary had been in Arabella Moulton-Barrett's care until her death in 1868, when she left it to her brother George. The excisions and obliterations are evidently his (*see* Introduction 6). In 1895 he left them to his brother Henry, and Henry's son left them in his turn to Lt.-Col. H. P. Moulton-Barrett. So, in 1924, the two halves came together, and, in 1937, again escaped a public auction to become the joint property of Group-Captain Edward Moulton-Barrett and Kenneth Moulton-Barrett. In 1965 the manuscript of the Diary was acquired by the Henry W. and Albert A. Berg Collection, The New York Public Library, Astor, Lenox and Tilden Foundation and acknowledgement is gratefully given to the Trustees of the New York Public Library. *Diary by E.B.B.* was published in its entirety, with the fullest of explanatory notes and Appendices by the University of Ohio in 1967, edited by Philip Kelley and Ronald Hudson, to whom I am greatly indebted for much of the information in the following pages. Readers requiring more detailed information about EBB's studies will find this in Philip Kelley's comprehensive work.

In its entirety the Diary, starting from June 1831 and finishing arbitrarily on 23 April 1832, runs to some 80,000 words. I had intended to cut this by half, discovering—in common with such distinguished editors as Betty Miller and Barbara McCarthy—that once EBB started to write, she found it difficult to stop. She herself admitted that she is like that 'bewitched broom in the story, which, being sent to draw water, drew bucket after bucket until the whole house was in flood'.

But as this is the only journal EBB ever kept—apart from a pocket diary in 1823—for a consecutive period, and that period such a vital and significant one in her life and personal development, cutting out days and weeks became more and more difficult. The ambience of her life among the circle of her Malvern neighbours, so typical of the 19th-century squirearchy, the day-to-day trivia of visiting, dining, talking, dispensing tea and gossip or high-minded conversation; the sermons and reading and expeditions, gradually enfold the reader, so that we find ourselves in the diaphanous web of someone else's weaving. Pen poised to make a cut, I often found that this or that passage led on to some dramatic denouement that would reverberate like the ever-prevalent thunder around the minarets of Hope End.

Some necessary cuts I have made, but none, I hope, is to the detriment of the Diary as a whole. I have cut out visits and talk about the acquaintances who drift in and away from the society around Hope End; and for the general reader I have omitted details of the Greek and Latin authors discussed by EBB and H. S. Boyd, and also the lengthy theological discussions which so occupied 19th-century Christians, but which hold little interest for us today. Explanations of obvious allusions to literary or classical works and authors have also been omitted.

Footnotes have been kept to a minimum in order to facilitate reading and to preserve the freshness of the original, which was written at a great rate, generally in the privacy of her bedroom at the end of a long day. Numbers in the text refer the reader to Notes at the end which will, I hope, clarify and expand several points of interest.

All necessary information about the members of the Hope End household, friends and neighbours is given in the *Who's Who* which prefaces the Diary.

EBB's erratic spelling has been kept, also her punctuation. Editorial additions are enclosed in square brackets, and cuts indicated by three dots. Two dots are her own. In the case of entries from January 1832, the excisions and obliterations made by George Moulton-Barrett are indicated by three dots within a wide-angle bracket ⟨. . .⟩. If more than one page is excised the number is shown thus ⟨. . 2 . .⟩.

THE BARRETTS AT HOPE END

The Early Diary of Elizabeth Barrett Browning

EDITED WITH AN INTRODUCTION BY
ELIZABETH BERRIDGE

JOHN MURRAY

Printed in Great Britain by
Butler & Tanner Ltd., Frome and London
0 7195 3106 3

I would like to record my gratitude to Mr Stephen Ballard and his daughter, Mrs Pat Hannah, the former for helpful information and permission to include several illustrations in his possession and the latter for showing me round the grounds of Hope End: to Mr and Mrs Geoffrey Harris, who entertained me at Ruby Cottage (now called The Ruby) and provided valuable information about the environs of Hope End and the Wyche: to Brian S. Smith, County Archivist of Gloucester, author of *A History of Malvern*, for information about the turnpike system; to Mrs Barbara Chaney and Mr Oliver Coburn for their practical help.

ELIZABETH BERRIDGE

February 1974

REFERENCES IN TEXT

EBB/HSB *Elizabeth Barrett to Mr Boyd,* ed. Barbara P. McCarthy (John Murray, 1955).

EBB/MRM *Elizabeth Barrett to Miss Mitford,* ed. Betty Miller (John Murray, 1954.)

INTRODUCTION

1

When, in 1809, a wealthy young gentleman named Edward Barrett Moulton-Barrett bought from Sir Henry Tempest the Hope End estate with its 475 acres of farmland, woodland and parkland, the county families who had lived for years on the calm borders of Herefordshire and Worcestershire did not expect to see the old 17th-century mansion pulled down and an extraordinarily flamboyant pile in oriental style rise up in its place.

Hope End, true to its old English meaning, lies in a hollow, encircled by low hills. Between the thriving market town of Ledbury and the village of Malvern, at that time gathering fame for its restorative waters, the Barretts' house vaunted its solid concrete neo-Turkish minarets. The cast-iron domelets, local people said, attracted all the lightning in the Malvern hills during the tumultuous summer thunderstorms. A massive glass dome covered the central staircase but, though threatened, never suffered any serious damage, although one year a large tree in the grounds received a direct hit. 'The bark rent from the top to the bottom—torn into long ribbons by the dreadful fiery hands.' The description is Elizabeth Barrett Barrett's, who was watching in horrified fascination from her window.

All this magnificence was of great satisfaction to the young landowner who was heard to declare that, if he thought there was another such house in England, he would pull it down. Perhaps he was attempting to reproduce among these green hills the lost splendours of the Cinnamon Hill Great House in Jamaica, where the Moulton-Barretts had lived since the 17th century among their extensive sugar plantations, in a style both opulent and licentious. Indeed, in 1794 his mother brought her children to England as a protest against the three different native households her husband maintained.

This devious family man died soon after, and Edward was made a ward of Lord Abinger and in 1797, at the age of twelve, was sent to Harrow. But there he could stand neither the fagging system nor the bullying and left after a few months. Cambridge did not suit him either. Regarded as 'a difficult, insensitive, self-willed and isolated young man', he did not derive much benefit from his time there, although he came briefly under the influence of a well-known classical scholar, Richard Porson, who was destined to mean more to his eldest daughter than to him.

Edward was determined that life should be lived on his own terms, and at the age of twenty he insisted on marrying Mary Graham Clarke, six years his senior, a gentle girl from another wealthy family. Lord Abinger, badgered into giving his consent, considered the girl far too good for him. Edward and his brother Sam had by this time inherited the vast Jamaican estates, and thereafter added another Barrett to their name.

The Edward Barrett Moulton-Barretts moved into Hope End in 1809 with their three children: Elizabeth, who was three, Edward, two, and Henrietta, not quite a year old. For the next six years alterations and enlargements were constantly being made. Was he perhaps influenced by the designs for remodelling the Brighton pavilion which had been published by Humphrey Repton in 1808—or recalling the eccentricities of William Beckford whose holdings in Jamaica a Barrett relative had handled? By 1815 Mary Moulton-Barrett was writing to her mother that 'the brass balustrades and the elegance of the hall really reminds one of the Arabian nights'. The circular-ended drawing room was decorated in the Italian style and took seven years to finish, the mahogany doors were inlaid with mother-of-pearl, and the billiard room hung with Moorish views. The library was stuccoed and the dining-room made gorgeous with crimson flock wallpaper.

In 1815 various prominent local families were invited to dinner, and again Mary tells her mother 'there is no parallel for this Event in the records of Hope End for the last four years. Lord Somers, Mr. Higgins, the Kearneys, the Commeline family . . . most lavish they all were of admiration for the house and furniture, which are indeed very *unique* and striking.'

The famous landscape architect J. C. Loudon was called in to do the gardens and the park in 1822 and may have put a few touches to the house, although Mr Barrett is thought to have planned this himself. Deer roamed the park until they threatened the rare trees and were excluded —a foretaste of his way with future suitors—there was a flamboyance of peacocks on the terrace; cascades, ponds and grottoes among stretching lawns set off the alien spires. At a discreet distance a great walled garden for vegetables and fruit was established, including a hothouse for grapes.

It was indeed, in the somewhat overblown language of the Sale Catalogue of 1831, 'adapted for the accommodation of A NOBLEMAN OR FAMILY OF THE FIRST DISTINCTION. A chef-d'oeuvre, unrivalled in the kingdom.'

That it was famous in its heyday is beyond doubt. George Moulton-Barrett, writing to Robert Browning in 1889, tells him of sightseers coming from Malvern in the summer. 'I remember one afternoon going up the park homewards with others, seeing a young girl on a pony coming from the house with a gentleman—that young girl was our present Queen and the gentleman Sir John Conroy.'

Was this the same afternoon's visit which Elizabeth noted in a letter to H. S. Boyd on 11 October 1830? If so, George's memory was at fault, for his sister wrote the following day, discussing the Duchess of Kent's visit to Malvern Wells, where she had brought the young Princess Victoria, then a delicate eleven-year-old, to spend the summer. In her letter there is no mention of Victoria.

'How many orisons did you make, that the Duchess of Kent might be inflicted on Papa? She and Prince Leopold and Sir John Conroy were here yesterday when we were at chapel—and upon Papa being announced to be from home, Sir John Conroy left his card and his compliments, and the Duchess rode thru' the yard, under the clock, and after having seen everything that was least worth seeing, went back to Malvern. Papa seems to be gratified that their Royal Highnesses did not ride over the grass, and asked with a little expression of anxiety what Sir John Conroy could mean by leaving his card. I suggested (out of spitefulness) that he clearly meant Papa to return the visit. Papa certainly ought to do so—and still certainly won't.'

A few weeks before, the *Hereford Journal* had noted that the young Princess Victoria had 'honoured John Biddulph Esq. of Ledbury and spent some time in viewing his grounds'. Elizabeth could not abide the Biddulphs, who make frequent appearances in her diary—and always to their detriment. This clock, under which the Duchess of Kent had ridden on that mellow autumn afternoon, regulated the lives of the family and the estate workers, its chimes marking the hours and days of what Elizabeth would in after years look back on as an idyllic childhood. It was set in place when she was nine years old and, perhaps feeling it incumbent upon 'the Poet Laureate of Hope End' as her father had dubbed her, to celebrate the occasion, she wrote a solemn poem beginning: 'Hark! what deep tones proceed from yonder tower' continuing in prophetic vein:

> Oh may its warning never cease to bring
> A useful lesson to our listening ear
> That hoary Time is ever on the wing
> To teach the value of each passing year.

The passing years brought the number of children up to eleven—three girls and eight boys. It seemed as if Edward Moulton-Barrett, having created his own kingdom, was determined (with the assistance of his obedient wife) to people it as well, and rule it on his own terms.

While his children were growing up and there was no

threat of any outside influence, he was a benign dictator who enjoyed family life. A sketch by Henrietta done one summer afternoon from the schoolroom window brings back vividly those childhood days. Papa playing cricket with his sons on the lawn, the obelisk in the grounds of Eastnor Castle visible above the trees. He allowed the older children the run of his library which, despite his own random education, was well furnished with a wide variety of books. On a forbidden shelf among 'improper' books were Gibbon's history and the novel *Tom Jones.* Years later at Wimpole Street, when his eldest daughter was in her thirties, he still kept *Don Juan* and *Héloïse and Abélard* locked up from curious female eyes. In an amusing letter to Miss Mitford Elizabeth explains that Hannah More and Wilberforce had joined the unmentionables, in a drawer and that if she were to ask him for a copy of the former 'he would as soon give me Prussic acid to drink if I were thirsty!'

That time was far off. At Hope End the Moulton-Barretts were in the fullest burgeoning of their family life and fortunes, no different, apparently, from any other family of landed gentry. The children were tended by nurses, governesses and tutors, and given a strict and religious upbringing; church or chapel three times on Sunday, and family prayers night and morning. No birthdays could be celebrated on the Sabbath (although the lucky one might be presented with an ode) and no books other than sermons or the Bible were read on that day. Despite their favourable circumstances it was driven in upon them by a succession of fervent preachers at the Wesleyan-Methodist Bible meetings, as well as at St James's Church at Colwall and the Chapel-schoolhouse by the south gate, that they were sinners and could be saved only by constant prayer and intercessions for divine mercy.

The first blow to the family happiness came in 1821 when Elizabeth suffered a series of illnesses which the doctors could not adequately diagnose. She was sent away to Gloucester for treatment. This took nearly a year, and it was another before she even partially recovered her health. During this time both parents felt they could not leave Hope End even to visit friends.

In October, 1828, when Mr Barrett was in London, his wife Mary died, and Mr Barrett did not speak of his grief, he merely shut up his wife's rooms just as they were. They were not entered or disturbed until the family moved four years later.

The last blow came when his financial difficulties, caused by litigation over his grandfather's will and trouble with the Jamaican estates, became so acute that the mortgagees foreclosed on Hope End. He knew in February of 1831 that they would have to sell up and leave.

Again, he did not communicate his troubles to the family. Instead, he wrote to his brother: 'I dread much the effect on my dear Children in tearing them away from all their most happy associations . . . say nothing on the subject of removal to the girls.' For a year and a half he kept his obstinate silence. When the end came, he acted quickly. With the sale a reality that could no longer be dodged, he travelled down to Devon to find suitable accommodation. Within a week he had found a furnished house at Sidmouth, rented it for a month and came back full of enthusiasm for the climate.

Still with a mask of good spirits set firmly in place, he played a last game of cricket with the boys on 23 August. The next morning Mr Barrett and his eldest son 'Bro' and ten-year-old Sette saw off the rest of the family, and turned back to the silent house to clear up the last details.

Twenty-three years is a long time to spend in a house. . . . 'Even now' Elizabeth was to write to Miss Mitford ten years later from Wimpole Street, 'Even now I never say "Hope End" before him. He loved the place *so*.'

2

Nothing now remains of what had once been a great show-place, for in 1873 the house was demolished. The weighty minarets had to be blown up with gunpowder. A Mr Hewitt, who had bought the house from the antiquary Thomas Heywood, preferred to build himself a new mansion in Victorian Gothic style on a hill which was once part of the deer park. This still dominates the site.

The gateway into the stables has, however, been reconstructed from an old print by Mr Stephen Ballard, father of the present owner. The Ballard family has figured prominently in the history of Malvern since the 18th century. Philip Ballard was an attorney in Malvern in the 1820s and it was his son Philip (Stephen Ballard's uncle) who painted the charming water-colours of Hope End (page 242). The Eastern ambience is caught by the domes and metal spires set upon the square tower above the archway. The empty stone circle in the turret once contained a great clock, which was removed when the family left, and by all accounts is now set securely in its new position in the court house of Brown's Town, Jamaica, where it still ticks away the minutes, regulating other lives and seeing justice done.

At the far end of the once-cobbled courtyard is a long Queen Anne building which had been there when the Barretts first came; by some lucky chance Mr Barrett had decided not to pull it down, but to turn the house (as it was then) into stables. A couple of minarets on the flanking wall give it an odd, jaunty air, the crescents curving against the grey sky. Here had been the brew-house, laundry and cellar, the cider-house, the cinder shed, the 'knife-and-shoe hole'. From this courtyard had once led 'a subterranean passage to gravelled walks through a shrubbery ornamented with magnificent timber trees, thriving evergreens, parterres of flowers . . .' which, when the present owner, Mrs Pat Hannah, tried to explore, she found partially filled in with rubble and bricks.

Beyond the low stone wall an expanse of wet grass flows to the edge of the choked lake. This was where the Hope End mansion had once stood. Under the grass the great lead cisterns lie hidden. It is difficult not to conjure up that pillared porch in Charles Hayter's painting, with the crop-haired child caught in unchanging pose, her King Charles spaniel behind her, carrying a beribboned straw hat in its mouth. Or to see again, with the mind's eye, those noble ground-floor windows out of which that same child had jumped, to relish the downpouring rain. Later, as a young woman, she noted in her Diary that, being frightened by 'a man with a coat', she had jumped in over the low sill to avoid him. Where, in the meadows around us, had she carved out that figure of Hector with 'a brazen helm of daffydowndillies' and gillyflowers and box for a nose? The 'lost bower' is lost indeed.

Strange to think, while walking over to what had once been proudly described as 'a fine sheet of water, fed by springs, cascades and well stored with fish', that one might, in another dimension and another age, be walking through that crimson-flock-papered dining-room, within sound of a vanished dinner bell.

Yes, an unquiet quiet place, set in a hollow not visible from the road:

Out of sight the lane was, sunk so deep, no foreign tramp
Nor drover of wild ponies out of Wales
Could guess if lady's hall or tenant's lodge
Dispensed such odours . . . behind the elms . . .

Walking there, it is impossible not to feel a frisson of the past. EBB herself never forgot it, and Hope End rises again fresh and living in her long novel-poem *Aurora Leigh.* She recalls the lime trees that had been murmurous with bees on honeyed mornings long ago, the 'overflow' of arbutus and laurel. And had figs once grown 'black as if by Tuscan rock' at the south angle of the house?

We do know from her Diary that once, on a summer afternoon, a Miss Steers had sat in the deer park painting a now-vanished ash tree, then said to be one of the largest in Great Britain and that, instead of coming in to lunch, she had had strawberries sent out to her. Later on Arabella sat with her on the bank while she sketched the house. The watercolour (page 51) might well have been one of the results of that afternoon's work, for both sisters (Henrietta and Arabel) were given drawing lessons by Miss Steers, and often sat in the grounds sketching. The day was remembered by EBB as one made fidgety by Mrs Boyd, who wore her out by her empty-headed conversation. 'What a woman to be Mr Boyd's wife!'

Today nothing remains of the gardens, which must have been as spectacular as the house. The Alpine bridge has gone, unless it was the crumbling one over which I ventured, grasping a handrail which plopped into the water below, rotten at a touch. Arabel (the family never used her full name 'Arabella') had once made a sketch of a little summerhouse thereabouts, now gone, except for a tile or two among elderberry roots and nettles. Even the ghosts of paths have vanished, along with the ghost of Lady Tempest (wife of the previous owner of Hope End), who had been seen by two workmen beside a bridge in a reputedly haunted field nearby. They had been terrified by the apparition of a woman whose 'face was of an ashy paleness, surrounded by long black frizzed hair; and the drapery white and confined by a white satin girdle reaching to the feet . . . indeed from the effect of terror, one of them was confined to his bed for several days. It leapt, he said, upon his back,—and when he shook it off, and looked behind, it seemed to lie and spread upon the road, and cover it all with whiteness, like a sheet of moonshine.' EBB's description in a letter to Mr Boyd is reminiscent of M. R. James. It is also a reminder of her lifelong fascination with the supernatural, 'I am afraid of only a few things in this world,' she wrote to her sister Arabel in 1848, 'for instance, of thunder and lightning, ghosts, musquitoes . . .' she could have added bats, which occasionally came silently swooping into her bedroom and filled her with horror. Or the deathwatch beetle, which she had heard the summer before her mother died, and was to hear again before she left Hope End.

The grounds would have been more open in the Barretts' day. A stand of Wellingtonia planted in the late 1860s to the south-east now cuts off the view of the obelisk in the grounds of Eastnor Castle, and a young larch plantation has been felled to let in more light. It is a lonely place, needing a large family and a host of workers to give it life and purpose. The 'grassy rock' above the upper and lower ponds, upon which the girls had sat to talk or read, is unchanged and solitary. The lawn on which Mr Barrett played cricket with his boys, grazed over by sheep; the long muddy drive leading to old Turnpike Lane lost in the parcelling-off of the estate. Elizabeth had once run along it in the rain, soaking her thin shoes, because Mrs Cliffe refused to drive her up to the house, for fear of encountering papa. The building at the south gate of the main drive from Old Colwall is the original schoolhouse-cum-chapel so often mentioned in the Diary. Here sermons were preached on Sundays and special occasions and the Barrett children met their friends. Today a small window shaped like a cross gives a clue as to its one-time use, although now it is a private house.

The lowering effect of a February morning was suddenly lifted by the sun splitting open the clouds and there, near the old icehouse, under a stand of fine Spanish chestnuts, was a flood of golden aconites and shining snowdrops.

Arbutus and laurel may have gone, but the great walled kitchen garden was still there. It had been ploughed up, and beyond, as in a bombed house, the huge flues of the hot-house were now exposed against an outside wall. Once it had been a little kingdom on its own, enclosing with its glass and ironwork the beautiful moist heat that ripened black figs and grapes and brought peaches to perfection in defiance of the weather outside. There is something very basic and reassuring about the self-containment of old country houses: dairy, laundry, cider-press, brew-house, stables and storehouses; harness rooms smelling of well-kept leather and polish, gunrooms and haylofts. They are the direct descendants of the old fortified manor houses, border castles and the great abbeys before the dissolution. Hope End even had its own springs of fresh water. Who would not feel safe here, wish to defend it, and be desolate at having to leave?

The silence of Hope End would never again be broken by the chiming of the clock over the stable-yard gate. EBB indicates the uncertainty and anguish of those last eighteen months in her own words:

'Papa was in very good spirits today at breakfast, most undoubtedly. He told Bro to put the clock half an hour more forward, and this sent my hopes forward—a little way. Would he think of altering the clock, if it were likely to strike so seldom before we are removed forever from its sound?'

3

If EBB is remembered at all today, it is by a handful of love poems, and the great god Pan chanted out by children in dusty sunlit classrooms, or as the invalid prisoner of Wimpole Street, brought back to life and liberty by a dashing young poet and snatched by him from under the nose of that terrifying tyrant in the shape of Charles Laughton, who insisted on her taking a tankard of porter.

Robert Browning's star has risen, hers has sunk. In the 1850s, however, both in England and America, he was known only as Mrs Browning's husband who surprisingly also wrote verses. In 1855 his *Men and Women*, a two-volume collection of fifty poems, won enthusiastic support from the pre-Raphaelites but otherwise sank without trace. Six years earlier, when Wordsworth's death left open the post of Poet Laureate, no less a quarterly than the *Athenaeum* had gravely proposed his wife for the position on the grounds that such an appointment would be equally satisfying for feminism and economy by helping two poets for the price of one.

Modern critics have wondered at her popularity. James Reeves refers to her 'voluminous but inadequate poetic gift', her 'valiant attempt to accommodate the problems of the day to a middle-class intelligentsia whose real literary needs were catered for by the prose novel'.* Certainly the bulk of her poetry is left unread today; but that is a fate shared by other, greater poets. Many ambitious works by Blake and Byron, Tennyson, Arnold and Browning himself, though they caught public and critical attention at the time, are now largely forgotten, while shorter poems to which perhaps they attached less importance, have survived. It is as if posterity stretches out a hand to break off one piece from an elaborate cake, leaving the ornate centre untouched.

In any case, when EBB came into contact with lively minds, her poetry often caught fire, as it did, too, when she felt there was a wrong to be righted. To a large Victorian public which revelled in deathbed scenes and moral dilemmas and was already feeling guilty and uneasy about the misery caused by the industrial revolution, such a poem as 'The Cry of the Children' brought immediate response. Published in 1843, the same year as Thomas Hood's 'The Song of the Shirt', it helped to create a climate of opinion which led to a reduction in factory working hours.

The Corn Laws, the Reform Bill, Catholic Emancipation and Slavery were the burning issues of the day. In EBB's formative years the Established Church had the last word, thundering out three times on Sunday its castigations of miserable sinners, sowing fear as the most important word of God. Women on the whole knew their place, although some were getting restive, and intelligent rebels like Mary Wollstonecraft, Harriet Martineau and Hannah More (referred to as 'the old bishop in petticoats') were duly mocked in the self-satisfied male columns of the respectable

* *A Short History of English Poetry* (Heinemann) 1961.

quarterlies. George Sand, by her conduct and her novels, secretly delighted and shocked a wide public.

In 1844 two volumes of EBB's *Poems* were published in England and established her reputation. It was in these poems that Robert Browning found his 'fresh strange music' and instantly took up his pen to write and tell the author so. Published in America the following year, under the title of *A Drama of Exile: and other Poems* her work excited a great deal of attention. Well-known writers praised her; James Russell Lowell wrote her a letter of praise, and Mrs Lydia Sigourney, known as 'the American Hemans', assured her that her poetry was 'stirring the deep green forests of the New World'.

At her very best, she was a very good poet indeed, and in 1856 she proved this with *Aurora Leigh*, a long novel in blank verse, which contains the best—and worst—of her writing. When this came out in 1856 the enthusiasm was so great that it went into three editions within a month, and lending libraries had to put a limit of two days on each loan. Ruskin found it unsurpassed by anything but Shakespeare; Landor, characteristically, was 'half-drunk' with it; Queen Victoria noted uneasily that it was 'extraordinary' and 'strange'; hardened American proof-readers wept over it; some shocked mamas kept it from their daughters: it went ultimately into twenty editions. The sober and perceptive William Bell Scott, in a letter to William Rossetti, administered one private pinprick: 'it is only a novel à la Jane Eyre, a little tainted by Sand'.

George Eliot, after a third reading, stated that it gave her 'a deeper sense of communion with a large as well as a beautiful mind'. Was she remembering Aurora, perhaps, in her characterisation of Dorothea Casaubon ten years later?

The intensity of her religious disposition, the coercion it exercised over her life, was but one aspect of a nature altogether ardent, theoretic and intellectually consequent . . . hemmed in by a social life which seemed nothing but a labyrinth of petty causes, a walled-in maze of paths that led no-whither.*

The portrait might well be that of the young Aurora-Elizabeth of Hope End days, who 'threw off her hunters' and escaped into books. What makes the comparison even stranger (since George Eliot could not have known such details) is that Elizabeth too, like Dorothea, devoted herself to an 'arid pedant' years older than herself, in order to help him in his work and also to educate herself—warming herself over somewhat synthetic embers.

> We were not lovers, not even friends well-matched
> Say rather, scholars upon different tracks,
> And thinkers disagreed.†

Aurora Leigh was certainly EBB's most ambitious work. She put into it not only her young self, but everything in which she believed, everything she had learned about life. It was a great cry of protest against the idea that women's minds were naturally inferior to men's and that therefore a woman did not merit equal education and could make no worthwhile career for herself. But the dual strands of melodrama and philosophical moralising which appealed to the Victorians, do not mix well for us today. Nor can we take the prolixity. Vivid, breathless, and acute as it is, it is ultimately defeated by its composite form, like a mermaid trying to walk, and few people today would enjoy ploughing through all its 11,000 lines.

This is a pity, for to read the first two books in conjunction with this Diary is both illuminating and exciting; they appear to complement each other. The countryside rises alive before us. The same repressed resentment that drove her to keep the Diary, to pour out her anguish, her fears and her love ('O the pain attendant upon loving'), drove her to formalise these emotions in *Aurora Leigh*. She had a long memory for slights. Robert Browning was

* From *Middlemarch*. † From *Aurora Leigh*.

to remark some years later tha too much tenderness masked insincerity, and certainly in this Diary EBB protests too much. In middle age she was able to pay off some old scores. Surely there is something of Aunt Bell (her 'dear, dear Bummy'), in Aurora's aunt with 'close, mild mouth a little soured at the ends' who tried 'to prick me to her pattern with a pin'? And H. S. Boyd, the blind scholar who meant so much to EBB, does not escape censure for displaying towards her the same kind of arrogance and condescension of which Romney was guilty towards Aurora.

Yet, among the poems that might well be rescued from the small print of her collected *Poetical Works*, there is one to the same man seen in a far more favourable light. 'Wine of Cyprus' is a deeply-felt tribute to Mr Boyd, and to their time of reading together in his Malvern cottage at a phase in her life when she badly needed such a friend.

4

Hugh Stuart Boyd had arrived in Malvern in 1825. He was a local scholar of private means, forty-five years old, with a wife unsympathetic to his studies, and a somewhat dizzy daughter, Annie. He came from a distinguished Irish family and had studied the classics under a Mr Spowers, who introduced him to a system of reading Greek by quantity. This method, together with his true ear and sense of rhythm and the practice of reading aloud metrically, developed a remarkable verbal memory for Greek lines which stood him in good stead when, as a result of ophthalmia, he lost his sight at the age of thirty.

While at Cambridge he had written a long, dull tragedy instead of working for his degree: it was never performed, but—and this is typical of the man—he had it privately printed. After his marriage to Ann, the daughter of Wilson Lowry the engraver, he published various translations of the Church Fathers because he liked their oratorical style. Throughout the years, despite his blindness, he continued to produce volumes which contained literal translations from classical and Greek poets, his own theological theories and comments and several original poems included for good measure. EBB, during the Hope End period of their friendship, took him at his own valuation, and only afterwards, when her intellectual and social horizons widened, did she realise how narrowly self-congratulatory and pedantic he was. Years later, when they disagreed on the worth of Wordsworth's poetry (which he considered, 'at best, *third rate*') she wrote of him in kindly exasperation to Miss Mitford, 'I asked him to read the sonnet on Westminster Bridge, among other passages—but the only thing that struck him in it was "the profanity" of the "Dear God". So he and I must talk and agree in Greek alone, for the remainder of our lives.' His pettiness, too, in small things, is very evident from EBB's innocent accounts of their meetings and conversations in her Diary.

Of his poetry, which apparently afforded him the same satisfaction as his now vanished Greek translations, one example will suffice. In 1826 there was a terrible summer storm among the Malvern hills, the one in which the tree in the Barretts' grounds was struck by lightning. Four people, two of them young girls, were killed on Pinnacle Hill while sheltering in an iron-roofed shack put up by a local benefactress, Lady Harcourt. Mr Boyd immortalised the event in 'A Malvern Tale'. Here is the first verse:

> Awhile they sailed on pleasure's golden tide—
> A storm arose; the lightning came: they died—
> If upon them Heaven's dart unsparing flew,
> Think that the next dread shaft may light on you.

Mr Boyd's habit, which one would think uncomfortable for his family, was to rent furnished houses in various places, so chosen as to be near to congenial people. His large classical library accompanied him wherever he went, and he had settled at Ruby Cottage, near Malvern, on account of the local vicar, Dr Card. The two men shared the same theological opinions, a dislike of Popery and an enthusiasm for campanology. Dr Card was engaged in restoring the priory of Great Malvern, whose ancient bells were famous for their sweet tone.

Ever on the look-out for intellectual companionship, which was scarce in and around Malvern, it was with alacrity that early in the year of that storm H. S. Boyd wrote to the young author, Elizabeth Barrett Barrett, hailing her as 'favoured daughter of the muses' and congratulating her on the erudition of her 'Essay on Mind'. He enclosed copies of his own work and invited her to call, as he was living scarcely five miles from Hope End.

* * * * *

In 1827 EBB was twenty-one years old. Her 'Essay on Mind', dedicated to and paid for by her father, stood in relation to her intellectual development as a pompous youthful thesis would to an undergraduate today. She had borrowed heavily from Pope's 'Essay on Man' which he had written in rhymed couplets to vindicate the ways of God to man, and to prove that the scheme of the Universe was best left unaltered in spite of apparent evils. Man's failure to see the perfection of the whole was due to his limited vision. It was a view EBB was to use again in *Aurora Leigh*, although she grew to hate her early work and honestly admitted its shortcomings:

> I poured myself along the veins of others, and achieved
> Mere lifeless imitation of live verse
> And made the living answer for the dead. . . .

and again, she accused herself of:

> counterfeiting epics, shrill with trumps
> a babe might blow between two straining cheeks.

By this time she had established herself, through ill-health, as the clever, delicate member of the family. Since early childhood, as is well known, she had written poetry and had a passion for her 'golden Greeks', and it was the greatest grief to her when her eldest brother, her beloved

Bro, was sent to Charterhouse and she could no longer share his lessons with the tutor, Mr McSwiney.

As a child, she had been violently active, headstrong and nearly ungovernable. Her passion was to be first in everything, in personal relationships, in learning. Time and again in her Diary she ruefully quotes Cesare Borgia's motto, *aut Caesar aut nihil* (either Caesar or nothing). She was indeed her father's daughter, with a strong autocratic streak, but being a woman she was denied any exercise of power. Her brother Edward could get his own way by divine right of his maleness. His sister was forced to work differently.

Biographers and psychiatrists alike recognise that escape into illness was a common enough loophole for frustrated and intelligent Victorian women, many of whom were aware that society was divided between those who had far too much to do and those who had far too little. The upper and middle classes employed other people to do jobs which they were perfectly capable of doing themselves. Only a sense of fitness, of status, kept them in their parlours or drawing-rooms, sewing the tick-pause-tock of long empty hours into bead slippers, pressing the time into seaweed albums, trilling vapid songs in off-key voices, watching the yellow fog drift up to the windows . . . and never being caught reading novels in the mornings. Those who actively resented this role had to be tough to survive. Some cast off their protective colouring and stood out boldly against the background like vulnerable animals to be sniped at. Others used it, and took cover in illness.

EBB chose the second way, although unconsciously. The fall from her pony at fifteen was real enough. It may have injured her spine. The accident certainly triggered off the fits of hysteria, the head or body pains, the fainting spells and the lack of energy from which she was to suffer (especially in times of emotional stress) all her life. It enabled her to opt out of the feminine role her age and position in the household demanded of her: now she need take no hand ordering it, for fear of over-fatigue, nor in sewing or embroidery, which she hated. Music, French, Italian, a little singing were available: she could now choose what she wanted, and discard the rest. In fact, she was to remain determinedly non-domestic all her life. She confided to Mrs David Ogilvy when she was living in Florence in 1858: 'It's a privilege on my part and an advantage on my husband's that I have never ordered dinner once since my marriage . . . what would become of me (and of the house) I wonder, if I had a house to manage. A positive blessedness is the smooth fashion of continental life—yes, I do think so.' She withdrew to her little green room ('the warmest in the house')—that essential room of one's own, grew her hair in ringlets, and divided her time between philosophy, poetry, novels and the Classics. Her only duties were to teach Latin and Greek to two of her brothers, Stormie and George.

She never forgot this full-stop to her education and it rankled. Years later she wrote to Miss Mitford, 'When I said lightly to Mr Boyd one day that the difference between men and women arose from the inferiority of the education of the latter, he asked me *why* the education was inferior and so brought the argument to an end . . . it is a hard and difficult process for a woman to get forgiven for her strength by her grace. You who have accomplished this know it is hard. Sometimes there is too much strength in proportion to the grace—then, o miserable woman!'

Her mind in these years must have been like a garden running wild, seething with plants and bushes and burgeoning climbers, paths leading nowhere but into a maze of brambles, brightened here and there by patches of brilliant colour: Pope and Aeschylus, Homer and Mary Wollstonecraft, Plato and Voltaire, all writhing round each other in choking embrace. No wonder that after her normal dutiful prayers each night, she breathed the words 'O God, if there is a God, save my soul, if I have a soul!' It was she, even more than her less clever brother Edward, who needed a wise adult to prune the excessive growth and clear the paths, and give her some direction.

It must have been a great satisfaction to her, when on the publication of her 'Essay on Mind', and its summary dismissal in the larger world, she received letters of congratulation from two local scholars. Apart from Mr Boyd, Mr Uvedale Price (later to become Sir Uvedale) of Foxley Hall, near Hereford, entered into a correspondence with her that lasted until his death at eighty in 1829. They discussed such questions as the accents, metre and pronunciation of Greek, and he asked her to make comments on his *Essay on the Pronounciation of Greek and Latin Languages*, which was published in 1827.

Up to that time there had been no one with whom she could discuss the things that interested her and, although the Barretts naturally exchanged visits with neighbours, friends and relatives, EBB hated the small talk and the tea and dinner parties. She sought solitude, but did not really relish it, for she was a great sharer, in the sense that she was always unconsciously seeking a guide, and a companion of like tastes. In Mr Boyd she hoped she had found one. Reverencing strong men, as she admitted doing, she was prone to mistake despotism for real strength: as witness her devotion to her father and—later on—to Louis Napoleon (which so outraged Browning).

Her first letters to Mr Boyd were self-consciously erudite, and it was not until she felt secure in his regard and affection that she dropped her scholarly pose and revealed herself as a young woman delighting to toss up ideas, play with words, and frankly confess to a voracious appetite for novels, as well as for weightier reading.

Once begun, the correspondence continued, although it was nearly a year before EBB was allowed to meet Mr Boyd. Papa had told her that as 'a female, a young female, she could not pay the first call without overstepping the established observances of good society'. By what one might call a lucky mischance they passed each other one morning on the road while she and her two sisters were paying a long-delayed call on their cousin, a Mrs Trant, who lived nearby. Mr Boyd was offended by his wife's report that Elizabeth had also gone into the house of Sir Charles Knowles. She had only done so to ask Lady Knowles not to call at Hope End, as Mrs Barrett was ill. However, Mr Boyd wrote a long reproachful letter accusing her of going into another man's house, and saying that as his wife was tiring of Malvern anyway they would probably move away, and that he would only drop her a note 'the day before'.

At this Elizabeth was so upset that she managed to persuade her father to give her permission to call. This time the pony bolted down the steep hill and threw the girls out of the carriage and a very dusty and shaken Elizabeth was introduced to Mr Boyd at last.

She described him as 'a rather young-looking man than otherwise, moderately tall, and slightly formed. His features are good—his face very pale with an expression of placidity and mildness. He is totally blind, and from the quenched and deadened appearance of his eyes, hopelessly so! His voice is very harmonious and gentle and low—and seems to have naturally a melancholy cadence and tone!—I did not see him smile once!'

The friendship developed rapidly. His guidance on Greek was just what she needed to stretch her mind and give her studies an objective. In return she read aloud to him.

In October, 1828, Mrs Barrett died suddenly on a visit to Cheltenham and, although she had been ill for more than a year, the shock upset EBB so much that she was unable to leave the house for nearly six months. During this time Mr Boyd lent her many books from his library, and she began to make real progress with her Greek. She started on St Basil and Gregory, Chrysostom and Synesius—the Church Fathers of whom Mr Boyd was so fond, and also read Euripides and Longinus. By June she was visiting him again and Mrs Boyd and Annie visited Hope End; Annie even stayed for a few days. Still, Mr Boyd and Mr Barrett did not meet. It was another of Mr Barrett's idiosyncrasies to avoid his children's friends; they could visit in his absence but he disliked their company at dinner. His daughter Henrietta showed the same choosiness; neither sought the company of people they did not consider important or socially prominent. Once only Mr Barrett told Elizabeth that, had she been available, he would have gone with her after chapel to call on Mr Boyd. Instead, in the manner of a *grand seigneur*, he sent Mr Boyd a present of game. Mr Boyd, not to be outdone, sent Mr Barrett a bottle of fine brandy, which vanished without comment into the cellar.

Mr Barrett was to encounter Robert Browning once only by chance. It seems as if he could not bear even to appear to share his daughter with a man, however innocent the connection. As if, by not speaking to nor seeing the person he instinctively feared and resented, he could annul his existence. The same instinct, perhaps, which, despite his pious words about not upsetting the children, kept him dumb on the subject of his financial disaster.

The following year (1830) Elizabeth was allowed to stay with the Boyds for two and a half weeks in the autumn, and during that time Mr Boyd recorded that she read aloud 2,200 lines of Greek, most of which he committed to memory:

And I think of those long mornings
Which my thought goes far to seek,
When, between the folio's turnings,
Solemn flowed the rhythmic Greek.
Past the pane the mountain spreading,
Swept the sheepbell's tinkling noise,
While a girlish voice was reading
Somewhat low for *αι*'s and *οι*'s.*

This was the highlight of their friendship, a happy time of shared harmony. Mr Boyd said that they lived in clover,

* From 'Wine of Cyprus'.

but Elizabeth preferred to think they lived in asphodel, as it sounded more classical. She did not even mind Papa's somewhat sarcastic comment on her return, that she 'might find it impossible to tolerate her family, after Mr Boyd'. There was even a proposal that Mr Boyd should be invited to stay at Hope End. It came to nothing, for Mr Barrett was given to sudden changes of mind.

That winter Elizabeth was ill for two months, with a persistent cough that kept her indoors, and in January her grandmother on her father's side died. Then in February came two more blows. The Boyds might be moving away from Malvern, for Mrs Boyd, after five years, desired a change of air and company. Undoubtedly she felt slighted by Mr Barrett's high-handed behaviour and hinted at a lack of a full social life necessary for Annie's sake.

The Barretts were threatened with financial disaster. 'How I remember the coming of that letter to apprize him of the loss of his fortune', wrote EBB to Miss Mitford in 1842 . . . 'and just one shadow passed on his face while he read it . . . and then he broke away from the melancholy and threw himself into the jests and laughter of his innocent boys . . . and in all the bitter bitter preparation for our removal, there was never a word said by any one of us to Papa nor by him to us, in that relation.' She always averred that 'he *suffered more*, of course, he suffered in proportion to the silence'. Years later, she confided to Browning that her father was a victim of his own system, he isolated himself.

'He bore up against the mortification and the anxiety, gallantly, admirably . . and the reserve in matters of suffering is a part of his nature and not to be disturbed by the most tender of those who love him.' This is a more than generous judgement on a course of action which appears to us today to expose Mr Barrett's utter lack of sensitivity and insight where his children were concerned—a not uncommon attitude on the part of Victorian parents. It simply did not occur to him that they would suffer far more by being kept in ignorance of their situation. A good deal of stress could have been avoided if the father had discussed the state of affairs frankly with his five eldest children who, with three of them in their twenties, and the other two in their late teens, were virtually grown-up.

It was ironic that for an avowed Liberal in his political views, an ardent supporter of the Reform Bill, advocating that ' "the cry of the people" be attended to, since all power emanates and ought to emanate from the people' (EBB quotes his actual words in a letter to Mr Boyd), such franchise did not exist in his own family. Like a Roman emperor he never explained his actions, nor justified his sudden whims, demanding absolute obedience and loyalty to such an extent that—later on—even marriage was regarded as an act of betrayal on the part of his children. Each one who married in his lifetime was disinherited.

When he sent for his sister-in-law Arabella Graham Clarke, to come and look after the family while he went to London to salvage what he could of his fortune, he did not even tell them when she was arriving: an extra place laid at luncheon was the only clue. He impressed on her the need for absolute secrecy (although she knew little enough), and Elizabeth noted bitterly that her aunt, affectionately nicknamed 'Bummy', was 'hermetically sealed'. In an uncharacteristic outburst to Mr Boyd at this time, she complained, 'It seems hard upon me that nothing of my childhood, except its tranquillity, should have passed away.'

One suspects that Mr Barrett was too proud to confess to a failure, even if it were not his fault (although he had made some unfortunate investments) and his mortification was so great that he preferred to ignore it. Years later he was to ignore the continued existence of his favourite daughter when she ran away, throwing himself into a round of dinner parties and 'frothing over with high spirits'. Hearing this, she must have realised that the mask was again firmly set in place. There is something terrible about a man who cannot, dare not, allow himself to crumble into human grief and doubt, even for a short time.

Was it fortitude then, or pride, that kept Mr Barrett away from June to December in 1831? Those who stayed at Hope End were the real sufferers, having to bear the constant intrusion of strangers come to stare, and the remarks of prying neighbours. On his return EBB noted in her Diary that when he saw Captain Johnson's cows in the park he changed countenance and turned his head away. Had this strange man vowed to himself that never again would he be humiliated, as he had once been—briefly enough—at Harrow? Or could it have been his early upbringing on the sugar plantations that made him so arrogant? Perhaps father and son shared the same passionate nature. And whereas in the father it had flowered openly into enjoyable promiscuity, in the son it had turned inwards, making him shun any show of emotion which could be construed as weakness or self-indulgence.

Whatever the explanation, Mr Barrett dared not admit any falling-short (and refused to accept any, either in himself or in those dear to him)—unless before his God, to whom one imagines he came clean in the manner of the day, robustly declaring himself to be a miserable sinner. That admission, however, remained a tight secret between the two of them, not to be taken too seriously by either.

5

The Diary opens on the fourth of June 1831. EBB was twenty-five years old, and the atmosphere at Hope End oppressive. It was a stormy month, the uncertain weather sharpening family tensions and the uncertainties of the estate workers and tenants. Rumours rumbled around them like the thunder. In May 'a fat gentleman with rings' had come down from London, said that the place was to be sold and ordered a farmer to plough up one of Mr Barrett's hop-yards. Instead of working in the fields, Papa's people were threshing grain and getting in wood, *for sale*. Papa stayed silent. The Boyds could not discover whether Hope End was already sold, or about to be sold, and whether the family were staying or going. Papa still remained silent, but ordered thirty-two gallons of beer. For whom? Fifteen-year-old George pulled up some boundary markers in a fit of indignation.

At last the fat gentleman returned to London. Aunt Bell (Bummy) arrived at Hope End. The Boyds, who had been on the verge of moving away, took a year's lease on Ruby Cottage, and Annie Boyd blamed Elizabeth for interfering and persuading her father to stay against her and her mother's wish. The overpraised yet undervalued EBB, so resented by the female Boyds for her influence and her cleverness, started, out of desperation, to write down all her fears; to lose both Mr Boyd *and* Hope End was scarcely to be borne:

'Once indeed, for one year, I kept a diary in detail and largely, at the end of the twelve months, was in such a crisis of self-disgust that there was nothing for me but to leave off the diary. Did you ever try the effect of a diary on your own mind? It is curious, especially where elastic spirits and fancies work upon a fixity of character and situation. . . .' When EBB wrote this to Richard Hengist Horne she had freed herself, and would have agreed with Jane Carlyle's dictum 'Your journal all about feelings aggravates whatever is factitious and morbid in you.'

EBB's Diary is more than a journal all about feelings, although she is much taken up with them. It describes a parabola from despair to hope to despair again. It marks in a curiously significant way, because of the absence of Mr Barrett throughout the major part of that year, the end of a total dependence on her father, and the tentative beginning of an independent intellectual existence. Although years of invalidism still lay ahead, when she was to be physically dependent, she was able, apart from a long period of guilt and despair over her brother's death, to detach herself from her father sufficiently to begin to see him clearly. Her understanding never lessened her love for him. Mr Boyd bridged the perilous gap between father and lover.

THE ENVIRONS OF
HOPE END
Redrawn from
the Ordnance Survey 1831
0
1
2
Miles
HEREFORDSHIRE
WORCESTERSHIRE
GLOUCESTERSHIRE
GREAT MALVERN
St. Ann's Well
Chalybeate Spring
Worcestershire Beacon 1394 ft.
Mathon Lodge
Mathon
Castle Frome
South End
Mathon Park
MATHON HOUSE
The Wyche
Malvern Common
Winnings Farm
RUBY COTTAGE
Essington's Hotel
The Admiral Benbow
MALVERN WELLS
Great Malvern Turnpike
Brand Lodge
Colwall Green
Colwall
St. James Church
Coddington Cross
Coombe Hill
Coddington
Bosbury
Leadon River
Upleadon
Upleadon Court
OLD COLWALL
Raycomb Wood
HOPE END
Hope End Farm
Cummins Farm
The Horse and Jockey
BARTON COURT
Old Turnpike
Wynds Point
LITTLE MALVERN
Chances Pitch
Chances Pitch Turnpike
Herefordshire Beacon 1114 ft.
Munsley
Wellington Heath
Petty France
Mainstone Court
Trumpet
Frith Farm
Frith Wood
Ledbury Turnpike
Walm's Well
Pixley
LEDBURY
Upper Hall
Eastnor Hill
Eastnor Park
Obelisk
Eastnor
Bronsil
Underdown
EASTNOR CASTLE
Little Marcle
Preston Court
Ledbury Canal
Donnington
Haffield
Donnington Hall
Court
Bromesberrow

Immature at twenty-five, EBB had undoubtedly developed the kind of 'crush' that a schoolgirl gets for a beloved teacher. In her restricted world he shone like a star of great learning. Hearing his name mentioned in the middle of a dinner party 'among a crowd of people whom I cared nothing about was like Robinson Crusoe's detection of a man's footprint in the sand'.

Growing anxiety, insecurity, suppressed aggression, desire for love on her own terms, a determination to get her own way—can one wonder at the turmoil of EBB's mind in those last twelve months at Hope End? That she was growing up fast is obvious. For the first time another man threatened Papa's supremacy. She dares to admit to herself in the secrecy of her Diary 'not to be shown to anyone else' that Mr Boyd is the only person outside her own family whom she loves. But she will not allow him to criticise her father and is very sharp when he does so, even obliquely.

It is tempting to see this period as a preliminary skirmish, a rehearsal almost for the Browning courtship. Had she not been through all the various shifts in order to get over to see Mr Boyd—middle-aged, blind, married and pedantic though he was—would she have been so ready to fight for a life with Robert Browning, however handsome and volatile? When EBB loved, she loved without reserve, being 'of an intolerably exclusive disposition'.

Her days were taken up with desperate plans of how to get over to Ruby Cottage. It was only five miles away, but the lack of a carriage or bad weather often prevented her from going. Permission always had to be sought from her aunt in her father's absence, and she had to fit in with the activities of the other members of the family, or the convenience of visitors. As it was she managed to get over about once a week.

The three-wheeled, light carriage was called 'the wheelbarrow'. Three people could fit into it, and in this Bummy and one or other of the girls would set off on their calls; to Eastnor Castle where Lord Somers' family lived, to Barton

Court to see the Peytons, the Martins of Old Colwall, or the Trants at Malvern. This suited EBB, for she could always be dropped off near Ruby Cottage, which could be reached in a variety of ways.

They could drive to the Wyche, for example, through Colwall Green; the Wyche was a pass through the long rocky spine of the Malvern hills, south of the Worcestershire Beacon. The road was so steep and rough that it was considered too dangerous for carriages and it was here that the wheelbarrow had overturned on her first visit to Mr Boyd. It was not improved and turnpiked until 1837. From the top of the hill, which rose 900 feet above sea level, fifteen Welsh and English counties could be seen, and according to a contemporary guide book, on a clear day, even the shores of the Irish Channel.

The longest, most sober and expensive route was along the road past Barton Court, and passing through Chances Pitch Turnpike on to the main Malvern road. The former turnpike cottage still stands near an RAC telephone box, although the gate has been moved further up the hill. At the road junction on Little Malvern was another turnpike. The cottage was demolished for road widening in 1962.

It cost half a crown to pass through these two turnpikes, a sum which concerned Elizabeth, who had to ask her brother for the money, and feared that her father 'might not like the bill'. Normally, a ticket bought at the first toll-gate would entitle the traveller to pass through other gates of the same Trust. The high price of this journey was due to the fact that EBB had to travel along the roads of two Trusts, first the Ledbury and then the Worcester Trust, so she had to pay twice.

She was always in difficulties over money, in spite of the legacy from her grandmother, 'Granny Moulton', who had left her £4,000. Evidently her father controlled this and presumably allowed her pocket money. She had to sell books in order to buy others. Clothes did not bother her, and she did not resent having to sit barefoot while her maid mended her only pair of indoor slippers—an incongruous picture to glimpse against the magnificence of Hope End, with its mother-of-pearl inlaid doors, its shining brass and solid mahogany, the great organ in the hall.

Sometimes, to save a shilling or so, she would tie the pony to the Great Malvern Turnpike gate and walk along the side of the hill, past Essington's hotel and the pleasure gardens, before scrambling down the steep slope into the Boyds' garden. Today, looking down from the path, the chimneys of Ruby Cottage can just be seen through the trees, and one can still make the 'descensus averni' and arrive out of breath at the bottom. Essington's Hotel is still there, but the extensive pleasure gardens have disappeared beneath concrete car parks and a housing estate. However, the view from the small garden in front of the hotel is the same. One can still see Worcestershire as EBB saw it: 'such a sea of land; the sunshine throwing its light and the clouds, their shadows upon it! Sublime sight. I must still call it!'

Going to the Wyche was a favourite excursion but Ruby Cottage was always EBB's goal. One of her most likeable characteristics was her utter disregard for material possessions or social consequence. It would never have occurred to her to notice the somewhat cramped circumstances in which the Boyds lived, compared to Hope End. Ruby Cottage was the house leased by Mr Boyd when EBB first visited him in 1828, and he returned to it (after a sojourn at Woodland Lodge, where she had stayed with the family for two and a half weeks) in May 1831 (map page 26/27). The nearby inn having been named after Admiral John Benbow (1653–1702), later renamed the Hornyold Arms, the house was named after the only ship of his squadron to support him in the action against the French in the West Indies in 1702, when the remaining five captains under his command mutinied. Today it is called 'The Ruby' and is very little altered apart from some necessary modernisation inside. It is a charming house, with two bay windows overlooking a half-moon-shaped front garden with a wide carriage drive linking it at two points to the main Malvern road which runs below. The house shoulders well back into the rocky hill, which seems as if it will burst through into the back kitchen windows. The garden is very steep and terraced, and EBB's footpath runs along the hill, some 300 feet up, to the boundary line.

Of the four rooms above the dining-room and parlour, one must have been the Boyds' drawing-room, judging by the carved lintels of the windows and doors and the elaborate fireplace. That left two rooms for Mr Boyd, a bedroom and study, and a bedroom for Mrs Boyd. Presumably Annie and the servant Jane occupied the upper rooms, for behind a baize door are back stairs leading up to the attics and down to the kitchens. One would think it difficult to house guests. Wherever did they tuck Miss Mushett and Miss Boyd? But it is an intriguing sidelight on 19th-century life that however stiff manners might be by day, teeming with niceties, girls who did not much like each other thought nothing of sharing the same bed at night. When Annie stayed at Hope End, she slept with Henrietta (who could not abide her). When Elizabeth stayed a night or two at Ruby Cottage she slept with Annie.

EBB's energy at this period of her life was remarkable. Only things which bored her—like binding music-sheets—tired her. She seemed able to undertake extremely energetic exercise. Running up hills, and slipping and slithering 'rolling presto, prestissimo' down them. A friend remarked on her high spirits; a Frenchman, guest of the Martins, complimented her on her temerity in riding a pony. She was able to get up at four in the morning in order to prepare lessons for her brothers before going off to Mr Boyd at eight; for Mr Boyd always rose at five in order 'to look down upon the rest of the world', and counted it a sin 'not to be up before the second cockcrow'. Often she would arrive at Ruby Cottage to be greeted by Mrs Boyd running downstairs to meet her, still in nightcap and flannel dressing-gown. They would talk in Mrs Boyd's bedroom while Mr Boyd was being shaved, Mrs Boyd eager to confide Annie's latest *amours*.

Her visits were not all pleasure. Mr Boyd was a cold fish. He refused to be leaned on, adjuring her to trust in divine support rather than human, and obviously had no patience with her 'fanciful' ideas. For, although he appreciated her devotion and looked forward to her reading to him, he was not above playing off one young woman against another. He made no bones about telling her that, had he been unable to bear her voice, he would have had to break off the acquaintance. Even more hurtful, was the information that this would have been done through his wife! Miss Mushet, Miss Borman, Miss Heard, they all imperilled EBB's exclusivity. She was tormented by jealousy. Sometimes they were praised by Mr Boyd, at other times denigrated, according to his mood. He could not do with hysterical young women like EBB, who perhaps tended to be tearful, nor young women who disagreed with him, like Miss Gibbons, on questions of philosophy and questioned his beliefs (which EBB sorrowfully found not 'scriptural'). All the same, with a wife who hated Greek and never read poetry, and a giddy daughter, he needed people to read to him. As EBB was to observe, many years later, blindness had sharpened his instincts like a prisoner in the dark, tapping round his dungeon.

Although he could be caustic on occasion, frankly telling her 'tho some of your letters have a good deal of wit you are not lavish with it in your conversation', he was genuinely appreciative of her abilities. He was evidently impressed to hear that she had read every play of Euripides. 'Funny girl!' he said, and observed that very few men had done as much.

He was as curious to know what was happening as EBB herself. Rumours and reports came in from different sources; Minny (the housekeeper at Hope End) heard from her maid that the family were not going to Jamaica. Mr

Barrett wrote blithely from the Isle of Wight, whence he has gone for a change of air after a violent attack of cholera in August, that he liked the clergyman at Ryde, and so threw the family into a turmoil. Would they be putting the sea between themselves and all their friends? He travelled to Eastbourne, was heard of in Brighton ('*not* rattling brick-dusty Brighton!' EBB confided to her Diary). Mr Boyd might settle near them if they went to Eastbourne . . . dare she write and ask her father?

In August there was a sudden reprieve from doubts and the intrusions of would-be buyers. A sale was held and Hope End bought in. Joyfully EBB wanted to drive over to Ruby Cottage at once with the news and was stopped by a furious Henrietta, who said she had no right to tell the Boyds their business. When EBB countered this by saying that Henrietta was about to call on the Martins with the news, Henrietta burst out that it was an impropriety in Ba to prefer the Boyds to the Martins. At once EBB's fearless loyalty showed itself and she noted in her Diary that her sisters, *and* Bummy, had, like most people, clearer ideas of the aristocracy of rank and wealth than of the aristocracy of mind . . . 'I love dearest B and H to the bottom of my heart, but without my pursuits they cannot have my tastes, without my tastes, they cannot be expected to understand them.' 'No confidences, no friendship,' Mr Boyd had once told her.

Throughout her life, EBB wrote a great many letters, and the best of them are delightful, full of humour and lively incident. Those dark, lambent eyes of hers (caught for us by Eliza Cliffe in the portrait she painted at this time) missed nothing of a neighbour's oddity. She could cut near the bone with a single phrase. It is this quality we constantly find in her Diary. She does not spare anyone—neither poor Mrs Hill, a local clergyman's wife 'who seems to have too many teeth and quite enough ideas', nor Mrs Drummond who 'talks like thunder' and certainly not the Biddulphs who needed 'stirring up with a long pole'.

Even if this were merely the account of a year in the life of an unknown but aspiring young woman of whom nothing more was ever to be known, it would still have its place as a curiosity, a tiny tragi-comedy of manners set among the Malvern hills, overshadowed by 'the pain attendant upon loving' and the imminent fear of removal. It gives us such an exact picture of the squirearchy in its petticoats: the endless visits, dinners at three, tea-drinking at six or eight (it seemed a moveable feast), the mild scandals, picnics, church-and-chapel-going. The performances of visiting preachers were as hotly discussed as those of actors or politicians in the broader London society. Current literature was read, novels and biographies were exchanged for comment. These country families might be cut off—apart from reports in *The Times*—from great events like the Reform Bill which was then being piloted through Parliament by Lord John Russell at Grey's instigation, or lesser ones, like the Paganini concerts and the 'speaking with unknown tongues' controversy, but life was far from dull. There were the choral societies, the missionary meetings, and the Bible discussion groups in surrounding villages on Wellington Heath. Also, in this time of unrest, rick-burnings to look out for. Both Mr Martin of Barton Court, and Mr Barrett, personally helped farm labourers whose wages were too low.

EBB herself never cared for 'localising' as she put it. 'Living for years and years a three-miles distance from Ledbury, I never had the opportunity of believing in St Catharine until Wordsworth gave me one.' She is referring to St Katharine's chapel in Ledbury church (where there is a tablet to the memory of her father and mother) which Wordsworth visited whilst staying with Sir Uvedale Price in 1827. His poem 'St Katharine of Ledbury' was published in 1835. She was, as Sir Uvedale called her, only 'a good indoor ferret'.

In the new year of 1832 the Boyds, tired of trying to fit in with the Barretts' nebulous plans, decided to move away when their lease was up in May. EBB, diving into her books for comfort, decided to translate 'Prometheus Bound' as a reminder of the happy time when she had first read it aloud to Mr Boyd. She finished it in thirteen days, and although Mr Boyd did not approve of such hasty work, she disregarded his judgement. It was published by Valpy in 1833, paid for by Mr Barrett, and dismissed by the *London Quarterly* in a gentlemanly fashion as 'a remarkable performance for a young lady but not a good translation in and by itself'. The *Athenaeum* warned that 'those who adventure in the hazardous lists of poetic translation should touch anyone rather than Aeschylus'.

Her choice of 'Prometheus Bound' as a kind of therapy for her mental turmoil is interesting. Prometheus is shown as 'relishing the pang of his chains' and refusing deliverance until Zeus himself descends to free him. 'I choose, with this victim, this anguish foretold.' In the same vein, shortly after the move to Sidmouth, she was to write 'A Drama of Exile', the story of Adam and Eve cast out of paradise.

6

The entries for 1832, as explained in the Preface, were made in another volume, which EBB used for making notes on her reading. This came into George's possession on Arabel's death and Browning wrote a troubled letter to him in 1887 expressing his fears about the possible publication of his and Elizabeth's private papers after his death. (He had evidently forgotten the little paper-wrapped manuscript, marked 'Diary of EBB', he had put aside for his son).

Browning had always dreaded future peeping-toms, and it is possible that he had been concerned about the scandal some years before caused by Simeon Solomon, a fringe pre-Raphaelite, minor painter and sexual deviationist, hawking round letters he had received from Swinburne. Browning's friend Dante Gabriel Rossetti had at that time written to all his circle warning them to vet their correspondence —and correspondents—carefully.

Not that anything in the Browning archives was likely to shock anyone, and certainly not a diary kept by a sheltered young woman in 1831. But Browning's letter evidently alarmed George Moulton-Barrett, who, at seventy years old, was still as upright and conventional as ever. He was a fair man and, although he had sided with his father when his sister ran off with a poet he thought of as a fortune-hunter ('He thinks it very immoral indeed . . . accepting a fortune from a wife', EBB once wrote to Miss Mitford), he warmed to Browning later on and the two men became friends. It was George with whom Pen, as a child, had been discovered laughing in the hallway at Wimpole Street. 'And whose child is that, pray?' asked Mr Barrett. 'Ba's child,' George had replied courageously. Mr Barrett changed the subject.

Did George's face take on its solemn judge-like aspect as he turned the pages of his sister's journal? His dismay must have grown as he read that flow of words, those terribly painful and to him indiscreet revelations of some fifty years ago. It must have conjured up for him those last months at Hope End, a time never referred to by the family since leaving.

To him, as a boy of fourteen and fifteen, learning his Latin and Greek with his sister and Stormie every morning up in her green room, she had appeared gentle and learned. He would have known of her friendship with the blind scholar, Mr Boyd, although he never met him, for she was teased about it. He might have wondered why Mr Boyd was never invited to the house, but in such a family certain questions were not asked, and he could spend his time fishing in the Bosbury brook with his brothers or mushrooming at Eastnor Castle, fighting with Henry, or riding over the hills, without bothering much about the under-currents of family life. He was too busy working to get to Glasgow University, to study law. He might remember the squirrel escaping from its cage while they read Homer, and leaping up the bookcase before it was caught. He did remember being scolded for taking his sister's copy of Heyne's Homer (a present from Mr Boyd) into the schoolroom without permission, and his pet jackdaw tearing a page, much to her grief.

To George, in his seventies, his sister's preoccupation with Mr Boyd, her tiffs with local families, must have struck a very sour note. He must have been deeply concerned for the good name of the Barretts as well as—with his legal training—possible repercussions from the relatives or descendants of the people mentioned in no good part by Elizabeth.

So out of the 144 pages he excised 56, and a further 18 were partly obliterated. By some poignant chance he left a fitting last line:

'Went away in the pouring rain. Left . . .'

The following nine pages are excised. This last entry is on 23 April.

Mr Boyd had been urging Elizabeth to spend a few days at Ruby Cottage. From a letter written to him two days later, she refers to Papa's displeasure at her leaving home in bitter weather, and accusing her of trying to kill herself, 'and *then* I might be satisfied'. In view of this she cannot bring herself to ask his permission though she wishes to bring the number of Greek lines Mr Boyd can repeat by heart up to a record 8,000. However, she paid her last visit to him on Monday, 13 May, and a day or two after that the Boyds moved to Bathampton.

'Even now', Elizabeth wrote to him on 17 May, 'it seems to me like a dream. It seems to me scarcely possible that if I were to go there, I should find nothing but even more painful recollections than I find here, that I shall never go there again to see you, and that perhaps I may never see you or read to you or write for you or hear you repeat Greek, anywhere. Forgive me, for saying so, . . . I have had the dread on my mind for three years, that you would go at last—and the feeling that if you once went away, we should meet no more . . Oh Mr Boyd! I thought it would all end in some way like this. I *deserved* it to end so—because when under the pressure of those heavy afflictions with which God has been pleased to afflict me since the commencement of our intimacy—I often looked too much for comfort to you—instead of looking higher than you. . . I have not deserved—and I think, never can deserve, that you should forget me or neglect to write to me or withdraw your friendship from me. And I entreat you, never, never, as long as you live, to do so.'

It was a long, heart-rending letter and I have not reproduced all of it, but it reveals the state to which EBB was reduced. The long nervous strain imposed on her by her father's silence as to his intentions added to the loss of intellectual companionship—the cutting off of her one escape route to a beloved friend and teacher—made her hysterical and ill. Bro took over the tuition of George and Stormie, and she was forbidden any serious study. Greek being denied her, she secretly took up Hebrew. Years later, writing from Torquay, she was to tell Miss Mitford her reasons:

' "Hebrew roots grow best on barren ground" and at painful times, when composition is impossible and reading *not enough*, grammars and dictionaries are excellent for *distraction*. Just at such a time . . when we were leaving Herefordshire . . I pinned myself down to Hebrew, took Parkhurst and Professor Lee for my familiars, and went through the Hebrew Bible from Genesis to Malachi, Syriac and all, as if I was studying for a professorship—and never once halting for breath.'

In August she was able to tell Mr Boyd that preparations for their removal were going forward; a hundred pounds' worth of timber alone went into the making of packing-cases; some of her books were to go with her, to Sidmouth, the rest to be left with Mr Barrett's library and the furniture, in warehouses in Ledbury. The plate was sent to

London, to the Bank. Henrietta had been visiting the cottages on Wellington Heath, 'on Bible business, the. . . women bursting into tears . . and calling down blessings upon Papa's head wherever he went, in a most affecting manner'. Five cartloads of furniture rumbled away down the drive, 'the noise of hammering and of men walking up and down stairs, from morning to night—and dear Hope End looking so unlike the happy Hope End it used to be. . . . I cannot bear to think that the rooms and walls in which we have not been in for so long [her mother's rooms which had been unaltered and unused since her death] will be inhabited and trodden and laughed in, by strangers.'

She is concerned that Mr Boyd should not be offended at the fate of the books he had lent her.

'With regard to your books, dear Mr Boyd, I hope you have not thought that in sending the large ones to Ledbury instead of to Sidmouth I was pleasing myself. We have sent to Sidmouth only one box of books, and not a very large one, as Papa particularly desired us to take as few as we could. In this box are a good many music books—and all the lesson books, which take up much room, but are necessary for the children. I have sent fewer than I have occasion for—and would have left Wolf behind, if they had not seen that I was sorry about it, and found out that it would lie flat and be very little in the way. Besides Wolf, I had sent Gregory, and the first volume of Heyne's Homer, which you gave me—and the first volume of Heyne's Pindar—and the two plays of Aeschylus which I had, edited by Blomfield—and two volumes of Sophocles in *8vo* —and six very little volumes of Euripides in duodecimo— a few duodecimo Latin books—my Hebrew and Greek Bibles—and your Select Passages and Agamemnon. That is nearly, if not all, besides your smaller books . . . [Papa] is packing his own, himself, with the assistance of the boys who dust them and fold them in paper and give them to him. Oh I do wish all this painful confusion were over! . . . Dearest Papa's resolution and cheerfulness are our example and our support. I exert myself in mind and body, as much as either will allow.'

On 24 August, in the morning, two carriages set out for Sidmouth. Although the house had been taken for a month, the family were to stay for three years, making three moves during that time. Bummy and the girls, six boys and five servants drove away down the drive for the last time, under the trees heavy with late summer, and out past the chapel-cum-schoolhouse by the south gate. While they made the long journey of 130 miles—to be broken at Bath, only three miles from where Mr Boyd was living—Mr Barrett, with Bro and ten-year-old Sette stayed behind to clear up the last details. The old days of Hope End were over.

EBB never returned, although Mrs Martin invited her when she paid a visit to England from Italy in 1850. 'We could not go into Herefordshire, even if I were rational, which I am not, I could as soon open a coffin as do it: there's the truth.'

The story has what may be called a happy ending. Mr Boyd asserted that the air of Sidmouth was absolutely necessary to his health, left his wife and daughter and settled into lodgings at a convenient walking distance from the Barretts, oddly enough, who had taken the house which the Grand Duchess Helena had rented the year before, and EBB must have been reminded of Dominick Trant's shocking story about her which had so put her out of countenance and caused 'a bedquake' of laughter when she relayed it to Arabel . .

Mr Boyd's family joined him four months later and they were to stay in the vicinity for a year and a half. During this time they met every day, and gradually, perhaps because now there was no difficulty put in her way, the excitement of meeting him died. In losing her feverish regard and romantic attachment EBB came to look upon him as a real friend rather than as a teacher. She saw through her perfect scholar, and came to regard him with gentle pity as a childlike man. He had been the one who:

> was looking for worms, I for the Gods.
> 'Tis well I should remember, how those days
> I was a worm too, and he looked on me.*

Mr Boyd had served his purpose. Now a younger man was supplanting him as mentor. The Reverend George Hunter, whose stimulating sermons at the Independent Chapel set EBB's mind off in new directions, was to become her jealous and devoted admirer for many years. When the Boyds moved away to Bath in 1834, the break was not so painful. The 'change of air' and scene which the Victorians regarded as the best medicine for every ill had worked wonders with the desperate young woman of the previous year.

But Mr Boyd had his revenge on Mr Barrett. He was the one not only to guess, but to support wholeheartedly the runaway marriage of his one-time amanuensis, 'Porsonia', with Robert Browning. It was to his rooms in St John's Wood that she went straight after her marriage at Marylebone Church on 12 September 1846.

Robert went home to New Cross to make his arrangements. Wilson, Elizabeth's maid, was sent back to Wimpole Street to allay any suspicions on their absence, and Elizabeth took a fly to 24a Grove End Road. There she was given Cyprus wine and thin bread and butter and rested until her sisters came to fetch her, knowing nothing.

'No confidences, no friendship,' Mr Boyd had once said, long ago. Now he, who loved secrets, had a real one. It was his triumph—and solace—after the slights put upon him and his family in Herefordshire fifteen years before.

* *Aurora Leigh.*

WHO'S WHO IN THE DIARY

The Family at Hope End

EDWARD BARRETT MOULTON-BARRETT. Born Jamaica 28 May 1785. Sent to England 1792. In 1798 he and his brother Samuel became co-heirs to the Jamaican estates of their grandfather, Edward Barrett of Cinnamon Hill, and assumed the additional surname of Barrett. Married 1805, to Mary Graham-Clarke. Moved to Hope End 1809, elected Sheriff of the County 1812, 1814; an active supporter of Local Bible and Missionary Societies. Death of wife 1828. Decline in fortunes necessitated removal from Hope End to Sidmouth 1832. 1835 moved to London, finally settling at 50 Wimpole Street, where he remained until his death on 17 April 1857.

ELIZABETH BARRETT MOULTON-BARRETT ('Ba'). Eldest child, born 6 March 1806. Early interest in writing poetry evidenced by first publication in 1820 of *The Battle of Marathon*. After a serious illness in 1821–3 her health was always precarious. *An Essay on Mind and other poems* published 1826. Move to Sidmouth 1832, and publication of *Prometheus Bound*, the first version, 1833. Her health improved at Sidmouth and deteriorated badly when the family moved to London. Recuperating at Torquay in 1838 with 'Bro', her favourite brother (who had accompanied her against her father's wishes and at her insistence), she was again made desperately ill after the shock of his death by drowning. Her guilt coloured the rest of her life and she could never bear to mention his name, and shuddered at the mention of Torquay and its 'ghastly merriment'. Returned to her room in Wimpole Street in 1841, tightly shut up against the outside air, with dust gathering under the bed, but kept up a lively correspondence with various friends: B. R. Haydon the painter, who committed suicide and wished EBB to edit his vast memoirs; Mary Mitford, author of *Our Village*, H. S. Boyd, F. G. Kenyon, R. Hengist Horne. Selections from these letters have been published.

Apart from contributing four papers on the Greek Christian poets to the *Athenaeum*, together with a series of essays on English poets from Piers Plowman onwards, she was busy with her

own poetry. Two volumes of her *Poems* were published in August 1844. In January 1845 Robert Browning, on his return from Italy, read them, and wrote at once 'I love these books with all my heart—and I love you too'.

A correspondence and courtship of twenty months culminated in their runaway marriage of 12 September 1846. They left for Italy where, in 1849, their only son Robert Wiedeman Barrett 'Penini' was born. 'Sonnets from the Portuguese', published in 1850, are regarded as her most memorable work. 'Casa Guidi Windows' was 'a personal impression' of the uprising in Tuscany in 1848, but was not published until 1851, and was received with indifference. Not so *Aurora Leigh*, her novel-poem, which was acclaimed by critics and public alike when it appeared in 1856.

Apart from brief visits to England, the Brownings lived in Italy until Elizabeth's death in Florence in 1861.

'For my part', she wrote to Mrs David Ogilvy, in 1852, 'this England will be as ever a load thrown off, and heart as well as lungs will be the better for crossing the sea.' And again: 'You know how I love Florence and Italy. It's like being kept prisoner on a diet of ambrosia, in paradise . . . Plenty of books, plenty of thoughts, health enough, love enough! Plenty to thank God for.'

EDWARD BARRETT MOULTON-BARRETT ('Bro'). Eldest son, born 26 June 1807. Attended Charterhouse 1820–6. On 11 July 1840 he was drowned while out sailing with two friends in Babbacombe Bay. His body was not washed up in Torbay for three weeks.

HENRIETTA BARRETT MOULTON-BARRETT. Second daughter, born 4 March 1809. Married 1850 to her distant cousin William Surtees Cook, who had courted her for five years. Disinherited by her father in consequence. She had three children, and died of cancer on 23 November 1860. Her death was a great blow to EBB and weakened her accordingly.

SAMUEL BARRETT MOULTON-BARRETT. Second son and fifth child (a third daughter Mary, died in infancy in 1814). Born 13 January 1812. Died of yellow fever 17 February 1840 at Cinnamon Hill Great House, Jamaica.

ARABELLA BARRETT MOULTON-BARRETT ('Arabel'). Fourth daughter. Born 4 July 1813. EBB's favourite sister. Remained unmarried and kept house for her father until his death. Worked for various charitable causes, i.e. the Ragged Schools. Was of great support to Browning when he brought his son Pen back to England after EBB's death. Browning made a note in July 1863, of a dream Arabel had had of her sister appearing to her. Arabel asked, 'When shall I be with you?' Elizabeth had answered, 'Dear, in five years.' Arabel died in Browning's arms on 11 June 1868.

CHARLES JOHN BARRETT MOULTON-BARRETT ('Stormie'). Third son, born during a storm on 28 December 1814. Suffered from a nervous stammer which caused him such agony of embarrassment that he was unable to read his Essays aloud at Glasgow University. He left 'much to papa's vexation' before taking his degree, although he was an able classicist. Sent to look after family's business in Jamaica, where he married in 1865. Died 21 January 1905.

GEORGE GOODWIN BARRETT MOULTON-BARRETT. Fourth son, born 15 July 1817. Became a barrister of the Inner Temple, retired after inheriting part of father's estate in 1857. Kept up a correspondence with his sister and Browning until their deaths; his letters to Browning throw valuable light on the Hope End days. Died, unmarried, 11 August 1895.

HENRY BARRETT MOULTON-BARRETT. Fifth son. Born 27 July 1818. Married the year after his father's death. Died 17 May 1896.

ALFRED PRICE BARRETT MOULTON-BARRETT ('Daisy'). Sixth son, born 20 May 1820. Married a distant cousin in 1855, and disinherited. Died in France 24 May 1904.

SEPTIMUS JAMES BARRETT MOULTON-BARRETT ('Sette' or 'Seppy'). Seventh son. Born 22 February 1822. In 1842 narrowly escaped death while fencing (without buttons on the blades and without masks) with his tutor on the leads at Wimpole Street. Spent latter part of his life in Jamaica and died there 17 March 1870.

OCTAVIUS BUTLER BARRETT MOULTON-BARRETT ('Occy' or 'Occyta'). Eighth son and last child (the twelfth), born 12 April 1824. Married twice, died 11 November 1910.

ARABELLA SARAH GRAHAM-CLARKE ('Bummy'). Born 27 June 1785, the fourth of nine children of John and Arabella Clarke. Sister to Mary, Edward Moulton-Barrett's wife. She never married and spent much time over the years with the family, particularly in times of stress: 1831–2 and 1838–41. Died in Cheltenham 30 December 1869.

Indoor Staff mentioned in the Diary

ANN. EBB's maid.

MARY ROBINSON ('Minny'). Joined household as nurse to Arabella in 1817. Later appointed housekeeper at Hope End and moved with the family to London. The Moulton-Barrett girls respected her opinion on childish ailments and EBB consulted her often after the birth of her own child. Died at Arabella's home in the 1860s.

Outdoor Staff

JACK COOK. Son of Thomas Cook, one of the tenant farmers. Worked on the estate.

DALY. The gardener at Hope End.

GENT. Worked in the stables and delivered messages, drove one of the carriages.

JOHN LANE. Groom and handyman, lived in a cottage on the estate.

WILLIAM TREHERNE ('Billy'). Son of John Treherne, a tenant. Employed principally in the stables, and drove EBB's carriage. He accompanied the family to London and was promoted to butler in 1837. In 1844 he secretly married Crow, then EBB's personal maid, and they set up in a baker's shop in Camden Town.

Wilson succeeded Crow, and accompanied EBB when she was married, and then to Italy.

BARKER, MRS. Gatekeeper. Lived in a cottage by the south gate and EBB in an early poem referred to her as 'sweet Madam Barker . . . with the sallow cheek / The lanky shape and with the long thin neck.'

MADDOX, MARY. A visiting dressmaker and seamstress. EBB also wrote a juvenile poem to her. In the Diary she describes her as 'A dear feeling creature'.

Relatives and Neighbours

BAKER, HARRIET. Unmarried niece of the Rev. Reginald Pyndar, from Worcester. 'A particular friend of Lady Margaret Cocks . . . a good deal past "the certain age".'

BARKER, EDMUND HENRY (1788–1839). Classical scholar, editor, friend of HSB, who at one time wanted to publish EBB's letters to HSB (*EBB/HSB* pp. 26, 103, 213).

BARRETT, SAMUEL BARRETT MOULTON- (1787–1837). Edward Moulton-Barrett's younger brother, co-heir to the Jamaican estates. His wife, Mary (née Clay-Addams), died in Jamaica in 1831 at the age of twenty-eight. EBB always refers to him as 'Sam', and he was devoted to her. When he died he left her £400 a year.

BARNETT, JOSEPH. Tenant of Winnings Farm, about three-quarters of a mile from the Wyche, on the Ledbury side (map ref. D7).

BEST, MRS MARY CATHERINE. Daughter of Mrs Cliffe. Married Thomas Best in 1827. Fanny is her infant daughter. Wrote *An Illustration of the Prophecy of Hosea* (London 1831) and continued to publish tracts on the Old and New Testaments until 1864.

BIDDULPH, JOHN. Banker, magistrate, Governor of Guy's Hospital and Treasurer of the Royal Geographical Society. One of the principal citizens of Ledbury: there is a large family tomb in St Katharine's Chapel in Ledbury Church. He and his wife had four sons and five daughters, none of whom EBB cared for. He kept a Diary which covered the last years of the Barretts at Hope End and his visits there are recorded. (Diary now in Hereford City Library.)

BISCOE, WILLIAM (1805–77), Rector of Donnington, near Ledbury. This may be the Mr Biscoe referred to throughout the Diary as one of Annie Boyd's suitors, whom she refused. There was, however, a Joseph Biscoe of whom little is known. In a letter to HSB (30 May 1834) EBB wrote in some excitement that Mr Joseph Biscoe had arrived in Sidmouth with his bride ('*Not at all pretty*') and that the couple had a large St Bernard dog 'which makes them celebrated people'. Mr Biscoe, she added, did not look well, and said that he found Sidmouth too gay.

BLOMFIELD, CHARLES JAMES (1786–1857). Bishop of London, edited five plays of Aeschylus. *Aeschyli Septem Contra Thebas.* (Cambridge 1812), *Aeschyli Prometheus Vinctus* (Cambridge 1810); EBB and Mr Boyd are much occupied with these works throughout the period of the Diary.

BOHN, HENRY G. London bookseller advertising a *Catalogue of Very Select Collection of Books English and Foreign* in *The Times*, 2 September 1831.

BORDMAN, ELEANOR PAGE (1815–78), later Jago, daughter of the Rev. James Bordman, curate of Ickham, Kent. The friendship was to last until EBB's death. Occasionally in the Diary EBB misspells her name as Boadman.

BOWERS, CAPTAIN. Friend of the Biddulphs, 'a vulgarissimus' who once called with Miss Penelope Biddulph. He had returned from America after nine years abroad and was appointed in 1832 Superintendent of the Seaman's Hospital ship at Greenwich.

BOYD, ANN, née Lowry. Daughter of Wilson Lowry, Fellow of the Royal Society, and a well-known engraver. Married Hugh Stuart Boyd in 1805. Had one daughter, Ann Henrietta. Died in London, October 1834.

BOYD, ANN HENRIETTA. Daughter of Mr and Mrs Boyd. After various unfortunate attachments, married a Catholic, Henry William Hayes, in 1837. Mr Boyd, who had spent his life refuting Papists, did not attend the wedding (at Marylebone Church). It was left to the three Barrett sisters to support their friend. EBB wrote the next day to say that the bride had looked lovely and cautiously congratulated him 'on the appearances of happiness which seem to have gathered about her path'. To Miss Mitford, however, in 1843, she wrote more fully: 'Once indeed I was at a wedding . . poor Annie Boyd's—but we met at the church and separated there: *that* was enough of it—and too much for her, poor thing, who has had reason to sit in ashes ever since . . .' Annie is a shadowy figure, and her mysterious sorrows are unsolved.

BOYD, HUGH STUART (1781–1848). Greek scholar, blind for the greater part of his life. Committed to memory 4,770 lines of Greek verse and 3,280 of Greek prose. Author of *Select Passages from the Work of St Chrysostom, St Gregory Nazianzen, and St Basil. Select Poems of Synesius and Gregory Nazianzen*, and other translations from classical and the Christian Greek poets, rhetorical theological discussions, original poems. He delighted in Greek epigrams, some of which EBB sent to *The Times*. After his wife's death and his daughter's marriage he lived alone in St John's Wood, cared for by a maid and visited still by members of the Barrett family. EBB wrote a moving poem to him, 'Wine of Cyprus', published in her *Poems* of 1844, recalling their shared days of study both in Woodland Lodge (the house he first rented in Great Malvern) and Ruby Cottage. She wrote to him three times after her marriage, once describing Pisa for his pleasure, and when he died of a paralytic stroke in 1848, she told Arabel that it was as if a great black shadow had fallen straight on her. She wrote three sonnets to the memory 'of this excellent and learned man', one of which lists the gifts he left her:

> Three gifts the Dying left me—Aeschylus,
> And Gregory Nazianzen, and a clock
> Chiming the gradual hours out like a flock
> Of stars whose motion is melodious.

BRIGHT. The family lived at Brand lodge, three-quarters of a mile from the junction of the turnpike and a rough secondary road to the Wyche.

BROWN, MRS. Tenant of Cummins Farm, just over a mile from Hope End, on the road to Barton Court and Malvern (map page 26/27).

BULWER, EDWARD GEORGE LYTTON (1803–73). Later Bulwer-Lytton and (1866) 1st Baron Lytton. Editor 1831–3 of *The New Monthly Magazine and Literary Journal.* He did not publish EBB's poems.

BUTLER, LADY (née Frances Graham-Clarke) (1790–1868). Wife of Sir Thomas Butler, Bt. Bummy's younger sister, Fanny.

BUTLER, MRS CHARLOTTE (née Graham-Clarke) (1787–1834). Wife of Richard Pierce Butler of Cloughgrenan, Ireland. Another of Bummy's younger sisters. Charlotte ('Arlette') her daughter, married a Mr Reynolds, and spent the winter of 1849 in Florence where she gave birth to a son a few days after EBB had her child, 'Penini'. 'My cousin whom you saw is as amiable as she is pretty', EBB wrote to Mrs David Ogilvy.

BRYDGES. A local family prominent in county affairs, living at Canon Frome, a village about five miles N.W. of Hope End.

CARD, REV. DR HENRY. Vicar of Great Malvern since 1815. Author of *A Dissertation on the Subject of the Herefordshire Beacon* (1822). *The Uses of the Athanasian Creed Explained and Vindicated* (Worcester 1825). Card's View is a path over the hill near Malvern Wells; several local residents in the 18th and 19th century had walks made at their expense on the Malvern Hills, sometimes leading to the famous healing wells. Dr Card raised money for the continuation of the restoration of the Priory, and its bells. Friend of H. S. Boyd, and also the Wall family. EBB never forgave him for joining in 'a *mere* party of pleasure' to look round Hope End while the family were still in residence, and wrote a strong letter to HSB on the subject (*EBB/HSB* pp. 143–5).

CLARKE, DR ADAM (1762–1832). Wesleyan preacher and theological writer, friend and relative of H. S. Boyd. Author (with

Joseph Clarke): *Concise View of the Succession of Sacred Literature, Doctrine of Salvation by Faith Proved, Holy Bible . . . With a Commentary* . . . 8 vols. (London 1810–26). EBB discusses his commentary on Romans at length, and her father enjoyed his work. Died of cholera two days after the Barretts moved.

CLARKE, JAMES ALTHAM GRAHAM- (1791–1860). Bummy's younger brother. Again, EBB refers to this uncle by his christian name in her Diary.

CLARKE, JOHN ALTHAM GRAHAM- (1782–1862). Bummy's elder brother, who lived at Kinnersley Castle, twelve miles N.W. of Hereford.

CLARKE, JOSEPH. Author (with Adam Clarke) of *A Concise View of the Succession of Sacred Literature* 2 vols. (London 1830–2).

CLIFFE, MRS ELIZABETH (née Deane). Widow of the Rev. Allen Cliffe, of Mathon. The Cliffes lived in a large house in this small village near Hope End, either at Shipend House or Mathon House —the records are not clear. Today there is a public house called The Cliffe Arms, and in the tiny church are memorials to the Cliffe family. They left the district in the 1870s.

CLIFFE, REV. ALLEN ROBERT (1806–97). Curate of Coddington. He had recently graduated from Trinity College, Dublin. Son of Mrs Elizabeth Cliffe. Married Mary Brilliana Crane, daughter of Samuel Crane of Worcester. EBB refers to the Miss Cranes as 'the singing cranes! they sang like nightingales.'

CLIFFE, ELIZA WILHELMINA (1810–48). Youngest daughter of Mrs Cliffe. Married a Mr Giles in 1844. Closest in age to EBB, she was a warm-hearted, unimaginative girl whom EBB merely regarded as an 'acquaintance'. A talented amateur painter, she painted a portrait of EBB, which is mentioned frequently in the Diary. EBB wrote a poem about this. She exhibited at Worcester at the Society of Artists in 1831. In later years she grew fat, and EBB reported that she wore her hair 'in bandeaux'. Most of the quarrels reported in the Diary seem to centre on the Boyds' jealousy of Eliza, as EBB preferred her company to Annie's.

CLIFFE, WILLIAM BATESON (1803–85). Elder brother of Eliza and Allen.

COCKS, JOHN SOMERS, 1st Earl Somers (1760–1841). Lived at Eastnor Castle, three miles S.E. of Hope End (map ref. H5). Begun in 1814 to designs by Smirke, A. W. Pugin worked on it in 1851, and it is a splendid example of 19th-century Gothic. The ninety feet high obelisk in the grounds was put up by Earl Somers in 1812, to the memory of three members of his family. His other seat was The Priory, Reigate, Surrey. In 1834 he married a second time, his cousin, Jane Waddington (née Cocks). The Rt Hon. Margaret Countess Somers, his first wife, died in 1831.

COCKS, LADY MARGARET MARIA (1792–1849). Daughter of the 1st Earl Somers. Her mother's death in February, 1831, made EBB sympathetic towards her, though she found her somewhat cold and formal, with literary ambitions but little talent. Lady Margaret visited EBB in Wimpole Street, when perhaps because she was feeling ill at the time, she wrote 'I dread her like a thunder-storm!' (Letter *EBB/MRM* p. 181.)

COMMELINE, REV. JAMES. Vicar of Redmarley D'Abitot, six miles S.E. from Ledbury (map page 26/27). His wife, son and two daughters had been on friendly terms with the Barretts from their earliest days at Hope End. The family had a reputation for being sharp-tongued. EBB wrote to Mr Boyd (January 1832) 'Some of them are very amusing, sensible sharp-minded people—and as they don't spare their pricks in making remarks on their neighbours, they are considered not altogether as good-natured as they might be. A short time ago, at a very large and formal dinner-party at Eastnor Castle, Mr Martin said, "I can't help liking those Commelines, tho' I know I shall be damned for it." The compliment was of course repeated to Miss Commeline who told Bro that her family considered it the very highest they could under any circumstances receive.' (*EBB/HSB* p. 157.)

The Rev. James, 'unhappily fell asleep while reading Horace in bed and was burnt to death'. (Unpublished letter dated 8 March 1889, from George Moulton-Barrett to Robert Browning: Collection E. R. Moulton-Barrett Esq.)

Elizabeth Barrett Barrett, 1831, from an oil painting attributed to Eliza Cliffe

Hope End, 1831, from a water-colour by Arabella Barrett

CORRY, JAMES (1772–1848) of Cheltenham, a close friend of Thomas Moore since childhood, often visited the Peytons at Barton Court. The article referred to in the Diary entry for 19 November was written with a Dr Brabant on German Rationalism. An odd subject for Moore: he allowed it to appear anonymously in *The Edinburgh Review*.

COVENTRY, HON. and REV. THOMAS HENRY (1792–1869). Third son of the 7th Earl of Coventry, at this time Rector of Croome D'Abitot, about six miles from Great Malvern. This is possibly the man referred to in Boyd's verses (Diary entry 2 September). He was a bachelor.

CRANES, The. Samuel Crane of Worcester had two daughters. *See* Rev. Allen Cliffe. Friends of Eliza Cliffe.

CURZON, HON. and REV. GEORGE HENRY ROPER- (later 16th Baron Teynham) (1798–1889). Ordained Baptist Minister, 1828, appointed to Ledbury. Also conducted meetings in a building by the Hope End south gate (the Chapel, or School house). Married Eliza Joynes in 1822. One son, Henry George, (1822–92). Left Ledbury in 1832.

DAVISON, REV. JOHN. Prebendary of Worcester, and Rector of Upton-on-Severn. EBB may have written DAVIDSON. She was careless over the spelling of names.

DAVIS, MR. A preacher substituting for Mr Curzon, possibly from Cradley.

DEAN or DEANE, REV. THOMAS. Curate of St James's Church, Colwall, where the Barretts usually worshipped. He also ran a small boarding school for sixteen young gentlemen. EBB did not think highly of his preaching.

DEIGHTON, HENRY. Bookseller of High Street, Worcester.

DRUMMOND, COL. and MRS. Members of the local social circle, living at Underdown, half a mile from Ledbury.

EATON & SONS. Booksellers, College Street, Worcester.

GARLIKE, DR WILLIAM BENNETT (1756–1841) of Melton House, Gt. Malvern, described as 'a physician of great eminence' by Mary Southall in *A Description of Malvern* (1822) p. 10. EBB's misspelling.

GIBBONS, SIR JOHN (1774–1844) 4th Baronet, of Stanwell Place, near Staines, Middlesex. He and his wife were friends of the Boyds, and Annie stayed with them for long periods. She was sent home when there was danger of an attachment between her and one or other of the two sons, either Richard (who, in 1831, was twenty-four) or Joseph (eighteen). Of the three unmarried daughters, Eliza, the eldest, came to stay with the Boyds and was baptized by Mr Curzon. This caused a furore.

GLASCO, MISS. A member of the Barton Court household, probably companion to Mrs Peyton or Mrs Griffith, or governess to the Peyton children. Bro referred in a letter to playing chess with her in 1821.

GRIFFITH, MRS CHARLOTTE (1762–1837). Widow of Thomas Griffith, of Barton Court. Her daughter, Eliza (1788–1861) married Nicholson Peyton (*see* PEYTON). Barton Court is half a mile from Hope End, on the road leading to Malvern, and would be passed each time EBB drove to the Wyche or Ruby Cottage (map page 26/27).

HAILES, BERRINGTON. Owner of land immediately to the east of Hope End.

HATCHARD, JOHN (1799–1849), publisher, of Piccadilly, London.

HEARD, or HURD, MISS. Little is known of her. In 1842 HSB asked for EBB's help in obtaining reviews of a book Miss Heard was publishing, *The Shipwreck of the Dryad* (*see EBB/HSB* pp. 252–3).

HIGGINS, REV. JOSEPH (1771?–1847). Rector of Eastnor since 1795.

HILL, MRS CHARLES. Wife of the Rev. Charles Hill of Bromeberrow, a village about five miles from Hope End (map page

26/27). Friend of Mrs Martin. Unforgettable because of EBB's devastating description of her: 'a lady who seems to have too many teeth and quite enough ideas'.

JACKSON, RICHARD. Wesleyan-Methodist minister stationed at Ledbury for 1830–1. Bible meetings were held at the village of Redmarley D'Abitot (*see* entry for 8 June 1831).

JAMES, REV. JOHN ANGELL, of Birmingham, a celebrated preacher.

JOHNSTONE, CAPT. JOHN of Mainstone Court, near Ledbury. Present at the Public dinner at The Feathers, Ledbury, to celebrate the return to Parliament of Mr Hoskins, MP, a staunch Reformer. This was the same dinner at which Bro distinguished himself. Brother of Lady Knowles, and lessee of part of Hope End land.

JONES, MRS G. Mother-in-law of Mr Biddulph's daughter Augusta Eleanor.

JONES, AUGUSTA, née Biddulph.

KENDRICK, WILLIAM. Local farmer, appointed by mortgagee's agent as Farm Bailiff at end of March, to supervise agricultural affairs at Hope End, pending the sale of the estate.

KNIBB, JAMES. Bookseller, High Street, Worcester. Had been declared bankrupt on 6 May 1831 and business carried on under official Assignees.

KNOWLES, CHARLOTTE LAURA (1804–93). Eldest daughter of Admiral Sir Charles and Lady Knowles. Her eldest brother Francis Charles, married Emma Pocock on 26 May 1831. The Knowleses had recently lived in Malvern, and it was while calling on them that EBB first saw HSB.

KNOWLES, LADY (née Charlotte Johnstone). Wife of Sir Charles Knowles.

MARIZET, M. DE. A French guest of the Martins.

MARTIN, JAMES (1778–1870). Member of the banking family. Married Julia (née Vignoles, 1793?–1867?). Lived at Old Colwall, adjacent to the Hope End estate. EBB frequently refers to Mrs Martin as 'icing me all over' and avers 'we do not amalgamate'. She kept up a correspondence with her until her death. It was Mrs Martin who invited her to Herefordshire in the 1850s—only to be refused with horror. There were three unmarried sisters of Mr Martin's living near Overbury Court, about fifteen miles from Hope End.

MUSHET, HENRIETTA (1802–65). Second child of David Mushet, metallurgist. An old friend of HSB, she sometimes acted as his amanuensis. They had a serious disagreement in 1832, which is hinted at obliquely in EBB's letters. (*EBB/HSB* pp. 178 ff.) She later married the Rev. George Roberts, Curate of Coleford.

MUSHET, MARGARET (1799–1885). Henrietta's elder sister.

PEYTON. The family lived at Barton Court, with Mrs Griffith. Nicholson and Eliza Peyton had nine children. Charlotte Peyton was Nicholson's sister.

An interesting footnote to the Peytons—although we do not know which of them is involved—can be added in Florence nearly twenty years later. In 1851 the Brownings were having trouble with their manservant, and 'the Peytons' who were leaving Florence, recommended their own man, Ferdinando Romagnoli. He stayed with the Brownings until Elizabeth's death, and incidentally married Wilson (EBB's maid) in 1855. Pen Browning, after his parents' deaths, took them both into his service. Wilson died in 1897, a widow, still with Pen in Venice.

EBB wrote to Mrs David Ogilvy: 'The Peytons are the cream of the milk of good kind people.'

PORSON, RICHARD. Classical scholar (1759–1808). ed. *Aeschyli Septem Contra Thebas* (Cambridge 1812), a work which EBB and Mr Boyd were much concerned with during the period of the Diary. HSB called EBB 'Porsonia' as a compliment to her abilities. He never called her 'Ba', disliking the sound of it. In later years he adopted the name 'Elibet' for her, forsaking the formal 'Miss Barrett'.

PRICE, MISS CAROLINE (1783?–1853) of Foxley, the only daughter of the late Sir Uvedale Price, Bt. She lived with her brother, Sir Robert (1786–1857) MP for the County of Hereford 1818–41, and for the City of Hereford 1845–56. He succeeded to the baronetcy upon the death of their father, in 1829. Foxley was eight miles from Hereford, and four miles from Kinnersley Castle.

PRICE, SIR UVEDALE, BT. (1747–1829). Author of *Essay on the Modern Pronounciation of the Greek and Latin Languages* (Oxford 1827). EBB made detailed comments on the proof sheets before publication. HSB, who agreed with Price's (as he was then) theories, wrote a letter about them to the Classical Journal (June 1828) pp. 325–7.

REID 'the mortgagees' agent in London, handling the sale of Hope End.

ROBERTS, REV. GEORGE. Married Henrietta Mushet.

SAUNDERS, MR. Probably the local blacksmith.

SMITH, MRS MARY ANN. Daughter of Dr Adam Clarke and a close friend of HSB for many years. HSB dedicated his *Select Passages* (1813) to her, in a poem 'To Myra', and did not reveal her identity until 1834. He suggested to EBB in her Wimpole Street days that she should correspond with her, but EBB tactfully refused, pleading 'weakness' and 'fatigue'. Mrs Smith was with HSB when he died, and EBB wrote to ask her for the return of her letters to him. She refused, and it was not until forty years later that Robert Browning secured possession. In an unpublished letter to Arabel, (1849), EBB wrote: '[Mrs Smith] is, we must all confess, a vulgar, coarse woman . . excellent in her peculiar way . . & [I] am grateful to her for her faithful affection to my dear friend Mr Boyd. Robert only sees the indelicacy of keeping my letters.' (Collection of Miss Myrtle and Col. R. A. Moulton-Barrett.)

SPOWERS, MR (1764–1841). Tutor in Greek to HSB.

STEERS, FRANCES (1797–1860) of the Well House, Malvern Wells. There was a William Steer who accommodated visitors taking the cure at the Holy Well, mentioned by the Rev. J. Barrett of Colwall (whether any relation to the Hope End Barretts is not known) in 1796. He lived at the Well House, and later opened Rock House, near Essington's hotel, in 1817, with private apartments, referred to in the Diary entry for 12 January, 1832. The spelling of the name is different, but William might well have been Frances's father. She gave lessons in drawing and music to Henrietta and frequently made sketches of Hope End. She became a member of the New Water Colour Society (later the Royal Institute) and fifty-nine of her pictures were exhibited between 1846 and 1860.

TRANT, MRS MARY, née Barrett, widow of James Trant, first cousin of EBB's paternal grandmother. She lived at South Lodge, a mile south of Ruby Cottage, and EBB would normally call there when she took the route via Little Malvern. It is evident that EBB did not like her. Her two sons, DOMINICK and HENRY, often visited Hope End and joined in family outings. Dominick, standing with his friend Francis Knowles, unsuccessfully contested the Parliamentary election at Shaftesbury in May 1831.

VALPY, ABRAHAM JOHN (1787–1854). London editor and publisher. One of his assistants was HSB's friend E. H. Barker. Despite HSB's opposition, Valpy did publish EBB's translation of *Prometheus Bound*, together with *Miscellaneous Poems*, in 1833.

WALL, MILLICENT. A close friend of Eliza Cliffe, whose family held the manor of Cradley, Herefordshire. She may have been connected with the two doctors, John Wall and his son Martin. Dr John analysed the water of the Holy Well, St Ann's Well and Chalybeate Spring and published an account of miraculous cures in *Experiments and Observations on the Malvern Waters* in 1757. His conclusion that there was very little mineral content in the waters invited the following couplet:

> The Malvern water, says Dr John Wall
> Is famed for containing just nothing at all.

A bitter feud between the families of the Walls and the Barretts started when Miss Wall, Miss Wall's uncle and Mr and Mrs Card secured a ticket of admission from Bentley (the agent) and attempted to walk round the house. In a letter to HSB EBB tells him that Bro told Lane loudly to turn them out of the house or he would do so himself, and they then walked along beside it, looking in 'at the windows of the tent-room & drawing room where my aunt was sitting', with 'a good deal of loud laughing and talking'.

WOOD, THE REV. JOHN, Minister of the Chapel in the Connexion of the Countess of Huntingdon, Malvern.

DIARY BY EBB
1831–2

ROBERT BROWNING TO ELIZABETH December 19, 1845

'Ba—that is you! I tried (more than wanted) *to call you* that *on Wednesday. I have a flower here—rather, a tree, a mimosa, which must be turned and turned . . so I turn your name to me, that side I have not last seen: you cannot tell how I feel glad that you will not part with the name—Barrett—seeing you have two of the same—and must always, moreover, remain my EBB-—'*

Saturday. June 4th. 1831. Hope End.

I wonder if I shall burn this sheet of paper like most others I have begun in the same way. To write a diary, I have thought of very often at far & near distances of time: but how could I write a diary without throwing upon paper my thoughts, all my thoughts—the thoughts of my heart as well as of my head?—& then how could I bear to look on *them* after they were written? Adam made fig leaves necessary for the mind, as well as for the body. And such *a* mind as I have!—So very exacting & exclusive & eager & head long—& *strong*—& so very very often *wrong*! Well! but I will write: I must write—& the oftener wrong I know myself to be, the less wrong I shall be in one thing—the less *vain* I shall be!—

Eliza Cliffe rode here today with the Miss Cranes—singing cranes! they sang like nightingales. We had luncheon with them; & after they went, we had a thunderstorm to ourselves. Such a thunderstorm! I lay down on Minny's bed, & grew hot & cold for myself & everybody near me, & many bodies not near me; viz for Papa & Bro who were out,—& for Mr. Boyd who is at Malvern where the storm was travelling. Arabel dreamt last night that *he* was dead, & that *I* was laughing! Foolish dream—& more foolish I who could think of it in the storm!— After the storm had gone off, the post came in. A letter expected from Mr. Boyd! A letter received from Mrs Boyd! "Mr. Boyd says that I was a true prophetess about the verses, but that he would rather talk to me on that subject." Something of the kind. The verses are mine entitled "Kings," & my prophecy was that he would not like them.* "He wd. rather talk to me on that subject." That means, he would rather not write to me on that subject—or perhaps on any other. I am beginning to be wrong already—*perhaps*! He has often spoken to me of his difficulties in getting some one to write

* Printed in *The Times* 31 May 1831.

for him—and yet "he would rather not!!" Why should those words stick in my throat like Amen in Macbeth's? There was a note too for Arabel from Annie. She has never answered *my* note—a note as affectionate as I could make it. No! not quite *as* affectionate; but *very* affectionate. "Dearest Annie;" I said, "may we not be as we have been"? No! we cannot. She has not written to say "Yes—we can". If she were not Mr. Boyd's daughter, should I love her as I do still? In that case, my answer to that question wd. be again "No! I cannot." How very very very unkindly she has behaved to me! I cannot bear to think of it: I wish she were *not* Mr Boyd's daughter; for then some of my feelings would not clash in the painful way they do now. Not that I wish to be at ease to dislike her. Oh no! I wd. not do that! But it is painful to be *longing* to love a person who will not be loved, or to *love* a person who repays your love with such coldness—such unkindness!— And then Mr. Boyd likes me to invite her here. How can *I* like it, except for his sake, when she acts towards me as she does? I hope she may go to Sir John Gibbons's; for then I shall be in no difficulty about inviting her here. *I* would invite her willingly, & have her here as long as she could be happy here, even if this unkindness of hers were to be dashed,—cold as it is, against the warmest pulses of my heart every hour —but Henrietta does not like her being here; & Bummy will not like it; & I shall have a thousand difficulties as usual to contend with. Now I must go to dress for dinner.

Annie sends her love to me in her note to Arabel, but says afterwards that she wonders how I could *publish* such horrible verses, & that some of those on Warren's Blacking are as good.[1] I am *not angry* at her saying so. But considering these words of hers, together with other words of hers,— Oh I feel how it is!— What is my sin? Having *been* anxious, & *appeared* anxious for Mr. Boyd to remain near me. Could I help appearing so when I was so? Could I help *being* so? Had I felt a less strong regard for him, I should neither have *been* nor *appeared*: and now I should be bitterly regretting that they stayed longer in this neighbourhood. But I *cannot* regret it, as it is!— I do regret having printed those verses. Mr. Boyd does not like them: & I *suspect* that his regard for me is dependant on his literary estimation of me, & not great enough, for me to afford the loss of any part of it. We shall see!—& perhaps we shall feel!—

Taylor told Papa today that Bro was the best speaker at the Reform dinner last Tuesday,[2] & that considering the youth of the speaker, he could not have expected so much from him. Papa seemed pleased as he repeated it to us. Dear Papa! dear Bro!—

Sunday 5th. June

I went to church with Bummy & Arabel in our wheelbarrow; & heard such singing—& such preaching. Alas for my ears & understanding! And alas for Mrs. Peyton's eyes, which were red in consequence of the sermon. How *affected* she must have been! There seemed to me to be far more bathos than pathos in Mr. Barnaby's discourse: but it only lasted ten minutes, & so I forgive him *my* share of the weariness.

No letters today. I sent a note written last night, to Mrs. Boyd, in which I send my love to Annie, & make no observations. Arabel sent a note to Annie reproaching her for unkindness to me; & would not let me see it. What will the effect be? Nothing good I am afraid, & I am afraid something bad. If Annie does not answer it, Arabel says she will not go to see her on Thursday,—a day fixed for our going to Malvern. Fudge! said Mr. Burchell![1] Annie will *not* answer it: & Arabel *will* go to see her.

We were a part of Mr. Curzon's congregation at the gate. Able sermon—but nothing eloquent—nothing to make me *glow*. Met the Cliffes & Cranes at the gate. *Settled* —that Eliza shd. come here on Thursday to ride with us to Malvern, & bring a poney for Henrietta. Henrietta & Bummy are going to hear Miss Steers play.

I read some of Chrysostom's commentary on the Ephesians. I am getting tired of this commentary. Such underground dark passages before you get at anything worth standing to look at! Very eloquent sometimes: but such a monotony & lengthiness!— Sunday is not a reading day with me. Driving to church—driving back again—driving to chapel—driving back again—& prayers three times at home besides! All that fills up the day—except the few interstices between the intersections. Mr. Curzon told me that he saw Mr. Boyd on Friday evening, & sate an hour & a half with him.

Monday. June 6th.

I have heard this morning that Kenrick had another letter from that Reid on Thursday, & that instead of leaving off working on Papa's ground, he has begun to weed the wheat. No other particulars known yet. Suppose we should go after all:—Oh, I *will* not think of it! Papa's spirits are very good: & I am not presentimental—at least I think not! If we do go—why then I have more to suffer; that is all! —& Annie will repent her unkindness—& Mr. Boyd—what will *he* do? Will he be sorry—very sorry? Or will he only "regret" it, as I do when I decline an invitation I dont care about? But I ought not to think so much of myself. Poor Papa! *He* is the person to be thought of, & felt for!—

No letters. . . . Walked out with Bummy & Arabel. Read. Henrietta on the heath. I have heard that Kenrick went today into the garden! I mentioned his hoeing the wheat to Bummy, who expressed herself "vexed at it." She did however say that she *knew* something was doing. I wish *I* knew what it was! A note came from Eliza Cliffe enquiring about "our hopes & fears"; & Bummy being in the room, I was obliged or fancied myself obliged to read part of it. Bummy angry—indignant at my allowing Eliza to mention the subject to me! I angry on the other hand. I went into Bummy's room afterwards to make friends. Soon made. Dear Bummy expressed her affection for me. Was the expression of mine necessary? No! it was not necessary *to be made*; but it was necessary for *me to make it*. Papa in good spirits, & playing at cricket with the boys. He reports more commendation of Bro's speech. I wish I had heard it. Papa pleased—& I pleased, of course.

Tuesday. June 7th.

No letters again! It is quite clear that the "something bad" has been the result of Arabel's letter to Annie. Arabel certainly used one of her own feathers in writing it—one way of calling her a *goose*!— There will be no letter tomorrow: and I shall dread the interview on Thursday, not only on account of Annie, but Mrs. Boyd. And as to Mr. Boyd, even *he* may blame me for letting Arabel again turn up the green sod which had been turned down; tho' there was not a chance of its ever taking root. I let Arabel do it: because I could not *let* her *from* doing it. Arabel loves me; & *would* shew that she loves me. I wish she had not, in this instance.

Papa has gone to the Newent Bible meeting: & Bro & Sam, Stormy Georgie & Henry, to the Bosbury fishing brook. Bummy Henrietta Arabel & I dined at one; & then Bummy Arabel & I went in the wheelbarrow to the Whyche. We walked thro' the rocky passage, & sate down on the Worcestershire side of the hill. Such a sight! Such a *sea* of land: the sunshine throwing its light; & the clouds, their shadows, upon it! *Sublime* sight, I must still call it!— I looked along the Great Malvern road. Shall I ever travel along it again? Not with the same feelings! & I had some sad ones in thinking so: tho' I would not have it otherwise. I ran along the walk to *see* if I could *see* Ruby Cottage. No! it was too far off. We returned thro the Whyche: & I climbed the low hill, & Arabel the high one; & Bummy sate below each of us. I looked on each side of the elevated place where I sate. Herefordshire all hill & wood—undulating & broken ground!—Worcestershire throwing out a grand unbroken extent,—& more than Worcestershire, to the horizon! One, prospect attracting the eye, by picturesqueness: the other the mind,—by sublimity. *My* mind seemed spread north south east & west over the surface of those extended lands: and, to gather it up again into its usual compass, was an effort. If I had stayed there another half hour, I should have made verses —or shed tears: and if some circumstances had not happened, those tears wd. have had a different character—they wd. have been *bitter* tears. As it is, Malvern is associated still with happiness: & I do like to feel myself there.

I dreamt last night,—for night dreams are as well worth recording as day dreams,—that I was re-writing the Warren-blacking lines,—& inserted in some part of them the following—

> Fame o'er him flashed her meteor wing—
> And *he*—he was a King.

What king I was writing of, is out of my head. They caught no fish at Bosbury. Read as usual. Papa walked eleven miles.

Wednesday. June 8th.

No letters again. The "something bad" is certain. Arabel wrote to Annie, enclosing a note to Miss Steers from Henrietta. A good pretext for writing! for writing her wonder at the silence, her disappointment at it, & her intention of no more recurring to the subject. This is the best way. Recurring to the subject can avail nothing: and five words explain everything—*Annie does not love me*. I wish she were not Mr. Boyd's daughter: and I almost wish that I were not going to Malvern tomorrow. Oh no! not even *almost*! I meant, "I almost *thought* I wished it"! Why should I mind seeing Annie? Why should I feel embarrassed? What have I done to be embarrassed about? At any rate Mr. Boyd will be glad to see me: & nothing, except his not being so, could make me less glad to see *him*.

Bro dined at the Bartons. Papa arrived at home, just before he did, from the Redmarley Bible meeting. Papa's

Saturday.
June 4th. 1831. Hope End.

I wonder if I shall burn this sheet of paper
like most others I have begun in the same way.
To write a diary, I have thought of very often
at far & near distances of time: but how
could I write a diary without throwing upon
paper my thoughts, all my thoughts — the
thoughts of my heart as well as of my head?
& then how could I bear to look on them
after they were written? Adam made figleaves
necessary for the mind, as well as for the
body. And such a mind as I have! —
So very exacting & exclusive & eager &
headlong — & strong — & so very very often wrong! —
Well! but I will write: I must write.

Facsimile of the Entry of 4 June 1831

Ruby Cottage, date and artist unknown
Turnpike on the road to Ledbury, date and artist unknown

account of the discussion between himself & Mr. Jackson the Wesleyan Minister. I said as little as I could; thro' a recollection of past circumstances: but when Bummy expressed a general dislike towards the *Methodists*, it would have been something worse than cowardice in me, to have said nothing. Read as usual.

Thursday June 9th.

Eliza Cliffe & two ponies arrived immediately after breakfast; & we set off for Malvern at about half past ten: Henrietta & Eliza riding; Bummy Arabel & I in the wheelbarrow. I was nervous about Annie & everybody at Ruby Cottage all the way there. No use in it—"thinks I to myself". They drove me nearly to the gate, & then turning back, left me to make my own debut. I could scarcely stand *debout*. Annie, espied in the garden, walked away on catching a glimpse of the carriage. I was shewn into the drawing room—'sola cum sola'!—& was, while I was *consternating* myself, desired to go into Mrs. Boyd's bedroom. She dressing. To my astonishment, she told me that Annie was going that day,—& she herself as her companion,—to Sir John Gibbons!! In the midst of our talking, into the room came Annie. Cool reception—on *her* part I mean. Very very cool manner! Mrs. Boyd sent her in to Mr. Boyd to apprize him of my arrival; & in a few minutes, he was ready to see me. When I got into the room, I was at ease in one moment, & in a humour to forget all the worrying out of it. With regard to my Warren Blacking verses he told me, that he could not see the meaning of the line ending each verse?—& my explanation seemed to make darkness darker. He said besides that there was nothing of my usual poetical manner in them: but that, as he was aware of the inequalities of the productions of people of talent, there was one thing which surprised him more than my having written them; tho' *that had* surprised him. I guessed the one thing to be, my having published them. "No! you know, I am always blunt —I am very much surprised at the Times Newspaper having received them". He hoped that I had not blamed him for not writing to me! Mrs. B had seemed so much occupied, lately!

We argued as to whether engraving or painting was the superior art. Agreed at last—that if we compared the engraver & the painter who was a mere copyist, the engraver should stand first: but that the original painter should stand before the engraver. Talked of Reform. . . . The rain came on; & as my party was thus detained at Great Malvern until six o'clock, I in the meanwhile, dined *superficially* with Mrs. Boyd, that Mr. Boyd might not be detained from his dinner by my being in the room. After dinner, I went back again to him. Talked of Blomfield's Septem apud Thebas,[1] which I have ordered from Worcester, to read with him. Mrs. Boyd's carriage, & our wheelbarrow at the door at the same time. She is to remain away a week; & Mr. Boyd asked me to go to see him in the interim. Monday or Tuesday—cant you fix Monday? I agreed to it. Annie kissed me *affectionately* at parting; & when I asked her to let *us* hear sometimes from her, she said she would—that is, if I have time!— We drove home at seven, in a pouring *rain*: Eliza dined & slept here. . . . We talked a little; & *I* talked *boldly* about the Wesleyans.

Friday. June 10.

As I heard last night that Bummy had agreed to visit Miss Steers again on Tuesday evening, I saw it was impossible to take the carriage to Malvern on Monday besides. Therefore I wrote four lines in a text hand that Mr. Boyd's servants might read them to him, saying that I could not be with him until Tuesday. . . .

How unhappy I seem on the brink of being! While Eliza Bummy & I were sitting in the drawing room, talking & singing, in came Lane. He wished to speak with Bummy. She went out; & I felt breathless—dreading to hear something past supporting. In the meantime Arabel came into the room, & told us that a Gentleman a Lady & a little girl had arrived to see the house. Bummy returned, & pretended to know nothing about it. I ran up stairs,—& trembled until now. I hear that Bummy has sent Lane up to Papa! Those people are in the dining room. I will pray now. Will not our Father who is in Heaven, hear prayer for His Son's sake. And has he not often & often heard mine? Yes! & when I felt in more *certain* sorrow than I do at this moment—

I can take breath again. The people are gone. Their message thro' Lane to Papa was, that they were sent by Mr. Reid to see the house. Papa's message to them was—that nobody belonging to Mr. Reid was here to show them the house. So they went away. I hear that their name is Brydges, & that they have come from Canonfrome (how is the word spelt?)—& that their servant spoke to ours of having seen Hope End advertised to be sold this month. How is it to be? Are we really to go? I am sick at heart about it; but will hope on still. Something may be doing, still. Papa in bad spirits at dinner. Bro said something of my note to Mr. Boyd, which made Papa exclaim "What! you were there yesterday—& did you write today—"? So then I explained how he had wished me to go to see him during Mrs. Boyd's absence; & how I had first agreed to go on Monday, & afterwards put it off. No objections made. Papa is *not* in good spirits today. If *they* dont go to Malvern on Monday, *I* must & will do so by myself.

Saturday. June 11.

Sam told me that Hope End is advertised in the Sun newspaper, to be sold in August—no name, but a full description. He & Bro heard it yesterday from Henry Trant! I begged him to tell nobody, & to let me tell Bummy. Ran down stairs & found Bummy in the drawing room by herself. Told her. She shed tears—we both shed tears! When will tears cease to be shed? She seems to fear the worst: but mentioned that Papa had written to [Uncle] Sam, who, he says, is *able* to assist him. If he *is* able, he *is* willing—if he is still *Sam*! So there may still be hope in that quarter. There is fear in every other. In every other? Can I not still look unto the *hill* from whence cometh my *hope*?[1] That hope is a hope of spiritual blessing; but I have found & known it to be one of temporal comfort also! Walked out with Bummy & Arabel, on the bank on the other side of the water. Strangers may soon walk there, with other feelings than mine. Bummy asked why I seemed grave. I *felt* grave. Read as I have often done lately, not for the pleasure of thinking: but for the comfort of *not* thinking. Papa in better spirits. How often I thought of Mr. Boyd today! He is the only person in this neighbourhood, whom it will affect my *happiness* to leave. I shall be very *sorry* to leave Eliza Cliffe but not unhappy. Why did I scratch that out?— Let me be honest, if I cant be wise!

Sunday. June 12th.

Went to church in the wheelbarrow with Henrietta,—Henry driving. . . . Eliza rode home with us, & walked down to the school with Henrietta at half past two; while Bummy Arabel & I were wheeled in the wheelbarrow. Papa walked by our side. He *seems* in better spirits. . . .

Ever since hearing what I heard yesterday, I have been thinking—shall I ask Mr. Boyd if he *will* endeavour to go where we go, in the case of our going at all? It wd. be a comfort to me to know if he would make the endeavour; & yet after my past "intrusions", I scarcely like asking. And yet (again) did he not tell me, that if I *had* left Hope End, he "would have been happier at Cheltenham than at Malvern, for one reason—because at Cheltenham there was nothing to remind him of my going to see him". Must he not care a good deal for me, to feel *that*? And in the case of his caring *at all* for me, must he not wish, for his own sake, to live near me, wherever I am? I shall never get at any certainty, by this interrogative system. Hope says one thing; & Fear, another, in reply!— If we do leave this dear place, what a consolation it wd. be to me, *not* to leave besides, the dearest & most valued friend I have in the world!!— But God's will be done in all things. I wish those words were as clearly written in my heart, as on my paper —in spite of my alledged illegibility! . . . Henrietta told Eliza that they intended not to go to Miss Steers's on Tuesday; so . . . I shall go by myself to Malvern! After dinner Papa & we all walked hat-less out of the hall-door, & he led us among the shrubs, directing our attention, now to one, now to another. Is this "a good sign"? I dont know. He is not in good spirits; & I am not in great ones. Now I am going down to prayers! bell ringing!— Read nothing but the Bible today.

Monday. June 13th.

The gnats kept Arabel & me & half the house besides up half the night: witness my swelled finger—witness this *eccentric* writing. I will *gnat* sleep in that room again, until the weather changes. I will go into the Bamboo room. No letters on Monday, & if it had been Tuesday, I should have expected none. Mr. Boyd cant write, & nobody else will. Mr. Boyd cant write? I wish he would try to write with a pencil. Shall I ask him? How I should like to receive from him an undictated letter!— Henrietta on the heath. Bummy Arabel & I went out to walk, & sate for a long time on the rock, where we were joined by Henrietta. They have determined on not going to Miss Steers's.

Tuesday. June 14th.

Henry drove me to Malvern, & Daisy filled as much as he could of the back seat in the wheelbarrow. Papa in bad spirits at breakfast. After breakfast we were about to set off —when in consequence of Papa asking me to wait for something inaudible, I sent Henry in to the library, to ask what I was to wait for. Bummy & Papa there. "What were they doing"? said Arabel. "Crying"—replied Henry. I would not, could not wait. If there is anything to hear, it *must* be something painful: & then I shall ("*un man* myself", I was going to say) unfit myself for talking to Mr. Boyd. That was my "Thinks I to myself"—so we drove off. I got to Ruby Cottage before twelve. Miss Hurd was there,—& I was shown into the dining room, to wait while she read some letters to Mr. Boyd. Annoyed!— Took up Stewart's Resurrection, with notes in Mr. Boyd's handwriting. The poetry seems super-erogat*orily* written,—as far as words are concerned, but if it had been admirable, I was in a nil admiraris humour. Miss Hurd came to say that Mr. Boyd was ready for me. I dont like her. Found him in the drawing room, where he spends part of every day "now that Mrs. Boyd is absent". . . . [I] read as well as I could out of the Septem Apud Thebas, which I began today in his Porson's edition. Read 78 lines. I do like reading with him. He was annoyed by my note; & because I had said in it that "perhaps I could not go to see him until the evening", he had fancied that I was to be engaged during the morning by visiting Miss Wall at Gt Malvern in consequence of a request from Eliza Cliffe!!! Did *my* fancy ever take me so far . . . wrong? Very often! He said that he had felt "*I* wd. not have visited any one who had behaved about Miss Barrett, as Miss Wall has behaved about us". It is amusing to think that he could think so!— As if he were likely by *any* behaviour, to prove a regard equal to, or greater than, the regard I feel towards him!— Impossible —at least as feelings & conduct go at present. Talked of Mr. Curzon—Calvinism—Catholicism—Annie. A charge against Arabel with reference to the latter, warded off by me. Some talking of her coldness to me—attributed by Mr. Boyd, to jealousy of Eliza. Fudge, said Mr. Burchell.— No love—no jealousy! Some talking of Annie abstractedly & Miss Wall's opinion of her!—& my opinion of her manners. Told him of the unending uncertainty about Hope End. He seemed interested in what I said—& "*sorry*"! Preached Christian resignation & philosophy to me; & wondered how I could show as little as I did at Woodland

Lodge when the subject of our leaving Hope End was agitated: He had been told that I had shed tears & seemed much distressed. My tears did not fall then *because I was about to leave Hope End*; and that he should think so, brought them again into my eyes. Mrs. Boyd will come back, *probably*, she said in her letter at the end of this week. . . . I left him at 20 minutes to six—too late to call on Mrs. Trant. Henry & Daisy had been running & having luncheon on the hills. Got home in time for dinner, & heard nothing about the conference. Only that more people had been here to see the place, & were sent away by Bummy. Merick's from Ross.

Wednesday. June 15

Heard this morning that Papa yesterday discharged his women, & told them that they might work for Kenrick but must not expect him to pay them for it. They are all in the garden with Daly, Jack Cook, & a man employed by Kenrick. I will never go there again; unless we are to stay *really*. Sam has come into my room to say that Papa has called Bro down stairs, & is still speaking with him.

My hand & heart trembled as I wrote those last words: but nothing of the conference has transpired, except Bro's being sent to Ledbury. What for, I dont know. "What for" is an unanswerable question just now. Papa did not go out of the house until one; & talked a good deal with Bummy in the library.

The Cliffes & Mrs. Best passed several hours here, in consequence of attraction & repulsion, from us & an anticipated thunderstorm. Mrs. Best is going to send me a little tract of hers on Eden, in ms.—& I am to say exactly what I think of it. I hope I may be able to *say* civilly & conscientiously at the same time. Eliza told us, when I asked her why she looked grave, that she had seen Hope End advertised in the Worcester Herald: and I have since heard that the Hereford Journal has the same advertisement. Oh we shall certainly go. There can be no doubt about it: and

if some of my feelings were armed "in complete steel,"*
I should bear it better. I must fix my eyes upon it, & learn to bear the contemplation of it, by God's teaching. If Mr. Boyd were likely to follow us, the bearing would be a less hard task—but I must not lean too many of my hopes on that if. I wd. rather trust to another if—for *if* he cared for me as I care for him, he could speak & act only in one way. The Cliffes brought me The Seven Cheifs which Mrs. Best had ordered from Worcester at my request; and I have been reading over again what I read with him yesterday, & writing in the margin such remarks of his as I could remember. The last day's reading with him, must soon come, even if it be not *past*—but I cant bear to think *that*!—He gave me yesterday his letter from Mr. Barker, to read. Mr. Barker intends "soon to have the pleasure of writing to Miss Barrett". Miss Barrett never expected to hear from him again.

I did not go out to day. I had another kind of exercise in *crying*, this evening! I could not help thinking of yesterday which certainly does not "look backward with a smile" & of a thousand tomorrows which may not wear one.

Miss Penelope Biddulph called here with a Mr. Bowers—a vulgarissimus who said "no thank you Miss" to me!—Now I must go down to tea. Papa's spirits were good at dinner today.

Thursday. June 16th

Papa was in very good spirits today at breakfast, most undoubtedly. He told Bro to put the clock half an hour more forward; & this sent my hopes forward . . a little way. Would he think about altering the clock, if it were likely to strike so seldom before we are removed for ever from its sound?? I heard Stormy & Georgie read Homer & Xenophon—*as usual*,—tho' I have not yet commemorated them here—& I prepared a part of the first choral ode of

* John Milton's *Comus*: 'Tis chastity my brother, chastity: / She that has that, is clad in compleat steel.'

the Seven Chiefs for Mr. Boyd. He seemed to wish me to "sound dreadful note of *preparation*" before I read Æschylus with him in future; as in this way, the benefit to myself is likely to be greater. I looked also at the Greek verbs, which he wishes me to be more accurate about. After all, I am annoyed & discontented & disappointed by Mr. Boyd. He talked so *cooly* about our leaving Hope End—seemed so little disturbed by it—& that little, more on my account, than his own. I can bear anything from anybody better than coldness from some people—and coldness, coldness, coldness, is what I have to bear from them. If they could communicate a portion of this frigidity to *me*, they would reconcile me to its existence. The society of that Miss Hurd is as much valued as mine—as much! *at least, as much*! and yet is it probable or possible that her friendship is like my friendship? Friendship!—the word makes me yearn for the time, the past time, when it was not familiar to my ear!— Abused & vain word!—

Walked out with Bummy H & A half way down the road & round the walks till I was tired. Sate in the ice house & talked of the garden & all the painful et caetera. Papa in good spirits at dinner. The wholesale *stock* of the Biddulphs called half an hour before dinner, but was not unpacked. Henrietta spoke to them at the door!—

On reading what I have written . . . I am more than half ashamed of it. I have certainly *no reason* for accusing Miss Hurd of being as much liked by Mr. B as I am; & if I had the *reason*, I should be still without the *right*. And as to coldness—Mr. Boyd used not to be cold to me! Had he been so, I should not have thought him so on Tuesday. The fact is—the greatest regard, *far* the greatest, is on my side:—or rather the fact is—my disposition is far too exclusive & exacting. Both those facts are *operative* facts. When will they cease to be so?— Read, as I do every day, seven chapters of Scripture. My heart & mind are not affected by this exercise as they should be—witness what I have written today. I would erase every line of it, could I annihilate the *feelings*, together with the description of them; but, since I cannot, let the description pass! That Friendship should fade away before my eyes, as Fame did in my poetical vision, is too painful! And that the "skeleton" of Friendship . . . but I am getting wrong again! Oh I never never should have begun this journal!— No one should write journals, who is not wiser, on a hundred points, than I am! & stronger, on a thousand!—

Friday. June 17th.

Papa was in very good spirits at breakfast this morning; but when I observed it to Bummy, I saw plainly from her manner, that there was no happy cause for them. Hope is all in vain!— We shall leave this place!—& all that is dear, *in it*, & *near it*!— Where shall we go? To Brighton? To the neighbourhood of London? Anywhere but in those suburbs!— Anywhere where there can be a chance of my having at some time, dear Mr. Boyd's society. And yet is there any chance of *that*, anywhere, for me? . . .

After dinner, Papa unfortunately walked *after* me out of the room, because like "good Madam Blaize,"[1] I walked out *before* Papa. The consequence of this was a critique on my down-at-heel shoes; & the end of that, was, my being sent out of the drawing room to put on another pair. So while Anne is mending the only pair I have in the world I am doing my best to write nonsense & catch cold without any. I dreamt last night that I was staying at Mr. Boyd's house. Almost before the *tail* of the dream was out of sight, —& certainly before my eyes were *quite* open, I said "Never again!" I was too right. Never, never again!—

Very busy today. Reading Aeschylus & learning the verb *τυπτω** This is being *et Caesar et nullus*, [both Caesar and nobody], at once!— But nobody ever was so ungrammatical in Greek as I am, since Greek was spoken or written in any way. Tea is ready; so I must go—or something besides the heels of my shoes will be found fault with.

* To beat or smite. This verb was the grammarian's delight.

Saturday. June 18th.

Such a day! such a miserable day!— After breakfast which past as breakfasts usually do, I sate down in my arm chair to put the verbs in *μι* in *me*. Then Arabel announced Eliza Cliffe; then I ran down stairs to bring her up stairs; then she began to paint at my picture—& *then* the door bell rang! Those Brydges's come back again to see the house!— Oh to hear their feet walking all over it—even up stairs— even to my very door!— Arabel locked it, & burst into tears! And I—the tears which ran down my cheeks, seemed scarcely to unparalyze me: I felt stone everywhere except in my heart! Well! they went away; & Arabel went out of the room; & Eliza & I sate silent for about an hour. Then Bummy came into the room,—& tho' I tried to speak & seem as if I knew nothing, I could not!— Oh I *could not*! She said that Papa was going to London on Monday to settle everything, that there was no cause for uneasiness, (said *before* & *for* Eliza Cliffe) & that Eliza must promise to mention nothing of this annoying visit, to Mrs. Cliffe.

We went down to luncheon; & when Eliza had run up stairs (to seem out of the way) to mix her colours, Bummy H A & I talked of what had happened with melancholy voices. Bummy told us that Papa knew that it wd. happen, —that it cd. not be avoided,—that those London people had been enraged at the Meyricks having been turned away the other day,—that the place must be *seen* until the business is settled. James is to meet Papa in London. [Uncle] Sam has not noticed his letter!— Is Sam still Sam? What a wretched day we have indeed had! Every nerve in my body seems relaxed; & the trembling has scarcely yet gone out of my knees. But as Papa is going to London, something may still be done. This is the *last* effort!— He was in tolerably good spirits at dinner. I wish I had been at Malvern today! Eliza told me that Miss Steers walks out with Mr. Boyd whenever she can. So he is not as considerate to *her* as he once was to another person!! He is not afraid of disgracing *her* by his "slovenly appearance"!!

Will Papa be angry with Lane for showing the house to those people? He told him that if they wished to see it, they might see it; but that he would not make himself a party to its being shown, by allowing any one belonging to him, to show it. Lane certainly ought to have been passive. Papa was annoyed at Eliza being here today: but he wd. not let Bummy send her away, for fear Mrs. Cliffe should hear of after circumstances, & suspect him of being ashamed of them. Wrote to Knibb to propose an exchange of some useless books of mine.

Talked in the evening of my poem—that is, Papa talked to me about it. He said of the essay on Mind that the more he read it, the more he liked it. He advised me not to put "By the author of the Essay on Mind" on the title page of the 1st. edition of my next poem,—on account of my late intermeddling with living characters. If it comes to a 2d. edition I can do so.— Lane was right in what he did. Papa had given him other orders.

Sunday June 19th.

A far pleasanter day than yesterday. We did not go to church,—because—I don't know what. One couldn't,—& another would'nt, which was as effective. Papa in good spirits. Bummy told us that she had told him about our knowing of his going to London. "And what did they say," was his question. "They were very glad of it"!— Now I was half sorry to hear of her having said *that*; and yet our present circumstances are certainly such as must make us glad even of his absence, if by being absent, he can in any way change those circumstances. At any rate it is a last effort; & shd. be made!—

We walked down to the gate, & heard a substitute for Mr. Curzon. Not a bad sermon; . . . Read the Bible, & Horne on its critical study. I do not think enough of the love of God, graciously as it has been manifested to me. My thoughts are wandering ungrateful thoughts. How strange it is, that *I*, who can feel so very gratefully towards those who benefit me partially, & often from interested motives, (as one human being must benefit another)—, that *I*, should be so cold & lacking in thanksgiving towards Him who has given me *all*!— And how yet stranger, that in the midst of professed thankgiving unto this *unweary* benefactor, my mind should be turning towards some who seem weary of loving me & doing me good!— Oh Thou who lovest for ever the being Thou hast once loved,—oh Thou who doest good unto the unthankful & unworthy!—teach me to love Thee better—teach me to think of Thee more!—

. . . Sent up stairs again, on account of a hole in my stocking. Mem—to show a fair pair of heels whenever I go *into* the drawing room instead of when I go *out* of it!— Shoes & stockings have got me into scrapes lately; and yet I am not usually *fundamentally* untidy. . . . The last evening with dearest Papa!— He in good spirits.

Monday—June 20th.

Papa's last breakfast with us until his return; therefore a sad one— He however in apparently good spirits; tho' *not very* good! After breakfast I began to chew the cud of such *bitter* thoughts; about Papa's going away, & about our going away,—that I was glad to begin to *graze*, instead, on the verbs in *μι*. I have learnt them & *τυπτω*, too perfectly for Georgie to puzzle me, as I begged him to try to do when he came to read Greek with me this morning. Felt rather triumphant—no! not *rather* triumphant,—afterwards. It certainly was disgraceful that I who can read Greek with some degree of fluency, should have been such & so long an ignoramus about the verbs. And besides, I have done what *Mr. Boyd wished*; & that is, of itself, a pleasant feeling.

Sam called up at my window between three & four, to say that Papa had come down from the farm; so I went down stairs. But we sate in the drawing room (all but Bummy) while he dined in the dining room. What was the use of taking our crying faces in to him? He came to us &

kissed us before he went. "May God bless you" he said! May God bless *him*—dearest Papa—in all temporal & spiritual blessing!

Now that the parting is over, I am very glad he is gone. It is right, & it will be consolatory, to make every effort in this unhappy business; whatever the result may be. From Bummy's manner, I plainly see that he is not, & she is not, & we ought not to be, sanguine. But I am glad he is gone; & have now to long for him to come back!

We had not dinner today. Bummy A H & I had tea instead, at six o'clock; and afterwards we walked backwards & forwards on the bank opposite the drawing room windows. Such a lovely *green* evening! We sate down near the little island, & talked; & Bummy proposed that I shd. go to Malvern tomorrow. Of course I agreed! & of course I am pleased to think of going. I am going immediately after breakfast, & must be back to drink tea with them at six o clock,—& Bummy says that if I do not dine there I shall not go again. I hope Mr. Boyd will ask me to dine with him; & that Mrs Boyd may not be arrived; & that Miss Hurd may not be there!— There are *three wishes*; & every one of them as foolish as the black pudding!—

Quaere. Is it civil in me to go away tomorrow when Eliza is coming here?

Tuesday. June 21st.

Two of my wishes were gained: but I must commencer par le commencement. Henry drove me to Malvern; & Daisy & Sette took their inside places with me & a packet of bread & cheese. We set off at about half past ten—arrived at Mrs. Trant's, where I got out. Talked a little of Papa's going & our going; & Mrs. Trant expressed herself hurt by Bummys repelling manner when she asked some question on *the subject*. *Hurt*! If you break stone into dust, you do not *hurt* it!— I resolved on trying to persuade Mrs. Trant to call on Mrs. Boyd—did all that I could—said all that I could—begged her for *my* sake—all in vain!— She "intended no incivility to Mrs. Boyd"—"was a bad visitor"—"did not give dinners"—& "could not bear saying *how do you do* whenever she went out"—& besides "Mr. Boyd could not bear a noise"—& in short she would not go. I was & am provoked about it; & think Mrs. Trant . . what I have long thought her. Sette & Daisy I left there; & was driven on to Mr. Boyd's by Henry. *Mrs. Boyd not arrived*—Huzza!— The servent introduced me into the drawing room—"Miss Barrett is come Sir"— "Miss Barrett—how did she come?" I think there was an expression of pleasure in his countenance, tho' he did not know that I was by to see it. I am sure he received me with pleasure. We had not talked for ten minutes when that Miss Hurd was announced. "Miss H wishes to know Sir if she is to wait, or to go back on the donkey". "Ask Miss H to go into the next room". So of course as the conference was to be *secret*, *I* begged to go into the next room, & Mr. Boyd agreed, observing that he wished me to bring Barker's Lexicon out of it. I went away very quickly, & shut the door, & sate down, thinking little enough of Barker's Lexicon. In five minutes or less, Miss H desired me to "*please to go* in to Mr. Boyd!" Vulgar girl!— And yet—! Of course I regretted to Mr. Boyd that I should be the cause of his sending Miss H away. "She can come another day," was his only answer!— I wonder on how many days she comes, & on how many other days he wd. *like* her to come!— Well—but we began to read the Seven Chiefs out of Blomfield's edition; & were very happy. Presently Miss Steers called, & was admitted. She brought back my poem which Mr. Boyd had lent her, of which she said that she could not say all she thought, on account of my presence. In a few minutes she got up to go—she wd. not disturb us any more: but Mr. Boyd begged her to stay a little longer. Mr. B's begging annoyed me rather. Soon annoyed—*you know*; I shd. say, if writing for any other person's eyes but mine: as it is,—"soon annoyed—*I know*". Mr. Boyd attacked me & made Miss Steers attack me on the subject of science standing higher in the scale of intellect than poetry. We disputed amicably tho' animatedly. Miss Steers ended by being inconsistent, & agreeing with my poem & me, on the subject of a poet deriving more exalted enjoyment from nature than the painter or man of science. Mr. Boyd called it "absolute nonsense." After talking a little more on French poetry, Miss Steers not only got up to go, but did positively go. And when she was gone, Mr. Boyd said—"I hope you did not think that I wished Miss Steers to stay for my own sake. I was quite disinterested about it—" & then he went on to say that he had fancied it would please her to talk longer with me. So *that* annoyance vanished away: and for the thousand & first time I owned myself (to myself) a fool. He asked me to have luncheon: and I asked him to have dinner. "Not while you are here". "But I am going to stay later". Upon this he asked me to dine with him; & upon that, I agreed to do so. We read until four; & then went into *his* room, & dined very comfortably. And after dinner I tried to puzzle his memory in the oration on Eutropius, by reading two words here & there dodgingly. Puzzling him was out of the question; but cheating him was not; so I turned to another part of the book & read two words there!— He thought & thought; & then I laughed, & betrayed myself. Then I examined him in Lucan: & there he was not so omnipotent. After this, we adjourned to the drawing room, & I read the newspaper to him for a few minutes before & after the carriage came. I left him at past six— A happy day!—

Think of those boys having had nothing to eat all day—of their leaving their cheese & bread & Mrs. Trant's,—& getting nothing instead of it!— But they were only hungry —not ill!— We arrived at home at seven; & found tea in waiting. Nobody angry in spite of somebody deserving it. After tea, I walked out a little with Bummy Henrietta & Arabel; & talked of Mr. Boyd—& tired myself not with talking but walking. Thoroughly tired when I went to bed. . . . Mr. Boyd seemed interested in what I said of Hope End, & Papa going to London. He asked me if there was any chance of Hope End being *let* to Papa, & of our living there even in the case of its becoming another person's purchase. As he was hearing my answer, I looked to see if he seemed sorry, but his countenance said nothing decidedly.

I mentioned the possibility of Henry walking out with him while "I might amuse myself by reading". "And *you* stay here! Oh no! I wd. not do that." "Indeed I would not mind it." "But *I* wd. mind it." I liked that answer. Certainly I had a pleasant day. I found a parcel on my return directed by Papa to me. Opened it in a fright. Six pairs of black silk stockings sent by him from Cheltenham; & one line in pencil from him, to say that he intended to sleep there & proceed to London on the next day. My own dear kind Papa!— How very very kind to think of me & my pedestals at such a time!— How I ought to love him!— *ought*!—how I *do*!—

Eliza did not come today. I took my sketch of Mr. Boyd with me, & half spoilt it, instead of improving it.

Wednesday. June 22.

Very soon after breakfast Eliza Cliffe came; but still sooner Bummy said to me laughingly "Are you going to see Mr. Boyd today?" And laughing was my answer—"Yes! if *you* will come too." Then grave was her observation "But you know you can go tomorrow". "Go tomorrow. Oh I think not." (*Oh I wish I could*! was what my heart *assided.*) "Why certainly Mr. Boyd may not like your going quite so often." How cd. I help saying "If I thought Mr. Boyd did not like my going *very often*, I wd. not go at all."

Eliza arrived; & Bummy ran up stairs to give me pre-warning that in the case of any *horrible* visitors arriving, I was to keep quiet & say nothing before her. Eliza says that Knibb will give me books to the amount of only £2—10 in exchange for those I wish to part with. I wish so much to part with them, & wish so much *more* to get Heyne's Pindar &c that I wd. close with his proposal. But everybody thinks me a goose for *giving away* my books (as they call it); & Eliza insists on trying another bookseller at Worcester, which she is to do next Saturday per carrier. Well! she may do it!—but I *must* have Heyne's Pindar—*coute qu'il coute*!!—so if Deighton *wont*, Knibb *shall*, for EBB *will*—

Eliza painted me & dined with us at once, & drank tea with us at six, & afterwards we went down the carriage road with her, I riding her poney at a slow pace. I rode round to the old gate, & then dismounting, she rode on, & we walked home. A lovely calm soft evening!—

. . . I wrote a few lines to Mr. Boyd enclosing Paganinis criticism—or rather a criticism on Paganini cut out of the newspaper—for Eliza to take with her & read. . . . When Bummy heard this, she said—"Really *all* the young ladies in the neighbourhood seem to me to be in the habit of going to see that poor man". I did not say anything, but thought something.

This was an idle day with me—respecting study. Mrs. Peyton called here & stayed a short eternity, which seemed to me anything but short. In the midst of her visit, I heard Minny was come, & ran up to see her. Dear Minny is looking thin, & began to cry when I kissed her. But her low spirits seem more on our account than her father's, who is much better than she expected or could have expected to find him. Mrs. Cliffe wishes us to spend a long day at Mathon next week. . . . I wd. a thousand times rather go to Mathon than to the Bartons; & Mrs. Peyton was teazing us kindly about going to drink tea there. How they have beseeched us about *tea*.

Thursday June 23d.

At breakfast this morning, Bummy proposed that I shd. go to see Mr. Boyd in the evening. But I would not do it —Eliza Cliffe was to go!—Henrietta exclaimed "This is the first time I ever heard Ba refuse to go to see Mr. Boyd". "Ah!" but Bummy responded—"remember the *reason*!"—

I wonder if she will propose my going tomorrow. If she does, I *will go*!— And I wd. not go tomorrow or any day if I did not believe in my heart that he really does like to have me with him. Read as usual . . . and wrote a long letter to Papa. A long & cheerful letter without one allusion to *the* subject. At about six B H A & I went out to take a walk. We walked up coome hill & sate down nearly at the summit, & tried our fate by daisies—"il aime—un peu—beaucoup—point du tout"!— And there are the degrees of my philosophy—un peu—beaucoup—*point du tout*!!! Bummy mentioned the Malvern subject again; proposed that I shd. go there tomorrow, & that Gent shd. drive me. I am to go!—. We drank tea at eight o'clock, & Bro read the debates to us afterwards.[1] I irrepressibly sleepy; & they, —the debates, not the company,—inexpressibly dull. How much happier I am in having a seat in my arm chair, than one in the House of Lords. How they are brawling and quarrelling just now, about nothing *for* something, at once aristocratically & cacistically.*

Friday June 24.

Gent drove me to Malvern, where we arrived I shd. think very soon after eleven. I was shown into the dining room, & therefore of course took it into my head that Miss Heard was there. Of course consequently out of humour. She was not however there; & I was admitted into the drawing room & Mr. Boyd's presence, before five minutes had past. He said that it was very kind in me to come so often, but that he hoped I had not inconvenienced myself. How I do hate those set phrases. *I* inconvenience myself by going *there*!—Well! we sate down & began to talk about Paganini,—& Mr. Boyd thanked me for sending him the extract which Miss H had read to him yesterday, & which had very much interested him. Then we adjourned to Mr. Boyd's own room & read Æschylus. At two o'clock I was

* From Kakistocracy: the government of a state by its worst citizens (Oxford English Dictionary).

asked whether I would have any luncheon—& how long I would stay. "*No*" to the first question: to the second a little hesitation. I had ordered the carriage at a late hour,—but there was no necessity for my staying until a late hour—I could easily have the carriage at the door earlier. "At what hour have you ordered the carriage?" "At seven—but you know, if you do not like my staying—" "If you dont go until seven, will it not be very late for you to be on the road?" How impatient & surprised I felt; & how moderately I answered—"There is no reason why I shd. not go before, if you dont like my staying." "I was thinking only of your being late on the road, when I said what I did: you know very well whether I like your staying or not". The smile which spoke at the same moment, satisfied me—but still two years ago when so much used to be said about "moon light nights", nothing was ever said about *lateness*. We dined together at half past three; & afterwards went into the drawing room, & talked miscellaneously of novels & Romances—of how many thousands I had read in my life; & of his surprise at hearing me say so. . . . I was provoked to hear of his having advised Eliza Cliffe to read Tom Jones. If Mrs. Cliffe hears of it, she will like the adviser none the better. I wish he had not done it; & I said to him what I have written here. Afterwards we returned to Mr. Boyd's own room, & read Æschylus again. . . . While I was reading, I observed the closing of eyes & imperfect attention—what he calls "his heaviness" coming on. I may be wrong; but I cant help thinking that if he were *much* interested, he wd. not suffer in this way. I thought so yesterday, till my voice absolutely *trembled*. I may be wrong. When the reading was over, we talked of the Knowles's. He scarcely liked (evidently!) my having written any congratulation to them. He told me that Lady Knowles had misrepresented me in one thing. He had doubted my essay on mind having been my own unassisted composition,—& Lady Knowles had said "wait till you see her",—& had written in a letter, which is preserved in the box with my letters, that my "conversation was brilliant & witty". "Now" Mr. Boyd continued "as far at least as I have observed, tho' some of your letters have a good deal of wit, you are not lavish of it in your conversation". He is certainly right in that observation. Why should I blame him for being disappointed in me?—& why should I,—observing & knowing what I do observe & know,—seek farther for a cause of his colder manner & conduct, than the simple circumstance of his being disappointed in me?— But then *should* he have expressed such warmth of regard, if he felt only literary estimation or admiration? I wonder where he has put my *letter box*. It is invisible!

We talked, in conclusion, of Annie & *injudiciousness*, until the carriage came, & a little while afterwards. I went away at seven, at past seven o'clock,—& got home at eight. Just in time for tea. . . . I feel misanthropically this evening, on account of some things which past this morning.

Saturday June 25th.

Bummy said at breakfast, that driving to Malvern always seems to do me good. I hope they will try that panacea upon me again soon—

Read Æschylus—the part I read yesterday,—& wrote down all that I cd. remember of Mr. Boyd's sayings upon it. Heard the boys read Greek as usual; & examined them in *τυπτω not* as usual. That they shd. know no more of the verbs than they do, is my disgrace not theirs.

Dined at one. No going out on account of the rain. On opening my drawer I saw the ms of *Thoughts versus Words*, & a *Thought struck* me that I wd. address & send it to Mr. Boyd. Bummy came into the room while I was writing, & I showed it to her. She seemed amused & pleased—I hope somebody else will be *in statu illo*. I wanted to finish the transcription before Sunday morning came, therefore I finished in the drawing room, while they were reading the paper loud out. On the last page I have written a few lines from myself unallegorically to Mr. Boyd. Will he answer them? How long ago is it since he answered a letter of mine?—

No letter from Papa or anybody. If there had been good news, wd. he not have sent it? . . .

Sunday. June 26th.

Dearest Bro's birthday.* Not kept but thought of. As the clouds looked as if they *would* rain, we would not put ourselves in the way of them by going to church. Bro read prayers. Mr. Watts called at one o'clock, & Eliza rode up to the door at the same moment. Was she to come in or not?—a message sent up to Minny. Mrs. Best's baby has the measles—& Sette & Occyta have not had them. We admitted her. She brought me Heyne's Pindar as a present. How kind of her: & how yet more foolish in me to have said a word before her about that book. She brought Bummy a present, in the shape of an original drawing of hers—a lion springing upon an antelope. Beautifully executed, & well designed—but the design seems to me rather deficient in spirit & animation. We dined & walked down to the gate. Mr. Curzon preached upon faith, very ably but too loudly & energetically, as my headache testified. When we went up afterwards to speak to him, & ask him about Papa, he said "I have seen Mr. Barrett several times. He looks very well & is in good spirits. When I saw him last, on Friday, he desired me to tell you that he was going down to Eastbourne, & that you must not expect to hear from him until Tuesday". I felt the blood fly to my heart like a hot arrow. Going to Eastbourne? Then we are going from Hope End—there is no hope!— Going to Eastbourne. Close to Hastings, where Mr. Boyd wd. have probably been by this time, had I not brought forward my "vexatious opposition"! Going to Eastbourne!—

Well! I recovered myself, & talked on. Mr. Curzon is not to preach here again for four Sundays. Shall we ever hear

* His 24th. As it fell on a Sunday, a celebration was deferred until the following day.

him preach here again? He said "God bless you" at parting. *He* thinks that we shall not!—and I think so too!—

As Bummy H A & I walked home, & sate down upon the pillar at the water side of the house, we talked of Eastbourne & Hope End. It is plain that Bummy has little hope. Has she any?—

Bro read prayers. Afterwards he read Lord John Russell's speech on Reform, in the midst of which, I who am interested in reform & admire Lord John Russell, fell fast asleep. My politics were not strong enough to keep my eyes open. However I slept only over the calculation of populations. I am not of a *calculating* disposition, in any sense of the word. I sent my packet to Mr. Boyd. No advertisement in the Gloucester paper today.

A letter from Mrs. Boyd enclosing a note to Eliza & me, from Annie. Mine cool enough. But that she shd. have written at all, is more than I expected. Mrs. Boyd was prompter, most probably. She is not to return until October then with the two younger Miss Gs. *Then* I shall be here no longer.

Monday June 27.

After breakfast, I was surprised in my room by Eliza running up stairs . . & kissing me vehemently, with an exclamation—"The advertisement is withdrawn from the Worcester paper." Is that all? Her manner had excited me into hope about *something*. *That* is *nothing*. Papa went down to Eastbourne on Friday or Saturday. There is no hope. I obliged her not to go back in the rain but to stay & dine with us at one. After dinner she rode out with Arabel, & promised to return to drink tea here; a promise which the weather prevented her from keeping. Storm of thunder lightening & rain. I in my usual heroics on such occasions. Lay down on Minny's bed. Crashing thunder. Thought of Mr. Boyd who, when I had told him of my boldness during thunderstorms, admitted his own ditto,—& owned even that *he* lies down on his bed, as I do.

At about eight Arabel returned, escorted by Mrs. Cliffe's servent. In the evening, writing instructions for Bro respecting my books, which he is to obey tomorrow. Very kind of him to go to Worcester on purpose. His birthday both kept & thought of!— Mr. & Mrs. Martin came & drank tea with us.

I read Pindar's first Olympic today—& thought of tomorrow—tomorrow's fatal decisive letter. Will it not, must it not be decisive?—

Tuesday June 28th.

Bro rode to Worcester. I wrote a note to Mrs. Boyd.

Bummy H & I drove immediately after breakfast to call upon Mrs. Martin who lent me the two last Edinburgh Reviews, & Lamartine's poems. I have admired two of them already. No conversation about *us*. Then we went to the Bartons. Mrs. Peyton invisible. I wish Mrs. Griffith had been inaudible. My attention distracted both morally & physically, by the thoughts of Papa's letter & by the sight of the thunderclouds. However, the latter broke away. What will the former do? We came home. No letter. The boy did not go until 12 & had not returned. We had dinner. Still no letter. Struck three! Still no letter.— How my heart is beating *inwardly*, as it always does, when I am agitated!

Well. The boy came & brought no letters of any kind. Papa has not written as he said he wd. Are we to attribute this omission to a favorable or unfavorable cause? Bummy says the former—but *I*—I will not throw myself again into the agonies of hope. . . .

A battle fierce between Henry & Georgie. I dreadfully frightened. But I wont make my being hysterical, *historical*.

Read the second Olympic today.

Wednesday . . . June 29.

Distracted (in both senses of the word) by looking for stray books, & packing up a full box of inutilities, to be sent pr. coach to Mr. Eaton. When the letter-time came—*no letters came*! —Yes! one from Mrs. Boyd, containing a message!!! from Mr. Boyd, who likes the talent, & nothing else, of my "Thoughts," & wishes me to write something cutting biting shining on the anti-reformers for the Times newspaper. I have tossed her letter into my drawer—prestissimo—agitato!! I suppose he means to neglect me altogether, never to write to me again! & expects that I should show my *gratitude*! by continuing to write as I have written, & feel as I have felt!— Well!—I feel *bitterly*— —as I have felt—for some time at least. He has not written to me once since the 16th of May; and this is the 29th of June. I may be exacting & irritable & inconsiderate & passionate—but I *cannot* feel satisfied or feel that I *ought* to feel satisfied. I wish I had half the regard which I retain for him, impressed on this paper, that I might erase it thus [ink blot]Mrs. Boyd may throw difficulties in the way of his writing. She may be busy & be out of the way, & he out of the humour for it— But if he wished it—oh if he really & indeed *wished* it, there could be no lasting obstacle—none!! How was it during the first year & a half of our intercourse? Did he ever even *delay* writing, *then*?

Well! It is better far better that I should go away; better in everyway, & perhaps for everybody. Better for *me*, I dare say. I am not of a cold nature, & cannot bear to be treated coldly. When cold water is thrown upon hot iron, the iron *hisses*. I wish that water wd. make my iron as cold as itself. Perhaps it may—*in time*.

Mrs. B thinks that because I did not notice her proposal about coming here, I did not wish her to come. Judging of me by herself!!— . . .

Thursday June 30.

Met Billy Trehern in my dressing gown. Had a fright & a run in consequence!—

Wrote to Mrs. Boyd & sent the letter. Wrote to Annie &

did not send the letter. I shall send it tomorrow. I told Mrs. B. to tell Mr. Boyd of Papa's message; but it will not affect him. Oh no—

No letters today. What can be the reason? Bummy says she looks on the bright side. I look *for* it, but cannot do more. What miserable suspence we have suffered on this subject,—& no out-let from it, even now! My lord & My God! Unto Thee do I commit my earthly as my eternal happiness!—

Mrs. Martin called here just before dinner. I should think from her manner that her mind had a great deal of *repose* about it—I do not mean insensibility—not a smooth sea, not a rough sea, but an undulating sea. I wish I resembled her.

But some circumstances & some people make my mind & feelings foam all over. Can I throw chains upon them, as Xerxes did upon the ocean. Yes! as Xerxes did—ineffectually!—

Bro & Sam are engaged in the Colwall green cricket match this evening; & the minor boys are to accompany them. Good fun to them!—Now I must go & read Pindar.

As Bummy A & I were sitting on the pillar, up the road came an Irishwoman in distress. Her daughter was lying at the gate apparently dying.

We went down (I on the poney) to investigate the case. The poor girl very ill—allowed to sleep in the schoolroom. Much controversy pro & con imposture. No imposture, in my opinion.

I *cantered* up the road & up the hill, without holding the pummel. The poney carried me swiftly; but more swiftly did my memory carry me back to the far days when I used to ride, with the halo of happy reveries about my mind & heart. I enjoyed this riding today, in spite of everything. Tired. Bro & Sam did not return until I was in bed.

Friday July 1st.

After breakfast Henrietta came up stairs to propose to

me that we should drive to Allen's the overseer about the Irishwoman. As Bummy wished me to go, I went. At the gate however we found the poor girl better, but *indisposed* about the overseer; therefore instead of driving to Allan's, we drove to the Whyche. Before we arrived quite at the usual resting point, I proposed climbing the hill with Henrietta. So we commenced operations & Bummy suspended the same; she being left as garrison to our wheelbarrow. I climbed the hill quickly enough, but with so much fatigue!— At the summit there was the sight of the tops of Mr. Boyd's chimneys; & I sate down & looked at them. I sate down & looked at them. I could not do any more. I could not run down the hill as I wished to do —because tho' *facilis descensus*, how was I to get up again? My feelings today were not as pleasant as they were, when I was near this spot, nearly a month ago. Not so pleasant in any way! Whose fault is that? Partly the fault of circumstances, & partly—!! Henrietta & I slid down Bummy's side of the hill, & drove home. I was so tired & exhausted that attempting to stand when I got out of the carriage, was a vain attempt. Bro carried me to the sofa; & I soon got better—indeed well enough, for Bummy to propose our drinking tea with the Martins. I did not feel equal to it: but as she wished it, I agreed!— Henrietta & Sam walked; B, A, & I in the wheelbarrow. Bro had preceded us, in consequence of an invitation to shoot rabbits. On the way, Bummy said to me that she had a proposal to make for tomorrow which I was sure to like; but that before she made it, I must promise one thing. I was about to promise, when Mrs. Cliffe's carriage appeared. . . .

After Mrs. Cliffe had past, I, imagining that B's proposal might regard Mr. Boyd in some way, was anxious for her to re-mention it. *She did not.* Arabel even asked her what it was. She had *forgotten all about it.* For *forgotten*, read *changed her mind.* Had tea with the Martins. I & Mr. Martin *discussed* about Ld. Byron. The Biddulphs called while we were there. I annoyed—felt so. B annoyed—

looked so. Mrs. Martin proposed that I shd. drive to Malvern with her on Tuesday. Tuesday a long way off; but better on Tuesday than not on Tuesday. And yet why shd. I wish so much to be with a person, who certainly does not wish *so much* to be with me. Why shd. I take pleasure in lacerating myself, & kissing the rod? . . . Got home & to bed—at last! Intolerably tired! So tired as to lie awake instead of sleeping,—& to dream when I did sleep, of my teeth tumbling out.

Arabel told me today that there is to be an auction at the farm on Monday, of all Papa's crops. And that papers are printed & hung up at the farm & at Ledbury, to that effect.[1] Henrietta & Bummy do not know it,—& I swore Arabel to silence, for fear of distressing them. No letter from Papa today; & Bummy rather elated about *that*? Is there any reason why I should be elated about anything?

Saturday. July 2d.

Got up this morning, tired thro' & thro'. The dreams I had last night about my teeth, were ineffectual in refreshing me altogether. While Stormy & Georgie were reading Greek with me, a cry from Henry called my attention to his figure suspended by the hands from the roof of the dairy. I called out to him to take care; and the boys, to take courage. I was in a fright; & they, in a rage. I sent them down to carry the ladder to him, for which he was asking them. Stormie got upon the roof, & dragged him up, poor fellow, by the arms. How frightened I was!

But how yet more frightened, when the horse's hoofs in the yard announced the arrival of the post. No letters!!! How very extraordinary!— Oh if I knew when & how this uncertainty is to end . . I might be yet more uncomfortable perhaps than I am. Well! I shall know soon! Bummy has not said one word about her "proposal" for today. I think, tired as I am, I could go to Malvern; if there, she meant to go. No letter from Malvern again today. It wd.

be well for me if I could think of some things & persons, as little as I am thought of. I must go & read Pindar. I have not read a line of him, these two days.

Did not read Pindar after all—but read.

I wonder why Eaton does not write. Impatient. Henrietta's protegèes* transferred from our gate to a lodging near the wyche on the poney. Maddox came.

Sunday July 3d.

H A & I drove to church, where we heard Mr. Deane preach a sleepy kind of sermon. Mrs. Martin there. She asked me to drive with her to Eastnor [Castle] on Tuesday, in the case of Mr. Martin not accompanying her on Monday. I wd. rather have gone to Malvern, but it is right for me, & indeed it will be a satisfaction to me, to visit poor Lady Margaret. Has she not felt for me? And can I not feel for her? Too well!—

Eliza was at church, & quite inclined to go home with us. But I thought of the letter, the expected letter; & begged her not to come here until Wednesday. . . .

How hot & cold I grew as we approached the house! Is it possible? No letter!—

B & H drove to church. Arabel & I walked to chapel. A man, some heads shorter than I am, preached! and if his voice had been in proportion to his size, I should not have had the headache. Vox, et præterea nihil.[1] The sermon was very weak & bad. Its matter must however have been thought excellent by the preacher: for he repeated it again & again. The doctrine was scriptural—so I ought perhaps to have been better satisfied than I happened to be.

B & H did not get home until seven,—& then we had prayers.

Settled. That I am to go with Maddox tomorrow morning early, & be left at Ruby Cottage.

Read the bible of course; but thought the bible, far less

* The Irishwoman and her invalid daughter.

than I should do. I have left off praying for the specific object of remaining at Hope End. I pray now only that God may direct our going forth or our staying in: for the Giver of all Good must, surely, know better than I, what it is good to give. *Thy will*—Oh Lord!—

Monday July 4th.

Dearest Arabel's birthday. She is 18; and an interesting intelligent amiable feeling girl. I should love her even if she were not my sister; & even if she did not love me.

As Bummy told me to go into her room before I went away, I undrew her bed curtains before she was awake. I wondered what she cd. have to say to me, & was perfectly provoked when she asked me to promise not to mention at Ruby Cottage, anything of our unhappy business. I promised that I would not, if the subject were not mentioned to *me*.

How I do hate & abhor this reserve, so foreign to my nature, so contrary to my professions, to be forced upon me! What is the use of a friend, if my heart is to lock itself against him? "No confidence,"—as Mr. Boyd once said to me—"no friendships". I cd. have cried with mortification: but there is enough to cry about, without this!— Maddox & I drove away at seven, after my having had a partial breakfast in the nursery. Arrived at Ruby Cottage at 8. Mrs. Boyd in bed. Mr. Boyd up,—but he had gone back again into his bed room. So I desired that my name shd. be unnamed for the present: & when the dining room door was shut upon me, out of the window I jumped. My hat I left behind, & ran up thro' the grove to the hill where I let my hair blow about & my feet walk about ad libitum. But I was not there long. I ran back again & then came a message from Mrs. Boyd who wished to see me. I went into her bed room & sate down upon the bed, & talked. Presently Mr. Boyd wanted to see me, which I gladly heard. Found him at breakfast. He is suffering from a painful boil on his upper lip. "I wish," he said, "that I cd. get rid of my boil as well as Bently did, of his." He talked of the difference between moral and physical pain,—preferred as I have heard him do before, suffering the former to the latter. The fact is, he is singularly constituted—for the enjoyment of intense pleasure, rather than for a sensibility to intense pain. In general,

> Chords that vibrate sweetest,
> Thrill the deepest notes of woe.[1]

but his chords were not so strung. He asked me if I had heard from Papa and said little more on the subject. His anxiety about it, can scarcely be very great.

After I had been down stairs to breakfast with Mrs. Boyd, I came up again & began to read Æschylus. We read the 2d. chorus; & I felt *happy* while I was reading it. A kind of happiness which cannot now last long!— Certainly, which *may* not! My voice trembled once, as I thought so!— I wish I were constituted like Mr. Boyd.

. . . We talked comparatively about Homer Æschylus & Shakespeare: and positively about Æschylus's Prometheus —Praises of the speech in the Medea. After dinner, we had some politics; and indeed before dinner. Then I examined his memory in the chorus's of the Agamemnon, in Casandra's three speeches, & in Gregory's orations on Cæsarius & Basil. Then we talked about a fourth edition of his Select Passages, which I urged him to put in motion. No! he wd. not—he cd. not—nobody wd. take the trouble of being his amanuensis without being paid for it: & to anyone who was paid, he could not commit the task of correcting the press, without his own attention being strictly directed to every sheet; which wd. fatigue & make him nervous. I longed to beg him to trust *me* with the employment; but I was too afraid that he wd. say something I might dislike hearing: So I observed *first*—"I shd. think you might easily find somebody who would correct the proof sheets for you." "Easily! You dont know how difficult it wd. be. My sister corrected the proof sheets of the first edition of my Select passages: and attention was not paid to them. You see even my own sister did not like the drudgery".

I took courage & begged him to employ me, & assured him of my liking & wishing for the employment. "Ah! I am well aware that *you* would do it for me sooner than any body else would. But I should not like you to drudge for me. And suppose you should be ill—" "Ill! I am not going to anticipate being ill. Do let me manage it for you. I should like it so very much!" "But we must see first whether you leave Hope End or not". I said that whether I left Hope End or not, the sheets might be sent to me— & I said more—& he said more—& I think it will end by my doing what I wish to do.

My dear friend Mr. Boyd!— If he knew how much it gratifies me to assist him in any way (I wish . . . I cd. do so in *every* way) all his '*drudgeries*' wd. . . . devolve upon me. It pleased me to hear him acknowledge that I would do more for him than other people would! And is not that true? I think so.

I left Malvern somewhere between 7 & 8, & got home to the relics of tea. . . .

The auction of the *crops*, at the farm today. I am glad it is over. Oh if there is no chance of our staying here altogether; & I believe there is little chance: and if Mr. Boyd were not at Malvern, I would yearn to be away from the sight & hearing of all that we see & hear every day. But it is God's will!— And I have in spite of everything, felt happy several times today!—

Mrs. Boyd called me Miss Barrett. She used to call me Ba. Quære *why*? Another Quære—*Why should I care*? Certainly I dont care very much for Mrs. Boyd. Mr. Boyd (backed by Mrs. B's reported opinion) still maintains, that *jealousy* of Eliza Cliffe, is the occult cause of Annie's late conduct to me. Fudge again; said Mr. Burchell. . . .

Tuesday. July 5th.

I was up a little after seven this morning. So were the

clouds; and to make them more decisive, the rain is *down*; there seems no chance of my driving out with Mrs. Martin. Surely a letter, a decisive letter will come today! or else surely Papa will come!— If *it* does—or if *he* does—what will be the consequence? Nothing good, I fear, humanly speaking: but everything good, I know, by my knowledge of the providence of God. I have prayed for good—I have asked for fish, & shall receive no serpent.

The rain went off, & Mrs. Martin arrived before the letters. So I was forced to go without them. As she had heard of my visit to Ruby Cottage yesterday, she did not propose my going there; & we went *past the house* to Grt Malvern. I never thought it possible that I cd. be made to do such a thing. But as we returned, I cd. refrain no longer, & begged to be allowed to go & see Mr. Boyd for two minutes. Allowed. She was "just thinking of proposing it". As we drove up to the door, there was Mr. Boyd walking! I walked into the house, & he after me; & we talked for not one minute. I ran up to Mrs. Boyd who was dressing. Talked not one minute. Then went into Mr. Boyd's sitting room, & talked to him there, not one minute. Then Exit. Cool—cool—cool. Warm—warm—warm!!— As I came away without hearing of the letters, & as my writing about them, by this day's post, is out of the question—Mrs. Boyd agreed not to come here until Thursday. I am glad of it. We drove home. . . . Mrs. Martin has agreable conversation, & is a feeling excellent person; but she has not vivida vis enough about her, to please me altogether. Henrietta met me in front of the house. "Any letters." "Yes! but no good!! He says he has waited for some good, but has none to tell us". I got into the drawing room—& got the letter. Yes! There is no good, but it is written in good spirits. Thank God for that!— I could scarcely read it, I trembled so much.

Wednesday. July 6th.

Eliza Cliffe arrived; & brought a note from Eaton in which he agrees to allow £3 for the books exchanged. It is less than their value,—but it is more than their value to *me*,—they being to me value*less*: therefore I will close with him. There is a strong opposition of prudent people against me; but I will close with him.

By Bummy's desire, I left Eliza at 12 o'clock, & let Gent drive me to Eastnor. Was shewn into the dining room, to wait for Lady Margaret. A coldness & desolateness about the room; an exactness about the posture of the chairs,—which made me think that no one inhabited it, or sate down on them. *I* could not; but walked about, & looked out of the window, & worked myself up into an agitation in the fear of Lady Margaret's. However it was not so. She came into the room with a cheerful countenance & unagitated manner. She received me affectionately—said that she had given orders to be denied to everybody except Mrs. Martin & me—& seemed particularly glad to see me. "So much," she said, "has occurred to each of us, since we parted." Yes! So much!— She enquired immediately with respect to our present situation— "Are you stationary at Hope End?"— "But I fear you are likely to leave it?" She told me that she had heard of Papa's intention of going to Brighton & that both Lord Somers & herself very much wished it . . on account of Brighton's being near Reigate where they intend residing two months in every year. Lord Somers wished that we would pass some time at Reigate. That was kind: & I laid my hand on Lady Margaret's hand, & said so. But I told her my prejudice against noisy, rattling, brick-dusty Brighton; & . . my love of silence & quietness & a sight of the green trees & fields out of the window.

For an hour I sate with her, & when she had asked me to visit her once more before she went away on Saturday week, I said good bye. . . . Three o'clock—dinner over; & Eliza & Arabel out of doors sketching. Eliza painted at my mouth till she spoilt it,—& then had tea,—& then went home. I tired, too tired to be agreable,—all the evening.

I wrote this morning one line to Mrs. Boyd, to say that Papa's letter contained no obstacle to our receiving her.

Thursday July 7.

Up at a little after seven, & writing to Eaton. I have sent him a list of the books which I wish him to send me immediately. Wrote also a few lines (a very few) to Mr. Boyd, to tell him what he asked me to write about: i e Lady Margaret's opinion of the House of lords' intended *doings* about the bill. What an awkward sentence, that is,—but I am scribbling against time—& tune *ergo*. Prepared some of the seven chiefs, & heard Storm & George read Greek —in which I was interupted by Mrs. Boyd's arrival. Miss Steers she left behind *vis a vis* the great ash. When I had talked to Mrs. Boyd a little while, Mrs. Cliffe Mrs. Best Eliza & little Fanny arrived, on their way to call at the Bartons. Fanny is a pretty interesting-looking bambina,— but as to writing a poem on her, as Mrs. Best begged me to do—excuse me there. I never can write when I dont feel; & my feelings are not apt to rise extempore in consequence of an hour's visiting. Everybody dined with us at one o'clock—except poor Miss Steers who was constant to the ash. We sent her down some strawberries; and after the ash was painted in oils, Henrietta sate with her on the bank, while she was sketching the house. I longed to be παϱεδϱος [sitting beside],—but I could not leave Mrs. Boyd. And Mrs. Boyd, tho' goodnatured & kind in her manner,—is certainly nothing more. She is a very trying person to spend a day with! Empty minded, & without real *sensibility*—which extends to the tastes as well as to the feelings—frivolous & flippant. What a woman to be Mr. Boyd's wife!— But she *is* his wife; & therefore I wd. not be inattentive to her on any account. So I fidgetted about with her, from one subject to another, & from one place to another—from the drawing room to the front of the house —from the front of the house to the drawing room. Oh how tired I was!—

Miss Steers came into the house a few minutes before they both left it finally. She sate on the sofa by me; & we talked of Lamartine. She is not, I think, a clever woman of nature's making; but she seems to have refined tastes, & a cultivated mind.— There is a little effort now & then to *seem* to have more—

They went away at six; and the clouds which looked fearfully like a thunderstorm, went away soon after them. Not *after* them, I hope! Bummy had a letter from Papa today. I suspected the black seal* at dinnertime; but she did not tell us until after every body had gone, that the seal was his, & that he could not fix the time of his return —that on Friday he had an engagement—& that he wd. write to Henrietta before he saw us. So he is coming!— So there is indeed no hope. God's will—the wisest will—be done!

Eliza gave me a note to give to Mrs. Boyd directed to Mr. Boyd. What did she write to him about, I wonder! I sent a note from myself. Which will he read first?— There is no use in asking questions on this subject. It is *unquestionable*, that he prefers me to Eliza Cliffe.

Friday. July 8.

. . . Mrs. Martin urgent upon us all to drink tea there this evening, & meet the Miss Biddulphs. Henrietta Bro & Sam agreed: Bummy & I demurred. I was afraid lest the demurring might produce a recurring . . to the point: but Bummy assured me in an aside that she wd. not go. So it was agreed that she & A & I shd. go to the Wyche instead. Nature & the Biddulphs are a contrast, & I never could doubt about preferring the former.

(No letters.) Bummy wrote to Papa to dissuade him from coming.

Arabel walked down to Mrs. Barker's; & Henrietta occupied her place in the wheelbarrow, until we had conveyed her safely to the Colwall first gate. In the meantime it began to rain, which made Henrietta à la Henriette again. She wd. go & she wd. not go. I was angry & I was

* In mourning for his mother, Elizabeth Moulton, who had died in London 29 December 1830.

not angry. I was certainly provoked. She went at last. B & I returned to Arabel at Mrs. Barker's & dried our wet exteriors by Milly's extempore fire. The rain went off, & so did we, to the Whyche. Bummy sate in the carriage with the newspaper, on this side of it, while Arabel & I walked along the terrace on the other. We walked to the spot immediately above Ruby Cottage, & in five minutes, if I had descended, I should have been *in* Ruby Cottage. And in less than five minutes, I wd. have descended, if I had not thought of Bummy & the late evening. If I had not thought of them, wd. Mr. Boyd have been glad?— Wd. he *indeed* have been glad?

I enjoyed this walking, & the odours of the fresh evening & the sights of the superb expanse & majestic hills, very much indeed. We were not at home until 9 o'clock; & Henrietta was not, until ten. Bro & Sam arived at the same time; so we had prayers, & went to bed directly.

Saturday. July 9th.

Read Pindar's 4th. Olympic before breakfast—read & digested it. After breakfast, heard the boys read Homer & Zenophon; and at twelve, drove with Bummy & Arabel to Mrs. Cliffe's. . . .

N.B. *A Bull!!*

Talking of bulls, as we proceeded on our road to Mathon, we met one, coming to meet us in a narrow lane, & with a bellow. Out of the carriage we all three jumped, & took refuge in a field close by. But one gate seemed to me by no means a satisfactory go-between for us & our enemy; so I climbed a very high railing with a rather deep ditch at the other side—which, if I had not been frightened out of my senses, I could by no means have done. At last a man came to our rescue & drove away the bull; & we got miraculously safe thro' the frying sun, over the earthquaking roads, to Mathon. Mrs. Cliffe was at dinner at two, & we joined her by invitation. Afterwards I went into Eliza's room—indeed into every room in the house—indeed into every room *not* in the house, for I visited the hermitage. . . Then I lay down on the sofa and rested my body & mind with the Literary Souvenir. . . . We had tea,—& at seven Mrs. Cliffe *wd.* save me a shaking, by driving me to our gate in her carriage. And besides she *wd.* lend me the first two vols of the mysteries of Udolpho *before she* had *finished them* herself —a kind of generosity which quite dazzled my weak moral sense. I have read the mysteries; but am anxious to read them again—being a worshipper of Mrs. Radcliffe. Bummy drove Mrs. Cliffe's carriage a part of the way; so, *she* escaped a part of the shaking. Parted at the gate with the kind Mathon people; & found at home the Colwall ones. Henrietta had been driven by Mrs. Martin to call on the Biddulphs, & had persuaded her to drink tea at Hope End. Mr. Martin there too—playing cricket. Sate on the hay a little while,—& then went in to tea the second!

No letter today. I *scarcely* expected one, but *did* expect one. I believe Bummy's letter urged him not to remove his family until the last, & urged him not to return home now. If that had weight with him, we may have no letter again tomorrow. I hope we may not. And yet if there is no hope & can be no hope (—and whence are we to gather it?—) it wd. be better for us to leave this fatally dear place at once —to go at once!— It wd. be better for all but me—and better for *me*, for every reason but one reason.

The Martins stayed until twelve. I dont know how it is. They have not the key of my mind. They are superior & feeling people; and yet I can neither think nor feel aloud when they are present. Read more than a chapter of the Mysteries, between the acts of pulling off my stockings & going to sleep.

Sunday July 10th.

Uncomfortable night between the rush light & dark thoughts. This morning I refused to go to church, because, if I went, somebody wd. be obliged either to walk or stay at home; neither of which, they might like. . . . I am in a fever about the letters . . . if a letter comes I wish Eliza would not come.

Neither a letter nor Eliza came; but a thunderstorm! However the thunder grumbled courteously at a distance until we had done dinner,—& then it lightened until five oclock. Minny *protected* Bummy & Arabel in the library, —& I lay down on Minny's bed *meo more* [in my fashion]. No going to church or chapel of course.

A letter from Mrs. Boyd who tells me that whenever the weather has been good, Mr. Boyd has said "Well, I think Miss Barrett might have come on such a fine day." I was there last Monday & Tuesday; Mrs. Boyd was here on Thursday: therefore only on Friday & Saturday, was there a possibility of my going when I did not go. I am pleased, very much pleased, by his seeming to wish to see me. Mr. Spowers, Mrs. Boyd says, is coming on Tuesday—(provoking Mr. Spowers!) & Mr. Boyd would like me to come on Monday if I could,—if not early on Tuesday. He *must* like me to be with him, I think.

Now we are going to the Bartons to drink tea tomorrow evening,—& if I shd. not be able to have the carriage tomorrow morning—why then I must wait until Tuesday.

Arabel felt Bummy's pulse for me on the subject. Decidedly unfavourable. "Nasty Boyds"! she said—but Arabel did not tell me *that*, or I shd. have been sulky instead of goodhumoured. I wd. have said no word more about it—wd. have staid at home tomorrow,—& set off the next morning! But in my blissful ignorance, while B was curling her hair, I asked her why she objected to my going,—elicited that she was afraid of my being late, & making her so, at the Bartons; promised to behave punctually;—& got leave of absence. I am going tomorrow morning at *8*, & am to leave Ruby Cottage at half past *3*.

"Nasty Boyds"! Arabel said she was not in her *particularly best* humour at the time,—but what an expression! Why shd. she dislike them?—at least *Mr. Boyd*, whom she never saw, & has heard nothing but good of?—

I am very glad Papa did not write by this post. Now, he cant write (i e. we cant get his letter) until Tuesday, & cant come until Wednesday. And as his coming would be his dispairing, I am anxious for him not to come. Prayers —& read the bible,—& wrote about the Biblical *MSS.* of course. But *on* the whole, & *thro'* the thunderstorm an idle day.

Monday, July 11.

Up at six, intending to go at eight.

Went however, at half past eight—& not *my* fault. Breakfasted by myself, & found Mrs. Boyd breakfasting, & had from her, details about the thunderstorm, & influenza & Mr. Biscoe & a thousand other things not worth remembering. I went up to Mr. Boyd, & fancied he was glad to see me. I really believe he was. When we had talked we read the seven chiefs, and when we had read we talked, and when we had talked, I assisted him in learning some passages in the Prometheus. Happy day!— He said once "Is it really your opinion that you will leave this house"? "Yes:" I answered—"it is indeed". "And will you go away then next month—"? I thought there was in his voice an expression of dejection. The tears came fast into my eyes!—I wish he may miss me . . a little. He showed me a letter from the German booksellers, in which Wolf's folio Homer is stated to be either out of print or so rare as to have escaped the exertions of their correspondents. My feeling on reading this, was pleasurable. I wd. rather that he had not given me the book; yet I am glad he *thought* of giving it to me. I went away at half past three. Called for a minute at Mrs. Trants, & found her at dinner with Sam & Henry. She begged me to spend a day with her *as I do with Mr. Boyd.* What an idea!—what a misapprehension of ideas! On cross questioning, I found out that she preferred my going to her *by myself*—in other words, *without Bummy!* Selfish woman!— Is her want of courtesy towards my friends, to be remunerated by my superabundant courtesy towards her? For nothing but courtesy could force me to spend a day with her.

I got to the Bartons at half past four, before their dinner, & was obliged to dine & talk until tea. Everybody was emptied out of Hope End into Barton court, at six—and *our children* seemed to enjoy themselves very much. Dear little things!— How tired I was, & unwell this evening. As, on our return, I was sitting by myself in our bedroom, I heard what I used to hear in the summer of 1828, & only *then*—the *deathwatch*.[1] I grew sick & pale, & dizzy—& slept miserably all night—solely I believe from the strong unaccountable impression produced on me, by this circumstance. I have mentioned it to nobody, & dont much like mentioning it here. There never was a more foolishly weakly superstitious being than I am.

Tuesday. July 12.

Went into the library to try to rationalize my mind about the deathwatch,—by reading the Cyclopædia. Feel very unwell today, & nervous. Read the mysteries of Udolpho—by way of quieting my imagination? & heard the boys read Homer & Zenophon—& read some of Victor Hugo's & Lamartine's poetry—his last song of Childe Harold. Miss Steers kindly sent a packet of French poetry to Mr. Boyd's for me yesterday. *Le dernier chant* wants the Byronic character (—an inevitable want for a French composition—) and is not quite equal even to Lamartine. No letter!!—

Wednesday. July 13.

Much better day,—in spite of the violent rain last night which agitated me teeth & all!— Arabel & I got out of bed & ran to Minny (little dears!) and I was in a thunder-&-lightening fright; & my teeth did what my tongue does sometimes—*chattered*. Dreaming over Udolpho. My impression is that Mrs. Radcliffe's spell-word is "Tremble" not "Weep". She is not great in pathos.

Wrote a part of a letter to Papa. None from him. Grumbled & had my hair curled, & went to Colwall with Bro, to meet as I understood only Lord Somers & Lady Margaret. Found there Mrs. C. Jones & Miss Biddulph, & Col: Drummond & Mrs. Drummond. Provoked— But I can wear sackcloth, (sometimes), without making faces—so I made none on this occasion. Mrs. Jones & Miss Biddulph are unassuming & apparently amiable, & *not* silly; but their faces & manners & conversation want expression. "Stirring up with a long pole" would be as useful with regard to them, as to the wild beasts late of Exeter Change.[1] Col: Drummond "thinks himself an Adonis" according to the general opinion. As long as he does not think himself a Solon, I wont complain. A goose may plume herself; & so may he, . . . on his externals. Mrs. Drummond talks like thunder. Lady Margaret sate next me after dinner, & we had some interesting conversation, about German & Italian. I confessed that if ever I learnt German, it shd. be more for the sake of reading the Sorrows of Werter than Klopstock's Messiah. So it shd. We got home at half past ten; &c—

Thursday July 14.

At breakfast, my parcel of books from Eaton came up the road. Fresh from the carrier. Unpacked it eagerly, & read the title pages of Barnes's Euripides, Marcus Antoninus, Callimachus, the Anthologia, Epictetus, Isocrates, & Da Vinci's Painting. The last I had sent for, for Eliza Cliffe; but the externals are so shabby that I have a mind to send it back again. Finished my dream about Udolpho;—& began Destiny, a novel by the author of the Inheritance [Susan Edmonstone Ferrier] which Miss Peyton lent me. I liked the Inheritance so much that my desires respecting this book were "all alive". I forgot to say that I dont like the conclusion of the Mysteries. It is "long drawn out" & *not* "in linked sweetness". Read some of the Alcestis. Mr. Boyd wished me to read it; & I wished so too.

No letter!— Sent mine to Papa!—

Friday. July 15.

Wrote to Mr. Boyd. Glad of it—for I received afterwards a note from him announcing the arrival of Wolf's Homer! and desiring me to go for it. He seems disappointed about the paper, & about there being in this edition only 6 books. In the envelope Mrs. Boyd advises me to come soon. If the book had been a fine one she says, I might have appeared to come *on account of the book*: but as it is *not*, I shall *appear* to go, on account of the giver. Ah! if it were on account only of the book!— —. I will go tomorrow, if I can. Mr. Boyd's note is not— —what his note would have been 3 years ago. He certainly does *not* care *much* for me! not as I care for him!

Read the second volume of Destiny, & a little of the Alcestis.

Mrs. Cliffe & Eliza drank tea with us; & so did Mr. Martin; & so did Reynolds & Tom Peyton who had been invited to cricket. Agreed—that B H A Bro & Sam shd. dine tomorrow at Mr. Martins, & drink tea at Mrs. Cliffes. I rescued my expedition to Malvern, with difficulty: at least it was rescued *for* me,—for *I* urged them to take the carriage & let me prorogue until Monday. We drove to Mrs. Martin's this morning. & sate there more than an hour . . . Mrs. Martin is an intelligent & feeling woman; but I dont know how it is. She & I dont amalgamate.

No letter from Papa today!— Whenever I hear "there is no letter", I take breath. It is a respite.

Mrs. Biddulph & Mrs. Phillips [her sister-in-law] & Miss. Biddulph called here. I caught in the hall, when I was going up stairs to put on respectable shoes without ventilators. But I dare say they care as little about my feet, as I do about their heads.

Saturday July 16th.

Clouds but no rain. Dreamt last night of all the passengers of a West India vessel,—except two rescued by Bro,—being drowned. I hope *that* does not indicate a drowning for me in my way to or from Malvern today. Read a little of the Alcestis before I got out of bed,—I think I shall like it.

Went to Malvern, & called at the Barton door, about Destiny; & on Mrs. Trant on my way to Mr. Boyd's. She asked me when I meant to spend a day with her. I said I did not know, & *she* said— —nothing. Silence is eloquent; & silence on this occasion did not I think, speak on the courteous side of the question—of which I was glad. Found Mrs. Boyd in the drawing room; & was soon released to Mr. Boyd. Before he admitted me, I heard him say "You did not show it to her? You did not say anything about it?" About the book of course. Well! I was received into his room!— He asked me if I chose to look at the book there, or wait until I got home. "*There*", my answer was. So he sent me back into the drawing room, for Mrs. Boyd to show me the sight. Bad paper! Only six books!! Twelve books—and the most splendid paper & type. He had wished to take me by surprise; & the surprise was complete. It is the most magnificent Greek book I ever looked upon; &, what is better & more valuable; has *τηφιλτατη* [for the dearest one] written on one of the first pages, in his own hand. I shall often look on & think of that writing, when the heart that dictated it, kind & gentle as are its feelings, shall not be dwelling on the thought of my thoughts!—

I went back into Mr. Boyd's room, & expressed, how imperfectly!—what I thought & felt of his present to me. We then read the seven chiefs,— Yes! but he first asked if we had heard from Papa, & spoke a little about Hope End. Will he be *very* sorry, if I go away? I am afraid of answering that question. I wish I were more sure of his regard. And I wish that he had not made me so costly a present!— How little & yet how much is necessary to please me!—

His sister & a Miss Nelly something [Bordman] is coming to stay at Ruby Cottage. The young lady is 16; & was, when she was 6, a clever child. Her father had amused himself by teaching her the Greek character[s], & had made her read the Hecuba thro', without of course, her understanding a word. Mr. Boyd does not think that she understands Greek. I hope that she— —I hope he wont prefer her society to mine. I hope Miss Boyd will like me. I will take pains to please Mr. Boyd's sister.

He asked me to talk to Mr. Spowers at dinner: "on *his* account, he thought I ought to do it." I promised to do my best; and as I went out of the room, he said that I must remember what I had promised, & that he wd. ask Mrs. Boyd if I had been "naughty or good". I in a panic of course. Found Mr. Spowers solo in the drawing room. Exit I in a fuss, went to Mrs. Boyd's room, down stairs—no Mrs. Boyd—returned perforce to Mr. Spowers. Talked to him of Mr. Boyd—my best introduction. Down to dinner. I impelled myself to talk, whether I had anything to say or not—to talk about the country, & the newspaper, & the raven, & Joanna Baillie[1] & Lord Byron. So that when I had to answer Mr. Boyd's "naughty or good", I could say "good". Mr. Spowers is a sensible man; & gentlemanly & goodnatured. Before dinner, Mr. Boyd had walked out with him up & down the garden. Mr. Boyd said a good deal about leaving me—& begged me to believe that it was not his wish to do so,—that he went only on account of his health. It was certainly right for him to go. But could he not have asked me to go with him? He evidently dislikes my walking with him. What is the reason? Shall I ask? No!—

While we were at dinner Mr. Wood called, to tell him that a celebrated preacher Mr. James, is to preach on Tuesday, at the anniversary of the chapel. Mr. Boyd wishes me to go, & to write or speak to Eliza Cliffe about it, & to make her use her influence with Miss Wall—that every body may go.

After dinner we had a little more of the Seven Chiefs; & I heard him recite some of the Prometheus; & then we talked; and at half past 7 I went away. As I was taking leave of him, he asked me to tell Mr. Spowers to take the newspaper & read it to him. Is it possible that I shd. have forgotten this message until I got to South Lodge? Very near going back again,—but it wd. have seemed ridiculous.

Found, on arriving at home, that there was no letter; & that nobody except Bro & Sam had gone to the Cliffes, on account, not so much of the rain as the *clouds*. So I understand it. Made them all stare at my book—& promise to hear Mr. James preach on Tuesday. Not very well.

Sunday. July 17th.

Not well—& as an ergo, did not go either to church or chapel. Mrs. Cliffe & Eliza came & I displayed my Homer to them,—& settled about Tuesday. They will go, & take *me*. Not sure that I like it. If I go in Mrs. Cliffe's carriage, I may not see Mr. Boyd. I *must* see him, if I go at all!— No letter!— I wrote about the BiblicalMSS. Afterwards wrote to Mr. Boyd about my forgetting to give his message to Mr. Spowers—& also about the Homer. I told him that tho' I wished he had not given me so costly a present, I was "pleased,—in associating the most beautiful book I ever saw, with the kindest & most valued friend I ever had". Said a great many words besides, but not one word that I did not feel—more than feel.

Monday. July 18th.

Bro went to Worcester, & I entrusted him with a commission, about exchanging Da Vinci for Reynold's Lectures. He went at 8, with Mr. Martin. At breakfast time we heard a speaking in low voices between Bummy & Lane at the door. Something wrong,—but I wd. not be grave before my time. It wd. not have been before my time. After breakfast Bummy told us that Reid had come, & requested to look at the house. We all four got out of it as soon as we could, & walked down to Mrs. Barker's—& stayed there until Minny brought us word that the coast was clear. Such a trembling, I had in my feet—& within me. The suspension of the advertisements is nothing favorable, after all our strawcatching hopes. Well! it will be *well!*— Bummy wrote to Papa, to tell him,—& she let me write one page of the letter, in which I told him about my Homer. I sent too my note to Mr. Boyd. At four, she fancied that it would do me good to drive out; & as she could not go herself on account of wishing to write letters, she sent both H & A with me. We drove to the Wyche—& tied the poney to the turnpike gate; & then walked along the Worcestershire side walk. When we had reached the point immediately above Ruby Cottage, I sate down meditating a descent. But Henrietta remonstrated, & talked of fatigue & Bummy & Mrs. Martin & "what oclock is it", until my resolution to walk backwards instead of forwards was almost taken. At the instant that I was wondering whether I might see Mr. Boyd walking out, Henrietta imagined "There he is",—and Arabel confirmed that there he positively was. "I know the way to the walk which he has taken— Come & I will show you." So down the hill, she bounded; & after her, I bounded; & Henrietta, after me. Down the hill—down the perpendicular—steeper & steeper—into the wood—steeper than steeper! I ran because I could not walk, from one tree to another, half laughing & half crying & half scolding Arabel. For I was half inclined to imagine that she was taking me in; & had no more seen Mr. Boyd than *I* was likely to see him. At last we arrived at the entrance of Essington's gardens: & Arabel declared that he & Mr. Spowers were walking within them. But I had suddenly grown modest,— & declared that I would not investigate the point any further. I fancied that the gardens were private, & that Mr. Boyd— —in short I *shyed*. But as I was turning, a clear view was caught of him and his companion,—so I changed my mind, & went to meet him. Met him—I said "Henrietta & Arabel are with me". And then *they* said that they would go & find a donkey; & then Mr. Boyd offered me his arm, & we walked up & down the pleasant shady walk, until the donkey arrived. Talked about Homer & Virgil, . . . et cæteræ*s* & *a*. Donkey came—& I was obliged to go. Arrived safely at the Wyche, & from thence home at 20 minutes to 8—talking of our adventures—of Mr. Boyd—and of his not shaking hands with Henrietta when she held out hers & said "Good morning Mr. Boyd." How should he know about her holding out her hand?—

He had not received my note when I met him; of which I was glad.

Tuesday July 19.

At a quarter to ten, Bummy & I were down at Mrs. Barkers, close to Mrs. Cliffe's carriage. Eliza & Henrietta & Arabel followed us in the wheelbarrow—& we got to the chapel just in time. Mrs. Boyd took me into her pew. As soon as ever I saw the preacher, I thought he was not eloquent,—as soon as ever I heard him, I was sure of it. A most excellent sermon; but *not* the sermon of "the first preacher in England," according to Mr. Boyd. I should have been *much* pleased, if I had not expected to be *very* much pleased: as it was, I was *pleased.*

When it was all over, I began to meditate the subject I was meditating, before it began—"how am I to manage a visit to Ruby Cottage?" Mrs. Cliffe & Eliza were going to pay visits at Great Malvern—& Bummy H & A to see the library. Therefore I could have no carriage. Mrs. Boyd was going to walk home with Mr. Spowers. Therefore I decided in walking with her. There was a little remonstrance on the side of my party—about the possibility of my being tired; but nothing vehement. I walked & was tired—what with the walk & what with the wind. Mrs. Boyd placed me on the sofa, & would have bolstered & pillowed me if I had been passive. She is a good natured woman. After five or ten minutes, I began meo more to fidget, & wonder why Mr. Boyd did not send for me. After a quarter of an hour or half an hour, I could have cried—in thinking that I had exposed myself to all this fatigue willingly, & that he seemed to have no will or wish to fatigue himself by talking to me until the carriage came. I could have cried!— At last Mrs. Boyd who was reading the newspaper close to me, (just as if I had gone there to see her read it), observed "Are you not going to Mr. Boyd?" "Why he is not ready: is he?" "Yes to be sure he is! & waiting for you." And so he was. A mistake had kept *me* down stairs, & him in an expectation for half an hour or more. How provoked I was. He did not shake hands with me when I went first into his room. Forgot it, I suppose!!— He put his hat before his face, & talked—first of Henrietta, whom he did not know was with me yesterday until "a third voice" said "Good morning Mr. Boyd". He understood that Arabel & I had left her on the Wyche: and as to her offering to shake hands with him, he was ignorant of *that* until Mr. Spowers told him of it. Then he talked of yesterday's note. "I had said too much—it was not necessary for me to say so much about the book—but of course he felt gratified & obliged by the sentiments I expressed." '*Gratified & obliged!*'— Well!—

We talked about the book, which he advised me to have half bound *in russia*—not in *vellum*. It *shall* be russia. Even the binding shall remind me of the giver.

δεχομαι φιλον γε δωρον εκ φιλης . . . χερος

[I take them—precious gift from precious hand.]

That line from the Alcestis, wd. be a good motto for the first page: but no—I wont have it there. After a little talking of Mr. James & my disappointment about his eloquence & my satisfaction about his scriptural knowledge, Eliza Cliffe came in & announced the carriages!— Obliged to go. Was not with him a quarter of an hour,—& tired to death for it. Oh *so* tired. Got home,—but could scarcely get thro' dinner—& then to oblige Bummy, off to Mrs. Martin's. There I sate in the armchair more dead than alive,— certainly more disagreable than agreable—until tea-time. The tea was a collation for the cricketers & sinecure visitors; & it was hardly over, before I fainted fairly away. They dragged me out of the room, & packed me up on the sofa. I got better soon, & sate quietly till Miss Peyton went home;

& she had the mercy to take me away with her & leave me at Hope End. To bed of course—but Lady Macbeth's dreams were nothing to mine.

There was a letter from Papa today [addressed to Henrietta]. Henrietta was later than I, incoming from Malvern—& it fell into my hands first. They were trembling ones. But they need not have trembled. Not *one* word on *the* subject. Dearest Papa is well, & in apparent good spirits. Thank God thank God for this *best* news!—

Wednesday. July 20.

How the days of this month are coming to a close,—quickly quickly; & probably much of our happiness with them. Next month—oh!—next month!— My fatigue has not quite gone off,—so I have determined on not going to Mrs. Cliffe's,—& they have all gone without me. I liked my solitude, even tho' I had no one to say so to—& in spite of La Bruyère, & Cowper!— Nearly finished the Alcestis. I will finish it tomorrow, before breakfast.

Friday July 22.

I could not write in my diary yesterday. A new sorrow: a letter from Papa to Bummy communicating to us the death of dear Mary, [Uncle] Sam's beloved wife, whch. took place on the 3d. of last month in Jamaica. Lovely, loving, & beloved she was! She loved me—I am sure she did: and I loved *her*—how could I help it? Does it not appear, as if all those who have loved, or been loved by me, are to be separated from me? The Lord's will—the Lord's will be done. But I am human, & very sad at heart. Yet if He is my shepherd, will he not make me lie down, still, on the green pastures—either on the pastures of earth or Heaven? Let me not think now of myself. Poor Sam! I have prayed for him. Comfort him Only comforter— Support him Only staff— preserve him Only Lord!—

I have written to Papa today. It was an effort, but a necessary one. Oh dear dear Mary—was our parting the very very last? How many tears I shed that day!—and *then* there was a hand here, to wipe tears away!—I will not write anymore.

Saturday July 23.

. . . I have heard the boys read Greek today,—& feel more tranquil. Nay! I have read myself, a good part of the Enchiridion of Epictetus,—but I read the bible before—& it was *that* that did me the good. Epictetus's philosophy never could make a philosopher in sorrow: it approaches indeed wonderfully near to Christianity, but not near enough to catch the warmth, with the light. "Think", he says, "that thy pitcher is a pitcher; & when it breaks thou wilt be calm: think that those whom thou lovest, are human, & when they die, thou wilt be calm." Cold philosophy! weak philosophy! vain philosophy! Thou wilt *not* be calm. *Thou* art human too!—

I had a letter from Mrs. Boyd today, & wrote two or three lines to her this morning, telling her the reason of my not being at the Malvern Bible meeting & at Ruby Cottage last Thursday as I had intended. She wishes me to spend next Monday or Tuesday at Malvern. If Thursday's letter had not come, how happy I shd. have been in doing so! Miss Boyd is to arrive on Wednesday; & Miss Gibbons on Tuesday. No more happy quiet days with Mr. Boyd!—

Sunday July 24.

The month is coming to a close. Next month— They are all gone to church. I did not feel happy enough to mix with the many who are going there; and Mr. Dean's preaching is not worth disturbing one's feelings, that it may be listened to. But I may as well have listened to it, as have read Dr. Wheatley's Essays on Cowper Newton Heber &c —& far better. Dr. Wheatly disbelieves in the *total* corruption of human nature, & in the regenerating influence of divine grace; and yet Mrs. Martin admires & lent me his book!—& I have nearly read it thro'!! which I believe is neither to her credit nor to mine. Paul called himself the *chief of sinners*. Dr. Wheatly wd. call *that* an *orientalism*. Let him call it what he will. We *are* sinful, deeply sinful, sorrowful creatures; & if Thou Oh Lord most merciful holy & true, dost not wipe away our sins & our tears, oh Lord Who under Heaven, will cease to sin & weep? Speaking & feeling for myself,—the dye of *my* sin, & the stain of *my* tears, will last for ever!—Not all great ocean's waters could wash out that which one drop of the blood of Christ *can* wash out— Yea! *hath* washed out!—

I had a letter from Papa today. Its subjects are exclusively religious.

Monday. July 25.

I finished Epictetus, & began Marcus Antoninus.

I was urged to go out in the carriage, & agreed to it; & I was afterwards asked by Bummy to call at the Bartons; *not to get out but to make an enquiry about Mrs. Peyton.* Agreed to that. At our gate she proposed driving to drink tea with the Cliffes. Did not agree to *that*. Went on to the Bartons, & there we were entreated to get out & have tea. *I* answered decidedly that we could not. Bummy answered in a manner that made both me & Mrs. Griffith feel convinced of her wish to do so. She pushed me *visibly*,—& at last said positively that we wd. return after our drive & drink tea with them. The tears were in my eyes while Mrs. Griffiths was entreating, but they fairly & foolishly started from them when we had driven from the door. And then tho' I did not say much & not *one* word of reproach, & tho' I yielded the point, Bummy's manner was so *very* unkind! I told her that I had refused going even to Mr. Boyd's. "*That*" appeared to her "of no consequence". Well! we returned & had tea—made a more agreable Barton tea-drinking than usual, by Miss Glasco's conversation; And after all, on our way home & when we arrived at home, there was nothing for me but gravity & coldness & silence. After I had yielded—after I had said so little—& after that little had been extorted from me by natural, recently wounded feelings!—Oh it went to my heart. I ran up stairs, & suffered tears to do me good. And then I sate down to write a note to Mrs. Boyd in answer to her proposal about my going there today or tomorrow. If Mr. Boyd shd. hear of my having been to the Bartons, he will not think any excuse I can send him, reasonable enough not to be unkind.

Henrietta came up stairs while I was thinking so; and she strongly advised me to go to Malvern tomorrow.

We went down stairs together. No smile, no word for *me!*— I had a hearty cry afterwards.

Tuesday. July 26th.

This morning, at breakfast before Bummy came down, Henrietta & Arabel & Bro tried my persuadibleness by begging me to go to Malvern. It yielded—& partly, of course, because the feeling within, about Mr. Boyd, took their side of the question. When Bummy came down, Bro said something indicative of my intention. "What"! she cried "is Ba going to Malvern today. Then I hope, Ba, you have forgotten the impropriety of drinking tea with Mrs. Griffith yesterday."

I might have answered that if it had *not* been for drinking tea with Mrs. Griffith yesterday, I wd. not have been persuaded to think of going to Mr. Boyd's today—but my only answer was,— —bursting into tears. Nothing more was said; & I wiped them away as fast as my nature wd. let me. Foolish to cry—but I was nervous & weak & unwell,—& really could not help it.

The first thing I did after breakfast, was to counter order the carriage whch. Henrietta had ordered: and the next thing, to run up into my room & cry. I sent my note to Mrs. Boyd. Out of spirits all day, & B—out of humour. We climbed the hill to pick mushrooms in the eveng.; & then her manner to me became kind again, & I became happy —or *happier*—again.

No letters. I finished the first book of Marcus Antoninus;

& began the second. . . . One of the advantages which Antoninus derived from his brother Severus, was, *το πιστευτικον περι του ὑπο των φιλων φιλεισθαι* [A confidence in the love of friends.] I wish Severus had been *my* brother. But perhaps after all I shd. have been a duller pupil than Antoninus was.

In my note to Mrs. Boyd today, I proposed deferring my visit to Malvern until next week; as *Mr. Boyd* & Miss Boyd might like to be undisturbed on her first arrival. *Will* he like to be undisturbed by *me*?

A low-spirited day. I could not help thinking bitterly & sadly of the dear days for ever gone,—& of those dearer beings gone with the days! The Lord's will—the Lord's will be done.

Wednesday. July 27th.

Dear Bummy & I are quite good friends now! Could we ever be otherwise? Not in heart. This is Henry's birthday [his thirteenth], & a holiday; & it ought to be a very studious day with me—but I am without energies this morning. I have however finished the second book of Marcus Antoninus, & begun the third. Heard from Mrs. Boyd who proposed my going to Malvern on *Saturday*.

Thursday. July 28th.

Finished the third book of Marcus Antoninus. I am getting on . . Weak & unwell all day; at least feeling actually weak, and as if I *could* be unwell—a common feeling with me, & not an agreable one. A letter from Annie to me; written in her usual manner, both as to kindness & levity. She has quick perceptions; and it is to be lamented that she has . . . associated so much more with one of her parents than with the other. But I am glad very glad to hear from her; to know or to guess that I am forgiven. Bummy had a letter from Papa!! Arabel says it *was* a letter from him. She went into her own room afterwards, & without mentioning having received it, to one person! Something bad!!—

I was relieved by her consenting to call at Colwall with Henrietta. They will bring the carriage back: and then I *am*, volens or not, to take a drive. My very heart is shaken. I have no heart for driving—but I will go, as they wish it. Ann & I were covering some of my dumb Greeks with cartridge paper. How well they look—and how unwell I am!—

Henrietta Arabel & I drove out—up the rough road to Brand Lodge, round the rough road to the Whyche,—home. . .

Before Arabel came to bed, I was reverie-ing about Papa coming home immediately, & our going away almost as soon. But after Arabel came to bed, she turned my reverie from black to brown, by telling me that Bummy had mentioned to herself & Henrietta, having received the letter; & had assured them that it related in no way to our business, & was silent as to Papa's return. So I went to sleep quietly, & dreamt of a unicorn.

Friday. July 29th.

A hard day at Greek & philosophy. Began & finished the 4th. book of Antoninus. He repeats himself a good deal, & his style is not flowing or harmonious: but there is an elevation in his thoughts & an energy in their expression, which I very much admire. How I do wish that Gataker's system of reform had been *applied* i.e. introduced into the text. As it is, to refer constantly to the notes when you wish to understand the text, is like dipping this pen into ink every time you wish to make a single stroke, which by the way I am obliged to do—or like being forced to look at the sun before you can see any object by its light.

Some thunder & lightening today—not very severe; but sufficiently so, to prove what they might be. No letter.

Besides the 4th book of Antoninus, I prepared a part of the Seven chiefs for Mr. Boyd tomorrow. Not *very* much tired after all; and tranquil & comfortable in my mind. Thank God for that.

Saturday. July 30.

Set off for Malvern at a quarter to nine, with Ann who wished to visit her mother, & William [Treherne] in an official capacity. I had my breakfast at home, & found Mrs. Boyd at hers. She met me at the door, & after a few considerate words in the dining room, she took me *vol, nol,* into the breakfast room. There I was introduced to Miss Boyd & Miss Bordman, & shook hands with Miss Gibbons. Miss Boyd is old fashioned in dress manner & *countenance.* She has not Mr. Boyd's. Miss Bordman is pleasing & even pretty, & has a voice & manner even more pleasing than her face. She went up stairs to tell Mr. Boyd of my being there, & I was admitted into his room almost immediately. "Is that Porsonia?"* But how annoyed I was when he desired me to sit only a minute with him, & then to return to the majority. I pleaded conscience & inclination. He insisted, on the ground that I should otherwise make him appear selfish—that he had promised to give me up to his sister & Miss Bordman, for the greater part of the day—that I could not doubt its being a sacrifice on his part. I did not know what to doubt. There is no doubt of my having been in an irritation—not to say, an indignation. However I was obstinate as to remaining until the hair dresser came; & then I went away quite *nol.* He told me to talk more to his sister & Miss Bordman, than to Miss Gibbons. Of course, as he wished it.

Well! I did talk to Miss Bordman & to Miss Boyd as much as I could, *until past luncheon time*—for until then, I did not get back to Mr. Boyd. I could not help saying "I did not think that you meant to admit me again today". "How can you say so?" &c &c &c— — Stayed with him until dinner. Dined & discussed the Socinian, Bible-society question[1] with Miss Gibbons—& had, in my own opinion, not merely the best *side* but the *best of the* argument. If the Bible Society excludes the Socinians, it must be consistent & exclude all those who are not spiritual christians. Returned

* See entry for Richard Porson, *Who's Who.*

to Mr. Boyd, & sate with him until he proposed walking a little in front of the house, as he had not been out all yesterday. It is a shame that he shd. be allowed to remain in the house, from the want of a person to walk with him. Once more I begged him to let me do so. No! Now his objections could not effect my being his companion in the *garden*; as *there*, there can be no carriages or horses! But I did not like proposing it. *He* wd. have done so, had *he wished* it!—Before he went, I begged him to let me know of his return; & I sate meantime talking to Miss Boyd & Miss Bordman in the drawing room. We talked of French & Italian & English & German Literature—of much that I knew something about; & much that I knew nothing about. In a quarter of an hour, Mr. Boyd's voice said "Ann" at the door. "She is not here" answered Miss Boyd. In five minutes more the same voice said——what Miss Boyd thought was, "Ann" again; & she answered again as before. Nothing more from the voice! I sate & sate & talked & talked & thought & thought, until I was boiling over. Half an hour longer before they went down to tea, & before I was sent for into Mr. Boyd's room!! I determined to let myself be in a passion; but to say nothing passionately. However Mr. Boyd began to tell me that the second supposed "Ann" was "Porsonia"; that he had walked to the door a third time, but had soliloquized "I will not be selfish" & had returned to his room without speaking. "I knew how much my sister & Miss Bordman would like to talk to you". I could restrain myself no longer—& overflowed—gently with—"you seem to have thought a great deal about what *they* like—but very little about what *I* like!" Mr. Boyd exculpated himself, and said that his feeling was "If *I* can be disinterested, *she* ought to be so also".

He was *very* kind in his manner to me today; & spoke in an anxious manner of our unhappy business. He said "Well! it is not certain", with respect to my going away; as if the no-certainty were a relief to him. Well: if it *is* certain—if I *do* go away—nobody will be left behind who cares for him more than I care. *More!!!* He reproached me for not having come to spend a few days with him—"You might have thought that this might possibly be the last opportunity you wd. have, of staying with me—*at least while I am here.*" Does not that expression seem to look forward to a removal *consequent* upon ours. Oh! I hoped & hope so!—

No Greek reading today.

He seems to like Miss Bordman very much. So do I; but I hope he will not learn to like her society better than mine. I hope— — — —

What a narrow *heart* I must have.

Miss Bordman *kissed* me when I went away. Curtseying in the morning, & embracing in the evening!— But I never dislike such a general principle. It is the principle of warm hearts & unsuspicious heads. I went away at past eight, & got home at past nine. A *little* grumbling indirectly, about lateness; but nothing which demands grumbling in return. No letters. . . .

Monday. August 1st.

This day—this month! How & *where* will this month end, to *us*?— . . .

Vexatious work à la Henriette about "who shall go to Gt Malvern"? Gained my point at last. H A & B went, & I stayed at home. They did not return until past nine; & I meanwhile was hard at work at Antoninus. Finished his 5th book—read 7 chap: in the Bible, & then went out to walk in the dark. Frightened by a man with a coat. Jumped in at the drawing room window.

Tuesday. August 2d.

A note from Mrs. Martin. . . . She has got another copy of . . . Moore's Life of Ld. Byron,—& therefore when the other is "in a presentable state" I am to be presented with it. Very kind of her. A large packet from London of bombazeens silks &c—& a catalogue inside, in Papa's writing. Surely if he were coming immediately he wd. not write—

but Bummy & Minny dont say "*surely*". They have some certain knowledge I feel . . certain, of something unpleasant.

The boys, save Stormy, & the girls, save nobody, to Colwal this eveng. to play cricket & drink tea. I wish a little shyness & obstinacy cd. have kept me at home with the only *saved* person. Bummy in low spirits—nay, H & A apart,—with tears in her eyes, all the evening. Something wrong.

Mr. Martin showed us his drawings & read us some of his journal in & out of Africa,—so that we were amused. How very very odd it is, that Mrs. Martin, who, I think, likes *me*, & I, who, I am sure, like Mrs. Martin, should be oil & water together. Some want of conformity & sympathy, I suppose! Got home late—at past 11.

I read half the 6th book of Antoninus today—so I cant say, after all, perdidi diem [I have lost a day].

Wednesday. August 3d.

Read very little of Antoninus, before Eliza came. Painted at the picture, which never will be like me until I change my nose mouth & eyes. Yes! Mrs. Griffith (who called here today with Miss Glasco & Miss Peyton to be congratulated on the new Peyton [baby]) declared that the eyes & the forehead are "*extrame like.*" In which case, I must be extrame wrong. Miss Glasco is an agreable, very agreable woman; agreable without effort: but, as to her interesting me, or anybody else, that is out of the question. Mind—I *like her*.

Eliza stayed until quite the eveng.: long past eight. I amused her in the morning by telling the story of the White cat and the man with the nose. I thought or dreamt that my vanity had fallen to cinders: but it must indeed be easily *redivivus* if I could be pleased by Eliza & Arabel telling me that my storytelling was "admirable". And yet such was actually & deplorably the case. Am I more difficult to be reformed than the House of Commons? The Ayes have it!—

Eliza has seen Hope End advertised *by name* in the Worcester paper. I wd. & cd. ask no particulars. I was so afraid of her telling me on what day it is to be sold. To be sold!— How like a dream! But from this dream we shall not wake. No letter.

Settled. I am to go to Malvern tomorrow. When this was suggested Bummy advised me to do so—"Your Papa may be at home, you do not know when". Does *she* know when? I am sick of thinking. But I will go. No last opportunity of being with my dear friend, shall be lost "for want of thought."

Bro & Sam went with Mr. Martin, who breakfasted here, to the Hereford assizes. Mr. Martin had tea here, on their return. . . .

Thursday, August 4.

Ordered the carriage at a quarter past 8,—& it was not ready until a quarter past 9. I in a passion of course. But as soon as it began to flow, it began to ebb.

Got to Malvern at ten, & found Mrs. Boyd & *company* at breakfast; & after a consultation in Mrs. Boyd's bedroom on the case, Biscoe versus Boyd, was admitted into Mr. Boyd's room. Mrs. B showed me Mr. Biscoe's two last letters to Annie. One of them had as a motto, a quotation from a poem of mine—

> *Unless you can dream, that his faith is fast,*
> *Thro' months & years of roving—*
> Unless you can die when the dream is past—
> Ah no! this is not *loving.**

It certainly is not *loving*, in Annie Boyd; who calls his letter, expressive of the most passionate attachment, & utmost distress of mind, "another stupid letter". I never could understand how a delicate woman can even tolerate the attentions of a man whom she does not love: or how a

* 'Song, written for guitar.'

kind hearted woman can wound the feelings of a man whom she does love.

Mr. Boyd received me, as if he were not displeased to do so,—& enquired with an apparent interest about Hope End &c. Presently he desired the servant to beg Miss Boyd to *read the paper to him*, whenever it came. Would he have had the paper read to him, when he could have talked to me,—*at one time*? "*Yes! Change!*—"

I was desired, as soon as the paper came, to go & talk to Miss Bordman—to go down stairs into the breakfast room, & talk to her. I cd. not do it—immediately. I went for a few minutes into the drawingroom, to recover *the newspaper!* — Down stairs; & sent up again by Mrs. Boyd with Miss Bordman. We talked—as desired!— She told me that Mr. Boyd had heard her read a little of the Greek New Testament, as her father had taught her a little Greek—very little;—which she had neglected. . . Mr. Boyd had told me before, that he had written some verses upon her, *at her request:* that he mentioned them to me, because they might possibly be shown to me,—& that I might think him inconsistent in writing upon a person whom he had known for so short a time,—after his professed intention of writing no more. As to his *inconsistency—that* is not the word I should think of applying. . . The verses were *not* shown to me.

More than half an hour passed over the newspaper; & then I was readmitted into Mr. Boyd's room. I felt very unwilling to read Greek. I fancied that he proposed it as if it were a self infliction; originating from *a feeling of general benevolence inclusive of me*. I assured him that I did not wish to read. When I did read, my voice faltered in spite of my resolution. I am a fool.

Went down to dinner, feeling wretchedly out of spirits, out of a talking & laughing condition. . . . After dinner, when we were in the drawing room,—I could *not* talk; & the tears were in my eyes oftener than once. Mr. Boyd's voice first called for Mrs. Boyd; then for Miss Boyd: not at all for me. After nearly 3 quarters of an hour, Mrs. Boyd advised me to go in to him. I went. Heard him repeat some passages from Æschylus, which he was not clear . . about. I could not help it. The tears rolled down my cheeks. They should not injure *him*—not even by blistering his book: so they were wiped away very quickly. Perhaps this was the last time of our being together!—

Talking about Annie & Eliza Cliffe—jealousy & insincerity. I would not, & will not, attribute one to one, & the other to the other. He wished that I had never been intimate with Eliza. (She cares more for me than *he* does!) He told me that he was not aware of any single fault I had; & that Miss Boadman's disposition (it was paying her, he said, a great compliment) seemed to resemble mine, more than the disposition of any person with whom he was acquainted. I observed "I thought you had found out my faults long ago—particularly after my having been so cross about the Terence".[1] "Cross! you were not cross"—and then he repented viva voce having ever made the application to me, which I had considered in such a light.

There is no use in it. Of one thing I am convinced; that if, from any change of circumstance, *one* of his visitors were forced to return home immediately,—he would feel more *sorrow*,—than if *I* were to leave this neighbourhood for ever. And this is the weight of human friendship! Ashes! *Dust* is too heavy!—

I wish I had not gone today. I will not go again soon. I said something to him, about depriving his *sister* of his society: & he begged me not to consider her. He would always be "happy to see me"— I have scarcely patience to write all these details. They make me sick—& mad—

Left Ruby Cottage in the rain. *Not* a happy day. Oh no!—

I forgot to mention the remarks which were made on Arabel's no-visit the other evening. Mr. Boyd observed that "if we remained at Hope End, & if I were *to die*, it was clear to him that my family wd. break off all intercourse with his." If I were to die!— Not an improbable case; but supposed so coldly!—

Got home at 8. While I was away, they had been showing my Wolf's Homer to Mr. & Mrs. Martin. Black thinking before sound sleeping, in my room tonight. No letter.

Friday. August 5.

Finished & sealed a letter to poor beloved [Uncle] Sam before breakfast; & yet not up early. May it find him lying by the still waters of the peace of God; & on the green pastures of his love!— I pray for him everyday.

The darkness of yesterday's fancies has still left a cloud over my mind, today. It seems to me that I am reconciled, quite reconciled, to the prospect of leaving Hope End. I can bear any thing but "an *altered* eye". How profound Gray was, in selecting that epithet!— I read the other half of Antoninus's sixth book,—& half his seventh, besides. What a creature I am—to spend my time in this way, between philosophy & folly. Antoninus wd. not be well pleased, if he could know whom he has for a reader!— . . .

Except that Eliza Cliffe sent me a parcel of new walking shoes, a print of Paganini bespoken by Bummy; & a promise of the Last man [by Mary Wollstonecraft Shelley], which is far from being the last book I am anxious about seeing. Mrs. Martin is to send it to me tomorrow; & I must finish the 7th book of Antoninus before it comes.

Eliza is really an amiable girl,—& very fond of me. Which quality is most valuable in my eyes? I have an oath in Heaven to be altogether sincere in this journal of mine, —therefore—the *latter* quality. I am always apt, too apt, irrepressibly apt, to feel with an old poet—

> If she be not fair to *me*,
> What care I, how fair she be?—

Narrow, narrow heart!— It is this that makes me so—about somebody else—

Saturday August 6.

Well! I am really to go with Bummy & Henrietta to Malvern; & this afternoon!— I shall make myself miserable all the time, I dare say; & yet I am pleased at the thoughts of going. Bro & Sam have ridden to call upon Mr. Allen Cliffe, who is "too proud" not to be called upon . . ., *before* he calls here. How I hate this punctiliousness of mind which can only exist in a petty mind. Trees may be cut into peacocks, when they stand in a small inclosure: but who wd. think of cutting into peacocks, the trees of America's vast forests?— Who am I, who wd. be severe upon *littleness* in character? Have I not just been measuring my own?

I had time to finish reading the 7th. book of Marcus Antoninus, before we went to Malvern, which we did not do until four o'clock. . . . Mr. Boyd walking in front of the house. I preceded the carriage to beg him to go into the house while it past. He said with a smile, an apparently pleased smile, that he did not expect to hear my voice tonight. Mrs. Boyd was out; so when I had opened the opposite gate for Bummy & Henrietta, I followed Mr. Boyd into his room. "As they are all out, shall we sit in the drawing room; & will you go & shut the window"? But he heard Miss Gibbons' voice, & changed his mind, & did not change his room. We talked a little about reform, & Miss Bordman's illness, & mine; & then I was asked if I had brought my book—, my Æschylus? No! I did not think that, at that time in the evening, he would like me to read Greek to him. I "might have brought it, at any rate—he *would* have liked it". So I proposed reading, & did read, out of his folio Æschylus; but we did not read much. He could not have liked hearing me, *much*. Kind in his manner. Some talking of the Hope End business.

Bummy & Henrietta called on Mrs. Boyd when they called for me; & of this I was glad. It was past seven when we left Ruby Cottage. A happier visit than my last! Oh I would give anything if I could *know*—not think, not guess —but *know*, what the feeling is there, with respect to me. I *know* my own exclusive & exacting disposition; . . .

Sunday. August 7th.

Bro gave me a note from Eliza Cliffe, to say . . nothing! She feels very warmly & kindly: but she does not write well. Better than vicé versâ. As it is, there is certainly no *vice* in the case.

Went to Church with Bummy & Arabel; not with Henrietta—because a carriage that holds only three, wont hold four—which is remarkable. When we returned, Henrietta wanted to know if there was any *news*— None in Mr. Dean's sermon certainly! . . .

Maddox came from Ledbury this morning; & she has been talking to me in my room for the last two hours. I love her for the sake of past & present. She is a dear feeling creature!—& *that*, I always thought & felt!— But now I must occupy a little more time more profitably, than even in talking with her—or writing here.

Mr. Boyd said yesterday that from the four words "Good morning Mr. Boyd", which he once heard Henrietta say, he thinks her voice agreable & *clear & distinct*. "The best voice of the three"—alluding to Arabel's & mine!

My voice pleased him *once*. Well!—there is no use in thinking of it any more!—

Maddox is going in our carriage to Malvern tomorrow. Shall I go with her? If I had not gone yesterday, I would. . . . But as it is, I think—no! I will not do so.

Monday. August 8.

In spite of my "No I will not do so", when I got up this morning, & found Maddox 'going going' I took an irrepressible fancy to be "gone" with her. But will Bummy like it? I agitated, o'connellized,[1] about, in my flannel dressing-gown,—& at last decided on feeling her pulsations on the subject. If she is against it, I wont go: & in that case my staying wont be my fault. If this shd. be the last or almost the last opportunity—how painful the thought would be, that I should myself myself [sic] have thrown it away. Went into Bummy's room—"Bummy! shall you think me very mad if I go to Malvern today". The answer decided me. *No! I did not do so.*

I have had such a hard day's work today, that I am quite exhausted & can scarcely write. I have written a letter to Papa, read the first vol: of the Last man, which Mrs. Martin has sent me at last,—& read the *whole* of the 8th. book of Marcus Antoninus,—& prepared some of the Seven Chiefs for Mr. Boyd,—besides hearing Storm & George read out of Homer & Zenophon. I feel nervous all over—tingling in my hands & feet—& cant write a word more.

Tuesday August 9.

I believe I was more tired last night than was good for me; certainly more so than was good for my diary which I had to bring to an untimely end, without noticing Bummy & Henrietta & Arabel drinking tea at the Martins; & Bro & Sam dittoing it at the Trants. I was left to my soliloquies—, & my Antoninus, & my Last Man.

This morning I sent off my letter to Papa. None from him. One from Miss Price, in which she alludes for the first time & in a mournful manner, to our prospect of leaving Hope End. Dominick [Trant] arrived to dine & sleep; an unprompted honor— Arabel was so goodnatured as to walk to Colwall before breakfast for Mrs. Shelley's second volume [of *The Last Man*],—& I have read it thro'. And I have read besides the whole of Marcus Antoninus's 9th. book. He becomes easy to me, as I become familiar with him; & this, I am becoming by degrees, tho' he *is* an emperor & a philosopher.

I did not like Mrs. Shelley's first volume at all, & fancied that all her genius had exhaled in Frankenstein. But in the second volume, Richard's himself again! There is a great deal of power & originality about it—and yet I devoutly wish that the book had been unread as far as I am concerned. It has dessolated me! I wish I had the 3d. volume! There are two wishes—like what most of my wishes are!—

Shall I go to Malvern tomorrow? If I can. And I think I can.

. . .

Wednesday. August 10

Went to Malvern, tho' Bummy, when I proposed it last night, opposed it. In consequence of the opposition I withdrew my motion; after which, she herself brought it on again; & I went. But *after* breakfast, & the lateness out-of-humoured me.

I forgot to say that Dominick arrived yesterday, with a shirt or two—to pay what we imagined wd. be a morning visit; but which turns out to be several morning & eveng visits joined together. He asked me to bring back his newspaper & letters from Malvern. Accordingly I called on Mrs. Trant—did not stay long. Got to Mr. Boyd's about 12, & was received by Mrs. B who took me into the breakfast room to consult over the Biscoe versus Boyd case. Poor Mr. Biscoe. From my heart & heart's heart I pity him. He devotedly loves one who does not, & never will, love *him*. Well!—these things are to be borne. If they are not, they will destroy: & then they need not be borne. Wisely said, Marcus Antoninus! Annie observes in her letter to Mrs. Boyd, that there are many people whom she cd. like as well as Mr. Biscoe, & some whom she cd. like better!!!!!!—

Mrs. Boyd soon took me into Mr. Boyd's room, where Miss Boyd was sitting. He said "I had just been thinking of you". Miss Boyd & I were turned out, & then I was readmitted, & sate with him until dinner-time. I read some of the seven chiefs . . . & we talked. He sighed when I was speaking of Hope End: but people will sigh sometimes without sorrow. I may be wrong. If I am, I wish I knew it. Went down to dinner, which was considered "very long" in coming. At dinner something was said of—. I am ashamed of writing down my own feelings & the causes of them.

After dinner, Mr. Boyd was discovered walking in front

of the house; & Mrs. Boyd asked me if I had ever done so with him. "No!—" "Will you go & do so now?" "No. I think Mr. Boyd does not like it." "*I* will go & try?" observed Mrs. Boyd. . . . She went out—& walked backwards & forwards with Mr. Boyd for half an hour, before the windows. I fancied at first, that she might mean to ask him whether or not *I* shd. walk with him? If she did, his answer was like mine—"No".

Could I help saying, *no*? Has he not proved to me that he disliked my walking with him? If I had gone out, either he might have been forced to do what he disliked; or I should have been sent back to the drawing room to explain what I did not understand myself about this distaste which seems exclusively to regard *me*. Painful it was to me to say "I *think* Mr. Boyd does not like it." But what cd. I do? The tears are in my eyes as I am writing. Oh that people shd. be so kind—& so unkind!— He came in, & called at the door for Miss Boyd, who went up stairs & stayed there about a quarter of an hour. When she returned, Mrs. B asked if she had brought a message for me, respecting my going up stairs, "On the contrary, my brother sent me down that I might have the pleasure of Miss Barrett's company". So there I sate for half an hour; for an hour; for more than an hour; until Mrs. Boyd suggested that if I did not go to see Mr. Boyd now, I wd. not do so at all, as it was seven! Miss Steers was there, & we had been talking of Keats & Shelley, & Colleridge's Ancient Mariner—& Mrs. Boyd had been confessing that she had lost all her taste for poetry. Lost! Did she ever possess it? Can any one *lose* his taste for poetry? Can any one lose his life, & yet live?—

When I went into Mr. Boyd's room, I cd. not help being grave & silent. . . At last I said—I could not help it —"I am sorry that you wd. not let me come up stairs before"— And then came the assurance that he had never intended me to stay away; & an observation coldly enough made, that I was "fanciful". Tears again. They *would* come.

We talked, & talked chearfully,—but I went away sadly. My spirits are broken, by strokes of pain from every side; & I am become morbidly & foolishly sensitive. . . .

Well! we shall go away soon; & in the meantime I will not go as frequently as I have done, to Malvern. . . . *I* am not the favorite at this present time. And yet whose regard has been professed & proved as mine? There is no use in all this.

On my return, I found a parcel from Mrs. Martin containing Moore's Life of Byron, handsomely bound. A kind & valuable present. Oh I wish, I do wish that I had not left home this morning!—

Thursday. August 11.

What a weight there is on my heart today. It is like lead, only colder. I wish I had not gone yesterday, where I did. . . . I wish I had commanded myself sufficiently to avoid making that foolish observation! I wish I had *never* gone to Malvern! Vain wishes, all of them!—

I wrote a note to Mrs. Martin, to thank her for her kind present; & I hope she may send back the 3d. vol of the Last Man, by my messenger. If she had read as many books as I have, she must have been at least six hundred years old by this time. No answer! Mrs. Martin was out—& so was I.

On Wednesday before breakfast, I read the beginning of Antoninus's 10th. book, & I went on with it today, but not to the end. My energies felt dead within me: & how could I do anything without them? Nothing but reading the 3d. vol: of Mrs. Shelley, which I despatched in two hours—(which *did* come at last!!—) No going out today. Marcus Antoninus after Mrs. Shelly, & drinking tea after Marcus. Not a letter!—

Friday August 12.

A hard day's work . . I finished the 10th. & read the 11 & 12 books of my emperor. Done with him.— I wish I were as good a philosopher as he is, or was: but I wonder if he practised what he thought, as little as I do, what I read. . . .

Miss Glasco called here today,—& we walked back with her to the gate which ushers you in to the green path parallel with our road. She said "Where shall we meet next? Recollect where we parted." She goes to Cheltenham tomorrow, & remains three weeks away.

An agreable, a very agreable woman—and a kind amiable warm-hearted woman besides. Bummy Henrietta & I were met, on our returning hatless, by Lane who brought an open letter from Papa to Bro, sent by Bro to Bummy. She dared not read it before us—. I could see that very well. Bro met us in our tribulation . . He was riding down the road on his way to a pic nic party on the Malvern hills. . . So to Bro, Bummy applied—"What am I to do with this letter?" "Read it—all of you read it—there is nothing in it." Nothing in it? Then we may breathe. Yes! there was nothing,—except an order for the discharge of those workmen who could get situations. Nothing besides.

I did not go out again. I felt too unwell for it: but I finished Antoninus: & then I began & nearly finished the *Messeniennes* by Casimir De la vigne. He is an energetic poet for a frenchman; but does not bring with him the certificate of his baptism in Helicon.

Unwell, very unwell all the evening! A strange nervous depressed feeling, as if I were both soulless & boneless!—

Saturday August 13.

Miss Glasco told me yesterday that Eliza Cliffe was to be here this morning, so I suppose she will. Henrietta is going to Malvern in the evening—, & something was said of my going too, tho' I really really actually feel "*Nolo*"— But in case of the possibility of it, I prepared before breakfast, some of the Seven Chiefs for Mr. Boyd. Bummy said yesterday that she wd. not go. Now if *she* does not, *I* will: not so much because I desire it, as because my not seeming to desire it, might seem strange to everybody here. It almost seems strange to myself! And yet wd. it not be stranger if—?— There is not any use in writing of it. Feeling about it, is bad enough!—

How depressed I felt yesterday evening. How I hung upon the past, as if my life as well as happiness were in it! How I thought of those words "*You will never find another person who will love you as I love you*"— And how I felt that to hear again the sound of those beloved, those ever ever beloved lips, I wd. barter all other sounds & sights— that I wd. in joy & gratitude lay down before her my tastes & feelings each & all, in sacrifice for the love, the exceeding love which I never, in truth, can find again. Have I not tried this, & know this & felt this: & do I not feel *now*, bitterly, dessolately, that human love like her's, I never can find again!* . . .

Eliza Cliffe came, & I sate for my picture. The paint is beginning to crack from redundancy. In fact my features are now literally beginning to stand out from the canvass. I shall soon be a companion for the Roman Emperors, for Marcus Antoninus himself, in *bas*-relievo.

Such pro & conning & à la Henrietting about "who will go to Malvern"? & "shall we go to Malvern at all?" I am really wonderful. I began to feel a wish—yes!—actually a wish—to go. No going at last; & when it was decided I was glad; not merely that it was decided, but that it was decided *so*. H A & I in the carriage, Eliza riding, to Warm well. Washed our faces & wet our hair,—& then, I on Eliza's poney, we mounted the hill. "Round we went" & then "down we went"; for a black cloud in the distance frightened everybody but me. So "home we went". But oh how exquisite the hills looked, stretching forward before us, in the midst of that expansive & sunlit scenery!— Eliza parted from us, at our gate. I was unwell this morning, but well this evening. How some thoughts will hang about me!—

* EBB was, of course, referring to her mother.

Sunday. August 14.

Everybody except me, went to church. I stayed at home, & felt wretchedly unwell all the time, & read the Bishop of Salisburys (Jewel's) Apologia Ecclesiæ Anglicanæ. I got thro' more than half of it; lying now in my armchair & now on the bed, & now smelling aromatic vinegar. The soul must be a weak being after all, that it cant animate one's body without aromatic vinegar: and *my* soul has life & energy enough about it, as souls go. Jewel writes very well, very eloquently, very nervously. I like him very much. I bought this little book before I could read it, when I was eleven or twelve years old. I have read some of it, here & there, since then: but never so much as I have read today. I wish I could write Latin as well as Jewel!—

Eliza Cliffe came up stairs & found me inbedded. I transplanted myself immediately into my sitting room, —& then, up came Mrs. Cliffe, who looked at the picture & by asking a hundred questions about my opinion of it, put my conscience in jeopardy. We went to chapel, & hoped to find Mr. Curzon. In vain! A young man preached "indifferently well". I am in doubt up to this moment whether he or the sun made me feel sleepy. As Bummy Arabel & I were driving home we made a sejour among the cows for some time; & while they were studying the picturesque, my thoughts went away where they liked. I forgot to say that the preacher put a note directed to Miss Barrett, into Mrs. Cliffe's hand. The note was from Mr. Curzon, & proposed dining with us on Wednesday or Thursday. *Then I will go to Malvern on Tuesday.* I felt better, far better, this evening.

Monday August 15.

Henrietta asked me yesterday if I would go to Malvern today. No! Tomorrow, it will be nearly a week, since I was there. How heroic I am,—& vindictive too!—

I wrote this morning, a note to Mr. Curzon; a letter to Miss Price, & a letter to Annie!— I am in doubt whether to begin to read *Cebes* or Callimachus. Philosophy wd. do me more good than poetry, just now, I think. . . . Had I always studied philosophy exclusively of poetry, I wonder if I should have been differently & more happily constituted in some respects. I am afraid—*no*. I am afraid I resemble the student of Ossuna, mentioned in Don Quixote, who even if he had been educated at Salamanca, would have been nevertheless *mad*. Well! tomorrow may—oh may tomorrow, remove one mad symptom. It is too painful.

Solved my doubts, & read half Cebes's dialogue before I went to bed. It is rather a pleasing than a profound performance,—& on this account as well as on account of the extreme facility of the Greek, it can bear fast reading.— . . . Nearly the easiest Greek I ever read!—

Tuesday. August 16.

The rain, the provoking rain, prevented my going to Malvern as soon as I intended: but I went after breakfast & after doubting whether I shd. go at all. Met Mrs. Boyd on the stairs, & was detained by her in the drawing room for a little while, after which, I was dismissed into Mr. Boyd's room. He had expected me yesterday, & wd. have expected me today, if he had not heard that it rained. I like to hear of his expecting me!— He asked if I had any good news to tell him. Good news!— He said something about the 25th. of August, as if that were the day fixed on for the sale by auction. I would not enquire—I wd. not satisfy myself if it were. I will not know anything about it!— We read some of the Seven Chiefs—very little! Mr. Boyd proposed that we shd. read in future what he is familiar with, —as my voice is not always audible to him—that we shd. read Gregory's poems & Basil &c. I am sorry: but as he likes it, let it be so— Farewell to the Seven Chiefs— . . . I shd. have liked to have finished the play with him, which I suppose I cd. not have done, at any rate!— He said "We can read Basil together you know, if everything is happily settled". *If*!!— We shall *never* read Basil together!—

Mr. Boyd wishes to learn forty more lines out of the Prometheus: & in search of them, I read to him nearly the whole of the last scenes of the Prometheus. I quite love the Prometheus. It is an exquisite creation: & besides,—I was *so* happy when I read the *first* scenes of that play!

. . . We talked till dinner-time—thro' such a thunder-storm!!— If I had been anywhere else I shd. have been in heroics! Flashing lightening & crashing thunder! To add to the sublimity of the scene I took my metal comb out & let my hair "stream like a meteor".

We had dinner, & afterwards I went back to Mr. Boyd, without waiting for an ambassador. . . .

I asked how long his sister intended to remain with him. He did not know. I think he likes Miss Bordman as much as he dislikes Miss Gibbons. . . *I* like Miss Bordman too, & I shd. like her better still, if it were not for— . . .! When *I* go away, *I* shall not be missed!—

"I wish it would rain furiously all the evening". "Why?" "Because then you cd. not go home". I was pleased by that answer; & wish!— Got home in the dark, & found that poor Bro was gone to bed with an attack of headache & feverishness. Talking. I was goose enough to tell Bummy about Miss Boyd's secession from Mr. Boyd's room, on my last visit to him: & she was severe enough to call his conduct "ungentlemanly & disgusting." I was lighted up into a passion of course!! But there was no serious breach of the peace. I cannot imagine the *quia* of Bummy's evident aversion to my dear friend, & everything & body connected with him—

He told me to consult Mr. Curzon about the passage in Coloss: & in the case of its being given in his favor, to write to him about it.

Wednesday August 17th.

. . . Clouds—& an imitation of yesterday's thunder-storm. . . . Mr. Curzon came at three, & when I went down stairs to see him, I found Mrs. Martin in the drawingroom—, Mr. Martin at the window! A little talking. When we went in to dinner, they sate down near us—& were *not* very agreable. Mr. Martin dumb & deaf to Mr. Curzon. Mrs. Martin rather icy to me! At least I fancied it, & did'nt care!— Talking to Mr. Curzon all the evening. He wont admit Mr. Boyd's interpretation of Colossions—so I suppose I am not to write. I sighed as I wrote that; & *not* because I cannot send Mr. Curzon's receipt in full, of the interpretation. . . .

A great deal of conversation, with Mr. Curzon, altogether religious. He sleeps here, to our surprise!— No letter.

Thursday August 18.

I finished Keats's Lamia, Isabella, Eve of St Agnes & Hyperion, before breakfast. The three first disapointed me. The extracts I had seen of them, were undeniably the finest things in them. But there is some surprising poetry —poetry of wonderful grandeur, in the Hyperion. The effect of the appearance of Hyperion, among the ruined Titans, is surpassingly fine. Poor poor Keats. His name shall be in my "Poets Record." Like his own Saturn, he was dethroned from the seat which his genius claimed: and in the radiance of his own Hyperion, will he appear to posterity—in

"splendour, like the morn,
Pervading all the beetling gloomy steeps
All the sad spaces of oblivion."

I talked to Mr. Curzon until three, when we dined. Afterwards he went away;—& we went out. Gathering mushrooms. I am glad we were so employed. It gave me an excuse for rambling away by myself, & letting my mind roll itself out, as the chart of a sad voyager. I knew, poetry wd. do me no good just now. I knew right. My spirits are very very cloudy! . . .

Friday. August 19.

While we were at breakfast two men came up to the

house, & rang the front door bell. I knew very well what their business was, tho' Bummy talked about lion-hunters from Malvern. As we went out of the diningroom, Lane past her, & said something in a low voice. I was therefore prepared for what followed. We had to go up stairs, that the lower part of the house might be seen by these gentlemen —one of them dark & foreign-looking, the other apparently an agent. I have heard no other particulars,—not even their names. I wrote to my dear dear Papa today, & made an allusion which was scarcely an allusion, to his present distress—begging him to let none of his anxious feelings rest on *us* who loved him more than we loved anything else, & felt that we *must* be happy when we shall be all together once again— It seemed to me better to say this, that he might not suffer the additional pain of fancying us unprepared for the stroke which he knew to be impending.

No letters.

I finished the Endymion today. I do not admire it as a fine poem; but I do admire many passages of it, as being very fine poetry. As a whole, it is cumbrous & unwieldy. You dont know where to put it. Your imagination is confused by it: & your feelings uninterested. And yet a poet wrote it. When I had done with Keats, I took up Theophrastus. Theophrastus has a great deal of vivacity, & power of portraiture about him; & uplifts that veil of distance . . veiling the old Greeks with such sublime mistiness; & shows you how they used to spit & take physic & wear nailed shoes tout comme un autre. . . . Theophrastus does me no good just now: & as I cant laugh with him, I shall be glad when I have done hearing him laugh.

This evening B H & A went out to walk; & I was their attendant cavalry. The poney carried me beautifully, past Mr. Hailes & there was some delightful cantering as we came back. I ventured to carry Isocrates down to tea, that I might read while they played chess. As Bro remonstrated, I wont do so any more. . . .

Saturday August 20

I had intended to finish today, Theophrastus's Ethic characters; but Eliza Cliffe's arrival after breakfast, put all my good resolutions to the route. . . . She has finished my picture, which, tho' it is not the *picture of me*, does her infinite credit: considering her deficiency not merely in instruction, but experience. The white gown is changed into grey,—& the red background into green,—& the hair from black, into something nearer its "proper hue",—& the lips from scarlet into a human rosiness: so that altogether, Eliza & I are to be congratulated. Before tea, we went out to ride, & rode all round by the farm & Petty France. My estomac &c none the better for it; & I went to bed by myself, at ten o'clock. Never mind. I enjoyed my ride. And there is no kind of enjoyment which one can have on this side of the grave, without paying its price in pain—no flower that one can pick, without nettling one's fingers! Is not this an unthankful thought of mine? Oh yes! There are heaps of flowers, which my hand, even *mine*, has picked, & in joy! tho' they are now lying afar, lost, & withered—

I forgot to say, that I did read a little of Theophrastus, before breakfast this morning—& that I gave Reynolds's Discourses to Eliza Cliffe. No letters. Dear Bro convalescent.—

Sunday. August 21

All gone to Church, except me; and I am going . . to finish Jewel.

Mrs. Cliffe & Eliza came to have luncheon during our dinner. Mrs. Cliffe investigated the picture, & pronounced it to be extremely like. It is not *likely* at any rate. She took me down to the gate in the back seat of her carriage. Bummy driving,—& we had the satisfaction of seeing Mr. Curzon's congregation augmented by several of the Colwall people—*not* by Mrs. Martin. His text was from Amos "Can two walk together, unless they are agreed?" The first part very good,—the latter part straggling, & heavy besides.

A note from Mrs. Boyd, to say that somebody has formed an attachment for Annie, & that, in consequence, somebody's Mama, wishes her to be sent home.[1] I was foolish enough, to make a report of this note to Bummy: & now, more items are put down to poor Annie's flirtibility.

I am very much afraid that she will trifle away her ultimate happiness. May it be otherwise! Mrs. Boyd says "I have not told Mr. or Miss Boyd of the reason of her returning sooner". Mr. or Miss Boyd! An extraordinary manner of introducing Mr. Boyd's name: & an extraordinary silence to preserve towards the father of her child!—

I cant help being pained by Mr. Boyd not writing to me, & not sending even a message in Mrs. Boyd's note. Probably he did not know about her writing; but then he might have thought of writing himself— —he might have been anxious to see me, when soon he may be able to see me no more. I dare not trust myself to dwell on these points. One thing is too clear.

This week may decide, perhaps *must* decide, everything. If I can go to Malvern tomorrow, I will go. Only a little more strength of mind—a little more power of self controul,—& it will all be over. God give me strength & power!— I have not felt at all well today, with an occasional pressure at the heart, & sickness.

Better, however, now: & I must try to keep so.

No letter from Papa: at least none that I know of.

Finished Jewel, & admire Jewel, & will read some parts of Jewel again, if I live much longer. He is very eloquent & energetic & learned; & well worth reading. His references to the councils, are tedious & heavy . . . to *me*.

Monday August 22d.

It must have been nearly nine when I set off for Malvern where I arrived as Mrs. Boyd was breakfasting. So Mr. Boyd is going to scold me about something! But he wont be very severe; for Mrs. Boyd told me that he exclaimed

"Good creature"! when he heard of my having come. "A good kind creature" he called me, when we met. His manner *very* kind—"Have you any good news for me?" No, still—no, always! The scold was about my not having shewn him, my "disquisitions on Plato", which Mr. Davidson read in ms five years ago. Mr. Davidson is dreaming. "Have you brought your seven chiefs?" Why what a question! We read some of Gregory's poems . . . & then Mr. Boyd gave me Meleager's ode to spring, to read, while he "stretched his legs" in the garden. Very very happy!—Meleager's ode is beautiful tho' monotonous: but the monotony is much less felt in the concluding lines. Nota Bene Ba! Buy Wakefield's Bion, & Moschus & Meleager.

Mr. Wood disagreed with Miss Gibbons & agreed with Mr. Boyd about the passage in Colossions. So Mr. Boyd told me. He "*cant abide*" Miss Gibbons—thinks her "nauseous" —that is, he thinks her vanity & *deviations* nauseous. She seems a goodnatured person, & in her conversation, a religious person: but the spirit of man cannot search the spirit of man. After dinner, I was over-asked into playing on the guitar & singing— I sang Kathleen [an Irish ballad], very badly, in my own opinion. When I got again into Mr. Boyd's room, he told me that he had heard today what he had often heard about—that he had been standing at the open window while I sang, & thought that my voice was sweet tho' low!— If I had known his "whereabouts" my singing wd. have come to an end—or at least, to a trembling. An exhortation to practise!— I am glad he liked my singing. He seemed to like it, certainly! We talked— —I cant recollect all we talked about,—but we talked very pleasantly & on pleasant subjects. So Mrs. Boyd thinks that there is no use in his asking my opinion of any composition of his own, as I "*cannot* be impartial".!! When he reported this, I answered nothing. What could I answer?—

I begged him to be less reserved to Mr. Curzon than he has been, with regard to his religious opinions; & he half promised me that he would. I hope the promise may be binding. Why should Mr. Curzon "stand in doubt of him", as Mr. Curzon seems to do?

I told him that altho' Mr. C did stand in doubt of him, yet that he liked his society extremely. "Then", he observed, "Mr. Curzon is inconsistent. According to his own views he shd. not like the society of any man not decidedly & clearly religious". My answer made him laugh. "But Mr. Curzon ranks *you* with *anchovy sauce*"! He asked me to read the Epistle to the Romans, with a humble & attentive mind,—& proposed doing the same himself,—that we might afterwards compare notes, on calvinism & arminianism. I have agreed to do so. "I should like very much," he added "to read it *with* you, critically". Should *I* not like it? Yes indeed! But there may be no opportunity for *that*!—

I left his room at twenty minutes to eight: & neither of us imagined it to be so late. How happy I was today. Indeed I do him great injustice very often,—& believe at this moment that he has a true friendship & regard for me. But because I have a fault in one way, I am apt to accuse him of one in another.

"Miss Bordman says that it is a shame for me to pocket you in this manner." "It wd. be a shame if you did'nt"— He gave me Dawes's miscellanea critica, that I might ferrett out for him, Kidds notes on the digamma. Will this be the last employment of the kind, which he will give me?

One thing gave me pain. He told me that in the case of my leaving Hope End, which he *hoped* (said emphatically) wd. not be the case, perhaps it wd. be better for him to have back those books that I have in my care.— And not a word of his going where we go!— . . .

Got home, & heard of the Cards & Walls having been here in the course of the day. Their conduct when here, was more heartless than their heartlessness in coming! Miss Wall has no finely tuned & feminine feelings: & why should we expect the sound of the organ from the jews harp. Everything "after its kind"!—

I called at Mrs. Trant's for five-minutes—

The moon was shining exquisitely, one star by its side, before I left the open air.

Tuesday August 23.

Today was as unhappy as yesterday was happy. Wheels will turn round. My first doing, was writing a long note to Mr. Boyd, to tell him about Dominick's desire to consult him "upon the Greek historians", & beg him to be philosophical, if not historical, & receive his visit; & to tell him besides of Miss Wall's amiable conduct with regard to us. Heard Georgie's Xenophon,—& read a letter from Miss Price. Had dinner—afterwards Bro said to me "Ba: here is a note for you to read." From Papa!— It was to procure Bro's & my signature to some testamentary document of my dear dearest Granny—& it spoke besides of our dearest Papa having had himself a violent attack of cholera. He is in consequence weak & low, & is going out of town for two days, that change of air may recruit him. The note altogether made us all melancholy; & nobody thought until past three, that the document might be of consequence & should be returned by this day's post. Then, when it was thought of, what a bustle there was! Bro & I drove off to Mr. Deane's, as hard as horse cd. go! What might not depend on our being in time!— And Sam was in readiness at Mr. Deane's to gallop off with the packet, as soon as the signatures were affixed. He did gallop, & *just* gained the coach!—just as it was going to descend the Eastnor hill! Thank God! upon that packet, much may depend. Bro & I arrived at home safely; I very much tired with the mental & physical agitation. Hysterics kept off, however. Bro to the Martins, to dine! . . .

At six o'clock, a large party arrived to see the house. Henrietta A & I ran up into my room, & lay on the bed. Nothing but curiosity brought them; yet we must be patient. Very soon, *this* kind of pain will come to an end.

My parcel to Mr. Boyd, containing my letter to him & Keats's poems for Miss Boyd, was not sent in the confusion until seven oclock. . . . Glad, more than glad, to get to bed —& be tranquil. What a bustling thundering wretched day I have had. May God bless & preserve our beloved Papa!— Anything but anxiety on *his* account!—

Wednesday August 24.

I read a little of Theophrastus,—not much,—for a letter arrived from Malvern, & I had to write to Mrs. Boyd as well as to my friend. He wrote to me, but not many lines; kind ones, however. He calls the Walls' conduct, "brutal & unfeeling," but vindicates Dr. Card who was *asked* to accompany them. In my answer I told him what *I* thought of Dr. Card!—& think!—

He says that he felt . . on reading my letter how unworthy he was of the regard which I feel for him— Perhaps unworthy in *one way*.

I copied some music this evening, & did nothing else worth commemorizing.

Thursday August 25.

If this *should* be the day fixed on for the sale,—& I very much suspect—but I wont think or hear any certainty about it. The feeling has weighed on my brain & heart all day; yet I cant dwell on it by reflection.— Mr. Boyd said in his letter yesterday that he "cannot help indulging the idea of everything ending happily". I have prayed that it may end *happily*, not that it may end in a particular way, by our leaving Hope End or retaining Hope End; but that we may be led to do or suffer what is best for us. Lord Jesus hear this prayer!—

Since Mr. Boyd expressed his hope to me, mine has risen up in a presentimental form; but whether it be a spirit of health or Goblin damned, there is no saying, or thinking! Well: all things will be wisely ordered—if not happily for the very present moment.

I have dogged myself on in study today, that I might not be dogged by less pleasant thoughts than studious ones. I have finished Theophrastus, who is a spirited amusing writer. Something in his manner, might catch the popular ear, at least as well as the tinkling of certain fools' bells! Shall I try? There is time enough to think of it.

Friday. August 26.

Read some passages from Shelley's Revolt of Islam before I was up. He is a great poet; but we acknowledge him to be a great poet as we acknowledge Spenser to be so, & do not love him for it. He resembles Spenser in one thing, & one thing only, that his poetry is too immaterial for our sympathies to enclasp it firmly. It reverses the lot of human plants: its roots are in the air, not earth!— But as I read him on, I may reverse this opinion.

Will there be a letter today? If there is, it will be a decisive one. God give us strength!—I am afraid that dear Henrietta clings too strongly to hope, & that when it give way altogether, she may fall low!— God give *her* strength—

Let me consider circumstances, while I am calm, in a degree. I may have to leave this place where I have walked & talked & dreamt in much joy; & where I have heard most beloved voices which I can no more hear, & clasped beloved hands which I can no more clasp: where I have smiled with the living & wept above the dead & where I have read immortal books, & written pleasant thoughts, & known at least one very dear friend— I may have to do this; & it will be sorrow to me!— But let me think of it calmly. I can take with me the dear members of my own family, —& my recollections which, in some cases, were all that was left to me here: I can take with me my books & my studious tastes,—and above all, the knowledge that "*all things*" whether sorrowful or joyous, "work together for good to those who love God". And my dear Papa's mind,— (should *he* not be dearest to me?;) will be more tranquil perhaps when he is away from a place so productive of anxieties. There is *one* person, whom it will indeed pain me to leave. But he may follow us,—& in the meantime he will write to me & not forget me. Oh I hope not! To whatever place we go, I will seclude myself there, & try to know & like nobody,—but live with my books & writings & dear family. With them, can I be altogether unhappy? I am unhappy *now*. There is no use in disguising it from myself!— I will wait for the letters, & in the meantime, get on with Isocrates.

Thank God! Hope End, dear Hope End, is not sold. It was bought in by our antagonists themselves; & may yet go by private contract: but still, thank God for this reprieve. A letter from Papa!—

I was in the dining room. Bummy came in to me with overflowing eyes, & an exclamation of "Good news!" The good news were too much for me, prepared as I was for the worst news: and I should have sunk to the floor, if she had not caught me. Thank God for *this* blessed good news! Many tears were shed, & all for joy, at Hope End today.

Saturday. August 27.

I determined yesterday to be the bearer of certain news to Mr. Boyd today: and the news of my having proposed to do so, appeared to have excited a tumult down stairs. According to Henrietta's report, Bummy exclaimed "What has Mr. Boyd to do with it?" What has Mr. Boyd to do with it? Why if he has *nothing* to do with it, what must be the sincerity of his professed regard for me? H & B had sent to the Martins; and is *my* friend to be treated with less consideration than theirs? I said so to H, who irritated me by her reply about the cases being different, & about the impropriety of my feeling *more friendship for Mr. Boyd than for the Martins!*— It is extraordinary that more than one person in this house, should entertain such dispositions towards a person whom everybody knows, I, justly or unjustly, consider as my dear & intimate friend. I believe the fact to be this. They have, as most people have, clearer ideas of the aristocracy of rank & wealth, than of the aristocracy of mind. Therefore it appears singular to them,

& not very reasonable, that I shd. so obviously prefer Mr. Boyd's society to that of some other individuals. I love dearest B & H to the bottom of my heart; and they deserve my love, to the bottom of theirs: but without my pursuits they cannot have my tastes, & without having my tastes, they cannot be expected to understand them. It wd. be wrong in me to blame, a miscomprehension—or to go on scribbling speculatively in this way, when there are facts to be stated *memorabilialy*.

The poney wd'nt be caught, so I could'nt get away from this place until 9. N.B. Bummy thought me "quite right" in going, when I proposed it *to* her—& made no shade of objection openly whatever the darkness might have been in the private committee. Got to Ruby Cottage, just as Mrs. B's breakfast was in an incipient state. Told her the good news! She had the tears in her eyes, & kissed me again & again! & I cd. not help being affected by this kindness of manner. Uncomfortable account of Annie, upon which my annotations & reflections assume the brun foncè. I wish she were, or cd. be made, unlike herself in *some* respects. Not in all. There is much good in her,—& more might be elicited. If she cd. be married to a sensible man whom she entirely loved, she might be happy & make him so. But the love *must* be strong enough to place her altogether under his influence!—or the happiness wd. be beyond both his & her's— Mr. Boyd sent for me; & his first words were "Have you heard?" A smile was *his* answer after hearing mine, & I am sure, a pleased smile: but no enthusiastic pleasure was expressed!— We talked until shaving time, & then I was exiled for half an hour; & then readmitted. Read two poems of Gregorys, "I would I were a dove." & "Where are my winged words". They have both great merit, but the last is too much drawn out—too much Procrustianized. . . .

After dinner, while we were at desert, a voice at the door, said, "Porsonia, are you ready to come?" Yes she was ready & willing to come.

Read a little more Gregory, & talked about Burgess the Bishop of Salisbury, (who must be a benevolent man by what I heard of him),—& on several other subjects. At last I thought & asked about the Greek epigram on the Tories, which I was to have procured from Mr. Spowers. Mr. Boyd let me write it down from his dictation, & then manumitted me, to send it to the Times,—but without his initials. On the whole, I had another happy day today.

Agreed with Miss Gibbons, who wishes to hear Mr. Curzon—that she shd. go to Hope End tomorrow & dine with us. Got home late, (at half past eight) & got a scold, both for my lateness & the Gibbons business. If she were to come from any house but Mr. Boyd's, it wd. not be so. I was excited into complaining that no objection was ever made to the visitors of other people; but that whatever person *I* invited, on him or her, every objection was concentrated. Sorry I shd. have said so, tho' there's some truth in it. Long pauses, & sharp words down stairs tonight. None of them mine however, after that one ebullition.

Wrote to the Editor of the Times about Mr Boyd's Greek epigram.

Sunday August 28.

Did not go to church. Miss Gibbons arrived at one o'clock, & Mrs. Boyd with her; . . . Some playing at cross purposes; Mrs. B having walked down the road to *meet me as I came from Church*, while I was sitting with Miss G in the morning room. She seems to be a feeling kind hearted woman, tho' not a faultless one. Looking at me, she observed that I did not appear able to bear much fatigue; & when I said "I am stronger than, I was some months ago, & very much wonder at it", the tears overflowed her eyes in a moment, & she told me to trust that Friend who is more than father or mother, & "sticketh closer than a brother"—

. . . Dined, & went down to chapel— Mr. Curzon preached *very well*; & our visitors were delighted.

Miss Gibbons inclined to returning to Hope End,—so there she did return,—& she & Mrs. Boyd climbed our mushroomed hills. Collision with the Martin party; & fire struck between Miss G & Mr. M in consequence of my report to her of his report to me of her *controversial* conversations at Eastnor. The Martin party came down the hill & into the house with us; & then there was an exposè of Eliza's representation of me. Abused, nem: con: Mr. Martin proposes that as Eliza has not & never can attain to my mouth, she should paint a book before it. . . .

Miss Gibbons glued herself to me all day, & we talked eternally. She praised Miss Bordman, & told me how much Mr. Boyd enjoyed her society. Well!—I ought to be glad of this.

She asked me when I was going again to Malvern. "Whenever I can", I said, "for my Malvern days are my happy days—they are my holidays. . .But I must not go too often." "You *cannot* go too often. Mr. Boyd does so thoroughly enjoy the days which you spend with him! they are *his* holidays!" "I did not exactly mean that—I meant that I must not leave home & occupy the carriage too often. I like to dream that Mr. Boyd has pleasure in seeing me, tho' I know that whatever pleasure his is, mine must double it." "Indeed! I dont think it does! and how can you know this?" "By certain inward oracles". "But tho' you understand your own oracles, you cant understand Mr. Boyd's".

I am half sorry that this conversation shd. have passed: but passed it has.

Miss Gibbons considers that learning is standing between Mr. Boyd & God. I defended his religious state with my best powers. May God increase the grace, which I am certain He has bestowed. Mrs. B & Miss G went away at 8 oclock, & then we had prayers,—& then Bummy went up stairs & did not come down again.

No letters.

August 29. Monday.

. . . Henrietta to the heath: & B & A in the carriage to the Bartons. My company was asked for in a *dispensable* manner,—of which I eagerly took advantage by staying at home. Read a few pages of Isocrates. I wish I had a more readable copy than mine, which is dark & squeezy,—& printed in columns. My wishes are so miscellaneous, that I might as well be comprehensive, & wish for Aladdin's lamp at once.

Mushroom hunting. Bro was pick nicing today on the Malvern hills, with twenty eight other persons, besides Sam. It was proposed that they shd. meet "on the top of the monument".* In that case they might have also met at the bottom of a monument.

Tuesday August 30.

. . . A little of Isocrates—, & then Eliza Cliffe came. Went down stairs, & found her & Bummy discussing *cum furore*, the Walls. *I* said little, & meant to have said nothing. Poor Eliza shd. not suffer by hearing her friend spoken harshly of; when she has to suffer by knowing that this friend deserves it. She dined with us—and just before dinner, the letters came. One from my dear Papa, to me—& dated *the isle of Wight*— He seems pleased with it—delighted with the scenery & Mr. Sipthorpe. Oh if he shd. intend to settle there—if we shd. be separated from England by the sea!—Mr. Boyd will not follow us *there*— I hope, I hope, this dungeon in the air, will fall into ruins. Hastings, Eastbourne, Brighton—Portsmouth—any place but the isle of Wight!—

Dont let me fall into a Pythian fury, *yet*, at any rate. I thank God that my dearest Papa is better!—

BA & I went in the carriage to the Wyche, & Eliza was our cavalry escort. Bummy was heroic enough to walk along the whole length of the terrace as far as the great elm, without her head having any extra motion, circularly. I

* The obelisk in the grounds of Eastnor Castle.

rode Eliza's horse whch. Eliza led. Proposed—that I shd. run down to see Mr. Boyd. Down I went, & Eliza with me,—and yet not *with* me, for I was before her. I ran, slipped, rolled, presto prestissimo, to the bottom. Got into Mr. Boyd's room, & got scolded for being out of breath—the necessary result of such a *descensus averni*. Told him of Papa's letter. He hoped that we shd. not go to the isle of Wight, & recommended me to write tomorrow a petition that in the case of our leaving Hope End, Papa wd. settle at Hastings or Eastbourne. Now he certainly wd. not care where we settled, if he had no idea of following us. It is clear to my mind that he has that idea, & I have been made very happy by it.

Mr. Curzon was at dinner with the rest of the party. Mr. Boyd smiled when I said "I never thought until this moment, of his meaning to be here today".

Eliza came into the room—& immediately Mr. Boyd began with "I have to congratulate you Miss Cliffe, on the late amiable conduct of yr. friend Miss Wall." I interposed, but Mrs. Boyd's calling me out of the room, made void my interposition. An explanation of Annie's doings at Stanwell. She is *not* coming home. Back again to Mr. Boyd. I upbraided him for his attack on Eliza, & wished him good bye. He told me that he disliked my coming for so short a time; & hoped that I wd. visit him meo more "long measure", before long. Promised!— Miss Gibbons came into the room for a moment, & *embraced* me, & begged that of the two minutes I was going to spend at Ruby Cottage, I wd. spare a quarter of one to Mr. Curzon & herself!—after all I forgot it, & went out of the house without seeing him, or re-seeing her. A happy little visit. Ascended the hill capitally. If Horace had been there, nil admirari wd. never have been written;—so I am rather glad he was not. Bummy said "I will trust you again": & towards home we went. Met the Martins by the rocky seat—Mr. M in trepidation & consternation at my determination of riding by the horse which Mr. de Marizet was leading.

He begged me to get off in vain; & at length decided that "temerity & timidity were the characteristics of my sex". They wanted us to drink tea at Colwall & to wait for them at the turnpike, neither of whch. we did. Got home in the dark. So ends this chapter of my life, which is a kind of chapter of hats—& walking shoes!—

Wednesday August 31st.

A note from Eliza, while we were at breakfast, speaking of our going, & of Miss Wall's *not* going, to dine at Mathon on Friday. I *wd.* rather *not.* A discussion about it after breakfast—, & the nos had it. Bummy Arabel & I drove off with our refusal & my picture, to call on Mrs. Cliffe. Called in viâ on the Martins—& I had a french conversation with Mr. de Marizet. He seems to me—nay, he certainly is, an agreable & clever man!— An emphatic discription of his *horreur* yesterday in witnessing my *temeritè.*

Off to the Cliffes;—& got *off* the invitation. Rummaged Eliza's room, & read some verses of Miss Walls, & some letters of her's relating to us, & took a fancy to Goldoni's back. Miss Wall's letters are impertinent & heartless. Eliza ought not, strictly speaking, to have shown them to us,—but Arabel over-insisted.

Went down stairs. It was necessary as to courtesy to mention Mrs. Bests book to her: it was necessary as to conscience, not to praise it warmly. I managed the "betwixt & between" very dexterously—I flatter myself. "Mrs. Best I was pleased both to procure yr. book & to read it"; which was the absolute fact, & civil besides. But Mrs. Best required no one to talk about her book except herself. She is evidently extremely satisfied with both parties. "I consult Lowth Horseley Scott & Whitby; but they always leave me wherever there is a difficulty, & then I have recourse to my studyings & references". So those great [theological] commentators (vulgarly called great) can be nobody to Mrs. Best!— This degoutè—d me.

Got home at three. No letters. But Mr. Boyd's Greek

epigram in the paper. Very glad of it. I am tired, & have been resting my body in my arm chair, & my mind in Goldoni. Read his Pamela, & Pamela Maritata. The merit of the first, is Richardson's; & there is not much in the second, for anybody to claim!—

Tomorrow being the 1st. of September & a holiday, I will go to Malvern.

Thursday. Sept. 1.

Th'o today is the 1st. of September & a holiday, I do not go to Malvern, for it rains most past-bearingly. If I had my own way *quite*, I wd. go, rain or shine: but, as it is, . . I will comfort myself with Goldoni & Greek. Will there be a letter today? There may—& with an account of my dear [Uncle] Sam,—for the arrival of the packet was in yesterday's paper.[1] I am uncomfortably presentimental about the letters today: & feel the more angry with the rain, as something *may* prevent my visiting my dear friend tomorrow. I *feel* as if it *may*.

I dreamt last night that I was married, just married; & in an agony to procure a dissolution of the engagement. Scarcely ever considered my single state with more satisfaction than when I awoke! — I never *will* marry: but if I ever were to do such a foolish thing, I hope I may not feel as I did last night!—

"Of such *stuff*
My dreams are made!—"

Oh! I *hope* there may be no letters today!!—

No letters: & no paper also. What can be the cause of *that*? . . .

I wrote to Papa this morning before breakfast; & my letter was an accompaniment to two brace of partridges. . . .

Friday. Sept. 2d.

. . . Ordered the carriage at a quarter to 8: & *past* 9 when

I sate [sic] off!! If I had been Jupiter, Billy [Treherne] wd. have been thunderstruck, as sure as I *was* Jupiter!—

Got to Malvern at breakfast time meo more. The feminine gender observed that they, in their joy to see me, buzzed about me like bees. I hope there was no *humming* as well as buzzing!— But never mind, if there were! Mr. Boyd came to the breakfast room door, to call Miss Boyd, & Mrs Boyd cried out "You dont know who is here!!" After he had known it, he walked up & down in front of the house: but I was not angry at that! No indeed I was not,—tho' I have *memorabilized* it!— He knew that I always stayed & must stay for a few minutes with the majority, before the minority had me all to himself. I went up stairs very soon to his room, & we talked on religious subjects & several others, & I had scold the second, for running down the hill: and then we sate down to Gregory. I read two very long passages out of the hexameter & pentameter poem, beginning *Δυσμοϱος* [Ill-fated]. How happy, how *very* happy I was, when I was reading it! A thunderstorm came, & in the midst of it, Miss Bordman. She came to beg me to go into the drawing room that I might be protected by numbers: good generalship, Mr. Boyd said, to get me away. She wd. have gone out of the room, but he called her back to say something about the Socinians, & there she remained for a full half hour . . I abdicated my chair in her favour, & sate vis a vis to her & the lightening!— Now did Mr. Boyd *wish* her to stay or not?—or was it good nature in the abstract, on his part? I am a goose.

After dinner, before desert was finaled, a message came for me from him. I was very glad to obey the summons, & did so immediately. He showed me over again, some of his antiquities in the form of Editions of the Fathers. A Gregory whch. will be 300 years old in 19 years— A Basil whch. will be 300 years old in 18 years. Another Basil edited by Erasmus—but with his preface torn out. A Gregory Nyssen which will be 300 yrs. old, in one year! I offered him my Rivinus (the anthologia)— Rejected. Carriage came at 7; & as I went away I was thanked for coming so often. "I am very much obliged to you", Mr. Boyd said. Very much *obliged* to *me*!!—

That Dawes was certainly born to torment me, as well as to elucidate the classics. In the midst of my good intentions of conveying him back to Ruby Cottage, I let him slip out of the carriage. Ecce the effect of reverie-ing, which I was doing all the way from home to Malvern!—I am a goose—for the second time of affirming!— Enquired at Benbow's & both the turnpikes, in vain. Now what am I to do? Send to Worcester or to Papa for another copy?

Got home at 5 minutes to 8. Capital time—& good humoured reception.

Played on the guitar to please the people who asked me, till my voice was worn out.

I wish I were going to Malvern tomorrow!—

No letters today—

I forget the two first lines of Mr. Boyd's epigram on Miss Wall, repeated to me today. (N.B. She & Mr. Coventry *were* going to be married.) Did they run this way? (I dont mean Miss W & Mr. C)

Since of all women, I aver,
None can more heartless soulless be!
If Coventry wont go to her,
Why let her go to Coventry!—

another—

"Coventry weds, to please the eye"
Her vulgar mother's heard to bawl!
Then who can doubt the reason why
He thus delays to wed Miss Wall.

Saturday. Septr. 3d.

. . . I wrote to Eaton today to sacrifice my Origen which I had ordered there, & to beg him to send Dawes instead, & immediately.

Pro & conning about going to the Wyche. My opinion of course *pro*. At last Henrietta A & I agreed to go, that I might run down with the catalogue to Mr. Boyd's, whereupon Bummy changed her mind & agreed to go too. But the sight of my parcel did no good— "She wd. not have gone with us, had she for a moment thought that I meant to visit Mr. Boyd; & that I seemed never to go to the Wyche, without meaning to visit him". So I . . . promised not to mean to visit him, but to send down my parcel instead of taking it. It was tantalizing to see him in the road, & to remain on the walk, which I did & was good humoured besides. We walked past Essington's, & then I grew tired & proposed making a session of it until *they* were tired. They walked on to the well house, while I amused myself by vanishing. Vanished into the fern, just above the ash seat, & was discovered by my pocket handkerchief only. I wish Desdemona & I had kept our handkerchiefs in our pockets.

Got home at eight in the starlight, after spending a most lovely evening amidst most exquisite scenery. But I was tired, wretchedly tired, & had to go to bed prematurely to save myself from being ill. Slept uncomfortably. Dreamt of Mr. Boyd, & that he was going to have the walls of his room painted after the manner of a cathedral window.

Sunday Sept. 4th.

Went to Church,—& neither Arabel nor I particularly well. Mr. Deane's sermon was *issimo*, but not *benissimo*. Mrs. Griffith invited us, & me especially, to meet Mr. Corry [close friend of Thomas Moore] tomorrow evening, at the Bartons. Refused!— Mrs. Cliffe gave me the seat of her footman (thank her) behind her carriage: & she & Eliza dined here. An exposè of Miss Wall's letter. Most abusive insolent & unfeminine. I am glad I never knew her intimately.

Found Mrs. Boyd Miss Gibbons & Miss Bordman at the chapel. Mrs. B came an [sic] avant to beg me not to invite any of them to the house. Out of some hesitation, I extracted or think I extracted that Mr. Boyd was afraid lest any superabundant attention shd. be shown by me to Miss

Gibbons. Before we parted, I said to Mrs. Boyd,—"Tell Mr. Boyd that I am surprised at his being so *vindictive*". Perhaps he may be surprised at my being so impudent. His precaution arose from a feeling which is consistent enough with human nature; but not consistent with his nature. And yet, he is mint sauce after all, as I told him once.

I have just heard that poor Minny's father is removed from the reach of her affection & anxiety. May God support her! I have not seen her yet.

I have been down to see dear Minny. She is lying on the bed, crying bitterly. Oh! our very grief shd. console us for the loss of those for whom we grieve; seeing that while we feel its acuteness we may remember "such, *they* can feel no more". And yet how hard, how impossible, to remember or to reason when the heart is breaking!—

Monday Sept 5th.

Eliza Cliffe came here to breakfast according to the arrangement yesterday; & the morning was bright for our expedition to the hills. Before breakfast, I went in to see dear Minny, whom I found much more composed & comfortable. For this, I thank God!—

Clouds coming over—a few drops of rain; but the rain ceased,—& then we set off. Bummy Arabel & I in the carriage; Henrietta & Eliza on horseback. Before we had past Mrs. Brown's [at Cummins Farm], on the rain came again,—& we paused under a tree, a semi-colon pause. I was dreadfully afraid of a full stop. But we were eloquent & Bummy persuadible; & we made our way en avant to the wyche; while "The rain it rainëd all the *way*". But at the whyche, the clouds brightened up, & so did our faces: & after sending the horses down to Barnets [at Winning's Farm], we proceeded with our veal pye, much faster than ministers are doing with the reform bill. Encamped a few yards above the ash,—

& laughed & ate, laughed & ate,
Laughed & ate & laughed again—

As the silver knives & forks could not be left without protection, I took them under mine, in my slipping down to Ruby Cottage. Turned to the left hand side instead of to the right, as soon as I had past the Ruby gate, & elicited notes of admiration from Mr. Boyd & Miss Boyd who were walking in front of the house. Miss Boyd could not imagine to whom my black figure belonged, & had some doubts as to my being "a spirit." A black spirit! How infernal I must have looked! Mr. Boyd wd. go into the house, tho' I was hypocritical enough to remonstrate a little. A very little,— for I felt in my secret soul that if my remonstrance had had any effect on him, all my philosophy wd. have had no effect upon *me*. But I went in to the breakfast room for a moment or two, before I was summoned to his room. It was about three I suppose when I arrived at Ruby Cottage,—& I stayed until six. Mr. Boyd had his dinner at his usual hour— Until then we talked; & after *then* we read. Read a poem of Gregory's which has been translated by Mr. Boyd. . . . I was very very happy. . . . An explanation of his vindictiveness on Sunday. No vindictiveness in the case. I thought it *could not* be! But Mrs. Boyd's manner being a mystery, was a raiser of doubts. He objected to their going to Hope End, *only* on account of the intrusive appearance such a visit might have.

Mrs. Boyd came into the room, to tell me that she meant to search over the hills for my party, and ask them to drink tea with her!— "Why shd. you ask them?" said Mr. Boyd. "I hope they wont come". After she had gone, there was some kindness of manner thrown away, in the fear that he had "hurt or offended me, by what he had just said with so little premeditation." I assured him of my being in no degree hurt or offended. Began an elaborate apology for Arabel, who has not once called on Mrs. Boyd since they settled at Ruby Cottage—but it wd'nt do: I saw that plainly. I was telling him about Miss Wall's Bacchanalian letter, when Arabel & Eliza came for me. He shook hands with Arabel, at "their exits & their entrances"

—& did no more. Not one word, did he speak to her. We stayed only a few minutes—& then our good bye was said. "Must you go so soon?" he asked me!— I promised to go again *so soon*!

. . . Indeed *all* his manner was *all* kindness today: & I felt convinced from the beginning to the end of it, that my absurdities towards him, & his regard for me, were very great. Not that his regard & friendship are equal to mine. But as long as there *is* a reciprocity, I have no right to expect an equality,—and that he really has a real regard & friendship for me, I feel sure—at least today!—

Arabel is angry at his silence to her; but I persuaded her not to *speak* her anger at home. Foolish, that silence was! I will speak to him about it, whenever I see him next. He & I feel very differently upon some points, & this is one; that when people about whom I dont care, neglect me, I never *think* about their neglect. Now *he* certainly does not care much whether he sees Arabel or not; and yet he not only thinks about her neglect, but takes the trouble of avenging it. Besides she never intended any degree of neglect or incivility, to any person at Ruby Cottage.

Miss Bordman goes to Mr. Davidson's tomorrow, for ten days!—

We got home at eight, and send an escort to Mathon with Eliza. A delightful day. . . Food for dreams!—

Tuesday, Septr. 6.

Dear Minny is much better.

I have been unwell all the morning. Nota bene, never eat *new* honey. Lay in bed nearly all day, in consequence of that nota bene not having been noted yesterday.

A letter from Papa to Henrietta: and—thank God for it, —a happy satisfactory letter. He is perfectly recovered from the effects of his late attack, & is in good spirits, & does not talk of returning. Bummy is in hopes that he may be "doing something"; indeed she feels "sure that he *must* be doing something." I wont—I dare not trust myself to, hope for *more* than a respite!— . . .

Wednesday Sept 7.

Wrote a note to Mr. Boyd about the direction to Mr. Bohn, & about Papa's letter [referring to Mr. Bohn's catalogue of rare books]—No letters from anybody.

I began to consider Romans, as Mr. Boyd desired me to do. I read also a little of Isocrates. An invitation from the Martins to Bro & Henrietta to go with them down the Wye. Henrietta was heroic enough to resist; & was *good humoured besides*, as I say of myself sometimes.

Thursday. Sept 8.

Bro left home at 7 this morning, for the purpose of going down the Wye; but we hear that the rain has kept him shooting at Mr. Biddulphs— I dare say he will go tomorrow. I hope so, if it will give him pleasure. For my part, I should like to go down the Wye, but I wd. choose my company, & not choose the cold formal commonplace Miss Biddulphs, who have no sympathy in their voice countenance or conversation, with the wild graceful varrying excellences of nature. Mr. Martin is a clever man *naturally*; but I wdnt go with *him*; he is rugged & unpoetical. Mrs. Martin has some sensitiveness as well as sense; but I wdnt go with *her*—because . . . because, we dont amalgammate. Mr. de Marizet is a clever agreable man,—&, I hear, *admires me*, which is a sign of abundant judgment—but he is French, & essentially unpoetical I dare say. At least as I know nothing to the contrary, I am reasonable in believing so—so I wdnt go with *him*. Mr. Boyd!— Yes. I shd. like *that* very very much—if he cd. see!!—

I think I shd. like to go down the Wye with that fair Damsel who accompanied Thalaba on his last voyage—and then as

> Our little boat fell rapidly
> Adown the river-stream,

if she said to me with her "melancholy smile"

"Wilt thou go on with me?"

my answer shd. still be "I *will* go on with thee"—

What dreaming all this is!— Well! after all, I am as likely to go down the Wye with Thalaba's Damsel, as to go down the Wye at all!—

Poor Bro & the King! How it does rain!— Was it a fine day on the last corronation?[1] If it were, I wish Fate had changed the days. Never mind! Our patriotic monarch has sunshine *within*; which the "other sceptered thing" could *not* have had!— A letter from Mrs. Boyd to *answer mine to Mr. Boyd*, & desire me to write to Bohn. . . .

I have been hard at work all day, reading & meditating on the first eleven chapters of Romans. Dr. Adam Clarke is wrong, I think, about "the whole creation", & wrong about "who shall separate us from the love of Christ."

The close of the 5th. chapter, strikes me strongly as it has done before, as favoring the doctrine of general redemption. Why should any body of Christians struggle to deny it? Is it not enough, that redemption is by *free grace*, —& *only* of God who showeth mercy? I cannot believe that the christian church will ever have a united opinion on some passages of Romans; and if my opinion of those passages shd. ever become clearer & more decided than it now is, I could not look upon Christians who differed from me, less as brethren than I now do.

Guitaring in the evening, for Bummy. I have sighed to go to Malvern tomorrow. It wont do!—Lane wants the carriage, that he may consult Dr. Garlick!—and the clouds besides!!— I wrote to Mr. Bohn.

Friday. Sept. 9.

Lane has gone—so I shall not go! That is quite clear!—

Bro did not return last night. We therefore conclude that the Wye party proceeds this morning; & as the wind has changed, & the clouds are more scattered, the probability is greater than it wd. otherwise be.

I have been thinking over Mrs. Boyd's letter yesterday. It certainly does strike at the most sensitive part of me (wherever that is), that Mr Boyd shd. write to me only *when* he is obliged, & only *what* he is obliged—that he shd. not even answer my letters, but commission another person to do it!—and yet when I am with him, how can I doubt his regard for me? Sometimes it is actually & altogether impossible to do so: and if it is so sometimes, why not always? Can a person's feelings ebb & flow in the course of two or thee days? It seems evident to me sometimes, that to have me with him is his greatest happiness—or at least a very great one: and yet he grudges to write the few lines which he *knows* will give *me* happiness!— Well!—I cant understand it!—

I have been considering the Romans again today. I think that the 8th chapter *must* be *spiritually* understood—& that the 9th does not necessarily convey any doctrine of particular election. May God grant me more light & clearer knowledge.

I have made up my mind to go to Malvern tomorrow—if I can by any means. I want to talk to Mr. Boyd about Romans—, & a hundred other subjects!—& I want to *see* him besides!— I made a motion to the effect that there shd. be a party on the hills tomorrow, while we were gathering mushrooms on Coome hill. The ayes had it—

Think of Bro coming home, without going down the Wye. Adjourned sine die, because the clouds looked glum!—And now they are looking as bright with sunshine, as summer ever saw them looking. Stupid people!—

Saturday Sept. 10th.

We did not get away from Hope End until nearly half past ten, which provoked me: but, oh shade of Marcus Antoninus, be it known to thee, that it did not put me out of humour. Henrietta was on the high horse *literally*; & Arabel & Bummy & I in the wheelbarrow, having a basket of sandwiches & puffs under our immediate chaperoneship— Sent the horses down to Barnets,—& walked along the right side terrace. As soon as we arrived at the spot above Mr. Boyd's house, I & a little basket of grapes & geranium cuttings began our descent, by slipping. I got safely thro the first gate, when two little black & white dogs with open mouths, began to chase me,—& I, tho' I had never seen Diana, fell into a fright. I trembled from head to foot, when I got into Mr. Boyd's house. Was soon sent for by Mr. Boyd, who told me that he had fancied the probability of my arrival today. I always like to hear *that*.

. . . Mrs. Boyd came in to the room to give the weather a good character, & to propose Mr. Boyd's going out. I seconded her proposition. No!—he wd. not go out until after dinner. . . . Dined as soon as I could, à fortissimâ. Talked about the Romans,—& agreed about the close of the 5th. chapter seeming to lean to the general redemption doctrine—& agreed & disagreed on some other points. He asked me to read with attention the 17th of John, & the commentary of Chrysostom on some verses in Romans, & to beat Gregory's cover a little, on the subject of election.

To be sincere with myself, today was *not* so pleasant & happy a day, as many, I have spent with Mr. Boyd. He *does not*—but I *will not*!—I forgot to say that I observed to him—"So you were determined to be vindictive after all"— "What do you mean?" I soon told him what I meant—that I alluded to his reception of Arabel the other day!— She did not, when she came for me, go into his room,—for which she is not to blame, in my opinion. Mrs. Boyd & Miss Boyd walked up the hill with us, & accompanied us even to the Wyche. Got home at ten minutes past seven. I am tired, & not in very good spirits. I am very extravagant both in my expectations & feelings!—

Sunday. Sept. 11th.

A controversy between Bummy & me, on the subject of my going to church. Feeling convinced as I do, that the gospel is not consistently preached there, & that my time can be more usefully & scripturally occupied at home, am I right in going? I think not; but there was so much thunder & lightening about it that I yielded the point. "Very goodnatured & amiable of me," perhaps Bummy thought; for she kissed me with a smile: "Very weak & wrong of me" I doubted,—for her kiss & smile did not give me as much pleasure as usual.

Met at church, the usual concourse, the Miss Biddulphs & Mr. de Marizet among them. He spoke to me of Lamartine. Mrs. Martin held my hand in her's in an affectionate manner, which I liked. An affectionate manner certainly does go to my heart which is itself far too affectionate!—Far too affectionate! Oh I feel *that* whenever I feel pain; & almost *ever* when I feel pleasure.

Mrs. Cliffe Mrs. Best & Eliza & *Eliza's niece* dined with us, & went afterwards to chapel: Eliza drove me down in the wheelbarrow, & gave me in the way, Miss Wall's last letter to read. There is something in Miss Wall's impetuosity, which I like, because (what a very bad reason:) it resembles my own: and if she had less coarseness of mind, I could even like *her*. She is very angry with my expression regarding her own conduct here—"I wd. rather that it were done *to* me than *by* me"; & thinks that there was a want of delicacy in my making use of such an expression to her friend. Well! the subject was not introduced by *me*; & when it was introduced before me, tho' I said those words, I said no others. My own heart knows that I wd. not stand between friend & friend; or wound the ear of one by the accusation of another, for the gain of a great good—, far less for the gratification of a petty malice! I am sorry that I said even those words; tho' Eliza had previously spoken with more severity of the person they referred to, than was conveyed by them—I am very sorry!

We met Miss Gibbons at the chapel, & after the service was over, she & I talked together a little. She spoke to me really with kindness. Mr. Boyd on one side, & Bummy on the other, restrained me; or I wd. have asked her to go to the house. *Now* I almost wish I had done so, in spite of everybody. I hope she did not think me unkind for *not* doing so: because her manner to *me* is far from being undeserving of a kind return.

Mr. Curzon's sermon was shorter than usual. He grew very pale & could scarcely terminate it: but we cd. not persuade him to allow himself to be taken to Ledbury in either our carriage or Miss Gibbons's, notwithstanding his indisposition.

Read Chrysostom, & extracted from him—for Mr. Boyd! The bible besides, as usual!—

No letter today.

Monday Sept. 12.

Mr. Jefferson [a friend of Allen Cliffe] came to breakfast that he might shoot afterwards. It is very extraordinary: but I never was acquainted with a *young man* of any mind or imagination—except Mr. Knowles. I do except *him*. They went out to shoot afterwards: & B, H A & I had the honor of their company at dinner—that is to say they talked while we ate. A disagreable kind of non-sympathy. We went to the Cliffes, nearly as soon as they went to the cricket match. Found the Cliffes gathering mushrooms. Mrs. Best & I with linked arms, not souls, talked about her future & past publications. An amiable, not an interesting, not a very superior woman. I asked her opinion of the *general redemption doctrines*. She seemed to me to have undecided & indistinct opinions on this subject. She seems to believe that all *may* be saved; but that the blood of Christ was shed only for those who *are* saved. Her little girl is a delicate intelligent little thing which I could love. . . .— Got home in the dark, at least with no more than a quarter of a moon,—but such a soft moonlight air! You know—, I mean, I know—, it is possible to *feel*, as well as to see the moon.

The Greek testament was all the Greek which I read today.

Tuesday. Sept 13.

So Sam came home in an irrational unchristian state, from the Cricket match last night! Henrietta heard him carried up stairs, & was very much frightened. Neither he nor Bro appeared at breakfast; for Bro went out to shoot, & he went to Mathon—& the farther he goes the better. Henrietta is very very angry, & threatens not to speak to him for a fortnight, which wd. be, in my opinion, both wrong abstractedly speaking, & impolitic. Nobody is immaculate; & young men are more inclined to a fault of this kind, than to many others: & our sullenness wd. do no more good in such a case, than Xerxes's whipping did to the sea. I hate sullenness, whether it be the quality of the offended or offender.

I read parts of scripture with reference to the Calvinistic controversy, & little else today. I am going thro' all the epistles, marking with my pencil every expression that seems to glance at or against the doctrine of particular *exclusive* election.

Wednesday Sept 14.

Agreed—that we are to drink tea with the Peyton's this evening. A bore; but more tolerable than if we were to drink tea with them tomorrow, when my dreams lead me to Malvern.

Comparing scripture with scripture. Reading besides Self control [novel by Mary Brunton] which Henrietta has borrowed from Mrs. Martin. It is formed on the model of Clarissa Harlowe; but the heroine is more immaculate than even Clarissa, & more happy finally!— The book is well-written & interesting. A combination of fortitude & delicacy always interests me in a particular manner.

B H A & I to the Bartons! Met there Mr. Allen Cliffe & Mr. Jefferson . . again!! I wished to hear Mr. Allen Cliffe dissert on the Dublin university that I might report him to Mr. Boyd. No! he wd. abuse my picture, until my hopes of his entering on another subject, were gasping! . . .

Well! Mr. Cliffe talked on—& called Homer "rigmarole" & "stupid stuff",—& expressed an opinion, that "any stupid fool cd. be an elegant classical scholar" while a degree of "ability" was requisite for the mathematics. I have heard a low opinion of the D. university with regard to the classics; & he justifies it!— I observed (how cd. I do otherwise?) that "as Mr. Cliffe must speak from observation & experience, I was quite convinced & ready to admit the fact of *all the classical scholars of Dublin University* being stupid fools."

Mr. Cliffe is no exception to my general observation on *young men*. Vide September the 12. He rode with us to our gate. Half past ten, when we got home: & I employed the last moment of my sitting up to speak of going to Malvern tomorrow. Well received by everybody.

Thursday Sept. 15th.

I had a note on Tuesday from Mrs. Boyd, to desire me, from Mr. Boyd, to take with me on my next visit, Chrysostom's commentary on the Romans. Chrysostom Ann & I set off at about half past eight, & arrived at Ruby Cottage before their breakfast time. Miss Bordman did not go yesterday. I sate & talked with her & Mrs. Boyd, & Miss Boyd on her appearing, until Mr. Boyd's message summoned me. "Why how did he know of her being here," said Mrs. Boyd. "*I* told him",—answered Miss Bordman. "And why did you tell him? *You* who pretend to wish to have Ba with you?" "I did not think he wd. send so soon for her." "Why you know that he was sure to send immediately, when he knew of her being here."

Now I was pleased to hear this: and yet why shd. I be? He sent for me, because he thought that I should be *annoyed*, if he did *not* sent [sic]. Perhaps *that* was the reason!—

I wonder why they all like me so much at Ruby Cottage —I mean, why Miss Boyd & Miss Gibbons & Miss Bordman like me so much. It is always so!— I am liked most by those whom— —but such reflections are "vainest of all vain things". Went up to Mr. Boyd. "Is that *you,* Porsonia?" I read to him out of Chrysostom's commentary, & we agreed in the saint's heterodoxy about original sin. . . .

Miss Bordman came into the room, to say good bye. Mr. Boyd seemed sorry to say it to her. Well! if he likes her, that is natural; & it is natural that he shd. like her.

He went to his bedroom, & when he came back, observed to me—"I was thinking in the other room how fortunate it is (I am afraid only *fortunate* was the word, or perhaps *happy*) that I am able to bear your voice. For if your voice had been in that particular key which I cannot bear, I never cd. have associated with you." "I am very glad it is not. I certainly shd. not have liked to have been told on my first visit to you, that you did not wish me to visit you again." "Oh I wd. not have done it *then.* I wd. have tried two or three times, if I could bear your voice,—& if I could not have borne it, I wd. have told Mrs. Boyd to tell you about it." Just as he told Mrs. Boyd to *tell Miss Gibbons* about not coming into his room!! . . .

I did not feel so strongly while he *said* it; & I ought to consider now that Mr. Boyd's organs are in a very excitable state, & that it does not lie in his inclination, to controul & calm them. But still, when he was aware of the possibility—nay, of the probability, of not being able to endure my voice, he shd. not have urged me to go to see him in the manner he did, four years ago. And above all, to speak of making Mrs. Boyd the instrument of turning me away!—

I was kept down stairs at dawdling dinner, for more than an hour & a half—& sate with Mr. Boyd only half an hour afterwards.

I called at Mrs. Trant's for a few minutes, which were Procrustianized into twenty by Dominic's nonsense. Because I asked him the cause of his high spirits—, he accused me of "fishing for a compliment"; & I had to assure him that I was neither accustomed nor necessitated to earn compliments by the sweat of my brow. Then he began to insist upon my lending him Mr. Boyd's Chrysostom for two or three days. I yielded like a saviour of the capitol. [a goose]

Got home in time for tea, & found Mr. Bohn's catalogue, directed to E B Barrett Esqr, waiting for me!— No letters. Bro was at the Hereford M[usic] M[eeting] today, by the help of dear Bummy's ticket.

Friday—Sept 16.

I wrote a letter to Papa,—& a note to Mr. Boyd containing the palinodia of my folly in lending Chrysostom to Dominick. He *may* be angry with me; for I am sure that he *can* be angry with me, if I give him cause. I forgot to memorabilize his idea of sending to the Times newspaper, a letter upon *ʽοι πολλοι* [The many] & his having written to Mr. Davidson on the subject. He can write to *Mr. Davidson*! But with regard to sending a letter to the Times Newspaper, he thought of what I had once said, & that I might not like it. I said,—"never mind *me*". No! if *he* does not mind, the probable consequences of publishing such a letter in the Times—never mind *me*!!

As we were going out to drive today, Mr. Martin intercepted us with an invitation to drink tea at Colwall. So we drove round by Mr. Deane's, down the rough road, where we found a pure cool looking stream & washed our hands in it,—& arrived at Colwall before six. I wish I cd. have washed my hands of *that*!— Mr. de Marizet left it today. A still life evening, which ended by Mr. Martin walking home with our carriage. No letters.

Saturday. Sept 17

Today's account, will not end as yesterday's did. And yet, it is possible that there *may* be no letters. No letters. I have been reading the new Testament with its comparative evidences, today, all day. I cannot—the word is correctly said—I *cannot* make up my mind from Scripture, to do otherwise than embrace the doctrine of general redemption.

Perhaps the *cannot* may be reversed some day; and yet how is it possible to understand otherwise than I do at present, the latter verses of the 5th. chapter of Romans; tho' Mr. Boyd's argument on the *ʽοι πολλοι* is certainly rendered null & void by the occurence of that expression in the last verse of the second of the Second Epis: to the Corinthians.

Maddox came, which is the beginning of a pleasant dream; namely that I shall go to Malvern with her on Monday. Shall I *Can* I?

Sunday. Sept 18.

Went to church with B & A in the wheelbarrow. If this were likely *to last*, I wd. not go; and as it is, I am not clear —indeed I am afraid I *am* clear, that I am not doing right. But my disposition is a yielding one. I have a constitutional dislike of all contention; & therefore I suppose I prefer contending with myself, to contending with other people . . because I am weaker than they are.

On the road, Bummy observed, "Most likely, you are preparing for your journey on Monday." She had penetrated, not heard of, my dream about Maddox. Yes! I see that I *can* go.

A better sermon from Mr. Dean, than any I had ever before listened to, from *him*. Mrs. Cliffe & Eliza accompanied us home, because Mr. Allen Cliffe excommunicated them from his congregation. Bro & Sam wd. belong to it, & heard a very decent discourse on *responsibilities*.

We went down to our gate, where Mr. Moens was Mr. Curzon's substitute. "The Lord is my salvation." He is a converted Jew; & his sermon was most touching & interesting—& made the tears come into my eyes more than once. The simplicity which is in Christ, is in this disciple of Christ. There is something irresistibly winning in his very manner. Dear old man!— He met Papa in London, two months ago, on the morning on which he heard of the death of dear Mary; . . & walked with him for more than two miles. "Blessed are the dead", he exclaimed when telling us of this meeting, "who die in the Lord; for *they* rest from their labours." . . .

Monday. Sept. 19.

Off at 8 in the morning, with Maddox—after have [sic] tea'd & bread & buttered with her & Minny. Intercepted by Dominic & Henry, who wanted me to breakfast at Mrs. Trant's, & talked a great deal of *native* nonsense—Dominick especially. He accused Henry of making use of his ideas in conversation,—which, thinks I to myself, accounts for *Henry's* nonsense. Breakfast at Ruby Cottage not begun; but Miss Boyd met me at the door,—& Mrs. Boyd ran down stairs in a flannel dressing-gown & nightcap, to hold communion with me on the subject of Mr. Biscoe's distresses. Annie does *not* love him, & *therefore* is not worthy of his love. If I were a man, & had a heart, I wd. not covet the possession of her's—Oh! *no no*! Mr. Boyd sent for me twice, before Mrs. Boyd released me from letter reading & her bedroom. When I went to him, & explained my detention, he regretted . . not that it *had happened at all*, but that it had not happened later in the day; *because*—no very flattering reason,—the earlier he heard Greek reading, the better he liked it. I am making an anachronism. This observation was not made until after he was shaved, during which operation, I was of course exiled!—

He showed me his Benedictine edition of Gregory. It is in high preservation, & very beautiful. I will get one like it, whenever I have next the use of Fortunatus's purse[1]—or any purse, heavy enough. He allowed me to read a part of the Apologetic, . . . a high privilege, granted on solemnly enforced conditions of not leaning my arm on any part of any page. I liked & admired much of what I read. I do like & admire Gregory's prose!!—& I *enjoy* reading a beautiful style so much the more, when I can read it with one who enjoys it too—when I can read it with Mr. Boyd.

Because he went out of the room for a moment, Miss Boyd came in,—& when *he* came in, he hinted rather broadly I thought, that she shd. go out. "Sister". "What?" "Oh I only wanted to know if you were in the room *still*".

When her exit had taken place—, "What was my sister talking to you about?" "She was praising the old fashion of cutting trees into peacocks & towers,—& she was abusing Samson Agonistes." "Abusing Sampson Agonistes!! But did she not notice my Gregory?" "No! she did not." He was *not* angry with me for the rape of his Chrysostom, by D[ominick] T[rant].

We talked & discussed a good deal about the Romans, —& he agreed with me, not altogether I think, about them; . . . I *think* that he likes to agree with *me*. I am *sure* that I like to agree with *him*—particularly on religious subjects!— And yet the desire of agreeing with him, *never*, as far as I know myself, *never did* or *could* occasion any change or modification of those opinions of my understanding which are independent of my inclination,—least of all on religious subjects! We were only an hour at dinner!! How prestissimo. . . . Milo cd. not have been longer dining than Mrs. Boyd!* Mr. Boyd sent for me before we had quite had our deserts. Glad of it. He lent me Beverley's pamphlets, which I took away with me at six—intended to be a quarter past five. Billy [Trehern]'s *apologia* was, that clocks are different. So are tempers. I may get a scold when I get home. Called for a moment at Mrs. Trants, to take Chrysostom. Interrupted the finale of their dinner, & was importunated to stay. Dominick & the Grand Duchess Helena![2] He is growing very forward; & gliding into a taste which is most unmanly & ungentlemanly—that of exciting confusion of countenance, *in order to enjoy it*. There was an impertinence in his manner today, which was quite intolerable,—& which my want of presence of mind made me suffer from, more than I shd. have otherwise done. It is provoking . . that such a fool as Dominick, should have made me feel confused even for one moment. . . .

*Milo, an athlete of Crotona, who is said to have eaten the whole of a four-year-old heifer.

Found Mrs. Griffith & Charlotte Peyton, among the arrivals—and only half past six—& tea only just gone in—& everybody in good humour. My hair was wet, & Mrs. G. pigtailed it with my pocket handkerchief. Very fine effect, I have no doubt!

Told Arabel about the Grand Duchess & D T,—& made her laugh until there was a bedquake.

Tuesday. Sept. 20th.

So Bummy has agreed to join Mrs. Cliffe's pic nic today; & so I am to go!— Heigho!—

B A & I set off in the wheelbarrow: H & Sam on horseback, & arrived safely at the wind's point. [Wynds Point] Mrs. Cliffe & Co had begun their ascent, but Eliza returned to be *our* co. I mounted Henrietta's "high horse", & Sam took the bridle,—& when we had overtaken the other squadron, Mr. Allen Cliffe took the bridle, & talked very . . uninterestingly, until we had topped the hill. Glorious hills! How finely they seemed to overlook the great expanse, as if they exulted in their own beauty. But the wind blew away all reverieing! I got off the horse, & *ran about* a little in my allegro style, until dinner was ready. The exposè of Henrietta's lamb & tarts, threw her into an embarras! The *union* between England & Ireland wd. affect her much less!— Si *sic* omnia, I shd have been sick, instead of eating my dinner.

Mr. Davis who with Mr. C & Sam, made our trium*virate*, may be in love with Eliza Cliffe, as she seems to wish—, but I hope he will never be in love with me. They say he is clever. He may know something of antiquities, & *something* of many things besides; but as to his being a clever man, I cry you mercy!—

After dinner my high horse, & Eliza my leader, took me up to the summit of the Herefordshire beacon. Nota bene. The Worcestershire side *is* finest!! What with the rain & wind & height & sight, I grew altogether inebriated,—& after leaving the "high horse"; to Sam's guidance, began to run & slip down to the bottom. Quoth Mr. Davis to Sam, "What immense spirits your sister has."!—

Ah if he knew!— But I felt *then*, as if I were ten years old, & as if *that* were my birthday!

We were rained upon until we took refuge in Mrs. Clarke's cottage—& there we remained until our hair & stockings were dry. The excitement had gone off, & I felt quite exhausted!— Got home, where we found Mr. Jefferson who had breakfasted with us & shot with Bro. After tea, music began. I glided off to bed at eight, unwell with overfatigue. These kind of things do not agree with me.

I read only until twelve today. I wish I had stayed at home, tho' I did enjoy about . . an hour of the time, when we were on the H beacon. With a few abstractions, the party wd. have been pleasanter. As parties go, it was *very well.*

Wednesday Sept 21st.

Very unwell—could scarcely get down stairs, my legs trembled so much. On going into the dining room, a note was given to me from Mrs. Martin, praying me to meet her at the gate, & accompany her, together with Bummy, to Bromesberrow. I felt so unwell, that I negatived the proposal,—& this set B's combustible particles on fire. She spoke crossly to me,—& I who was on the very verge of hysterics, & required only a finger touch to impel me forwards, burst into tears, & had that horrible dead precursive feeling all thro' my hands & feet. But I made an effort—a great effort was really necessary—& got over it. I dare say Bummy thought it was all humbug. Indeed from her cool manner to me from morning to night, I have no doubt that she actually thought so. But what cd. I do!? I lay down on my bed after breakfast, because I cd. scarcely sit up—and yet when time drew near for us to meet Mrs. Martin, I sent Henrietta in to Bummy to carry my palinodia. I wd. go, if she wished it. No!—it wd. not do. If I did not feel equal to it, she wished nothing of the kind—, so she & Henrietta went instead of me. In the meantime, I read Mr. Beverley's pamphlets which Mr. Boyd had lent to me; the letter to the Archbishop of York, & the Tombs of the prophets.— They are clever & forcible; coarse enough, & in some places too highly colored. For instance, I do *not* believe that the body of the established clergy are as much opposed to the reading of the scriptures, as the papistical clergy are; and I *do* know instances of members of that body, refusing the sacrament to persons of immoral character. . . .

No letter today again. How very extraordinary it is.

Thursday. Sept. 22d.

The Jackdaw has torn one of the leaves of my Heynes Homer, the Homer which Mr. Boyd gave to me on his birthday. And why did he tear it? Because Georgie ventured to take the book into the schoolroom, & without asking my leave. Georgie was scolded of course. I had the philosophy not to cry.

Well! I have tried with gum & Ann & philosophy to make the best of the torn leaf. If it had but been a book which Mr. Boyd did not give me!—

I heard Storm & Georgie double reading lessons of fifty lines each, out of Homer & Euripides, on account of their idleness yesterday: and for my own study, I have been reading Isocrates—his panegyricus still!—

A letter from Papa to me! Very kind & very cheerful—but he has not heard yet from [Uncle] Sam! I wish he had heard, or could hear!— Not a word of the Hope End business; & Bummy & Henrietta augur *most* favorably from this silence. I am a *μαντις κακων* [Prophet of ill]. At least I think that if any happy change of circumstance *had* taken place, Papa wd. have told us of it; and I think it is foolish to look so exclusively at the bright side that our eyes are blinded to the darker side where our way *may* lead! *May* lead! That is putting it in the softest language. Probability says, *will* lead.

Mr. & Mrs. Martin called here today—& I was called

down to them. Mrs. M. said, she hoped that I was recovered from my real & *imaginary* fatigue. I answered that there was nothing imaginary in my fatigue, but I *was* recovered.

This has been Bummy's report. Not kind in her; but I will take no notice of it. It is not worth either irritating or being irritated about. . . .

Friday. Sept 23.

I mean to go to Malvern tomorrow, if I can peaceably, & *obligingly*. Finished the Panegyricus, at last. What is the reason that I have been *able* to dawdle over it? There must be some reason. A long passage near the end, has a great deal of eloquence; & vivida vis besides: and the general style is very flowing & beautiful.

In general, perhaps, more *flowing* than *glowing*—which may account for my "reluctant indolent delay". Another thing which materially blunted the edge of my interest, is, my deficiency in historical information. This I really must correct.

Read some more of Lamartine. He is certainly verbose, & apt to mistake "words that burn" for "thoughts that breathe". There is much lengthiness together with much picturesqueness & *Goldsmith*, in his mille, ou la terre natale; but le tombeau d'une mere, is perfectly exquisite. I read also some of Shelley—the whole of his Queen Mab as extant "free from the objectionable passages." It is not in my opinion, written in the highest vein of poetry; & it is dull & heavy. . . .

Saturday Sept 24

Henrietta went out to drive at twelve oclock with Mrs. Martin. I heard the boys read Greek—& Latin on account of Bro being at Worcester. By the bye, I hope he may bring home my shoes & combs & Theophylact.

I wonder if Mr. Boyd is expecting me; & if he will be disappointed at my not coming!—

Shelleys *Adonais* (the Elegy on Keats) is perfectly exquisite. Oh! it is *so* beautiful! He walks in Bion's footsteps,[1] & thinks about Adonis, evidently; but who would quarrel with an earthly piper for imitating the music of the spheres? Shelley was one of the *Θεοι παρεδροι* [Those sitting near the Gods] without any doubt. Finished Lamartine who is a poet too—tho' he is a frenchman. *Can any good poetry come out of Paris?*— My answer today is quite a different one from what it wd. have been a year ago.

Mrs. Martin—yes! & Mr. Martin,—came to dinner; & afterwards I talked to the latter, about the pleasure of writing letters. It *was* a pleasure to me! And indeed, while my dear Papa is away, it *is*. What is the *quia* of Mrs. Martin icing me all over, as she undeniably does? . . .

Sunday. Sept 25th.

Went to Church, & took the sacrament. I wish the sacramental service were shortened, & weeded of its expressions "*holy mysteries*" &c. What mystery is there, can there be, in this simple rite? Are there not many weak brethren who shrink back from holy *mysteries*, and who wd. hurry on with a trembling joy to "do this in remembrance" of their Lord? Blessed Lord Jesus! Thou who are the strength of the weak, strengthen *my* heart—& let the remembrance of Thee, outlast, within it, the affecting rite which I, in my unworthiness, performed this morning.

The Cliffes dined here as usual. Afterwards we waited more than half an hour at the chapel where no Mr. Moens appeared. Returned disappointed, & *not* wet; tho' the wetness seemed the more natural & probable consequence of our expedition. I hope it may be fine tomorrow, at least until I get to Malvern. When I do get there, it may rain newfoundland dogs & Tom Cats,—& be *welcome*—if any rain cd. *keep* me there.

So Bro met Mrs. Boyd yesterday, & she complained of my not going to Malvern!

No letters. How it is raining!—

Monday Sept 26th.

A splendid day; as if earth as well as Heaven were all sunshine. Breakfasted in the nursery; & off to Malvern before eight oclock. Called at Miss Steers's, with Shelley's poems. Could'nt get in on account of her being unwell, & not up. Mrs. Boyd, whom the sound of my chariot wheels, disturbed, emerged in her flannel robes to the top of the stairs, & received me very graciously indeed. But after talking with me a little, in her bedroom, she dismissed me into the drawing room, *not* into Mr. Boyd's room—because, she said, he was breakfasting!— In a few minutes however, I was *per*mitted, to try to be *ad*mitted. "How do you do, Mr. Boyd." "Why Porsonia! *can* that be *you*?" "Did you not know of my being here?" "No! to be sure I did not. Have you been here long?" And when I explained about the breakfast, he remonstrated with me for delaying going in to him on such an account. I was glad to hear that remonstrance. Well! we talked a great deal, principally on religious subjects—, & I read to him some passages from St John's gospel referring to the doctrine of Election & perseverance. . . .

Mr. Boyd walked out *a little* with Miss Boyd; but when Miss Boyd returned into the drawing room, I did not immediately return into his sitting room, because she brought me no message from him. There I sate for a quarter of an hour—twenty minutes—& no message came. I was beginning to be *offended*, when Mrs. Boyd proposed my going to him. "Wd. he not send for me, if he wished me to go?" "No! it is disinterestedness that prevents him from sending". So I went, & found Mr. Boyd beginning to be offended too. "He had shortened his walk on purpose that he might hear me read on: he thought that I liked reading. I knew that he had gone out only for exercise,—& therefore it seemed unnecessary to him that he shd. send a message to me, when I cd. not be ignorant of his having returned". Then *I* was sorry that he had shortened his walk on my account. Then he "certainly liked walking; but he liked hearing me *read too*". Not very flattering—I was obliged to be satisfied. "Since my return, I have been amusing myself in making observations on you,—on the manner in which you have arranged my books. You certainly are the most careless creature about books, that is possible."

After our long Milonian dinner, he went out again. Mrs. Boyd walked out with him *then*. What can be the reason that *I* am *never* asked to walk out with him?— I should like very much to know; and yet perhaps it is as well that I do not know it. Ah! It is *that*, that I fear!—

We talked till the carriage came which it did at half past five; & Mrs. Boyd drove with me to nearly the bottom of the great hill. The last time I was there with her, was the first time I met Mr. Boyd!— So Miss Bordman returns on Wednesday!—& has sent her "very very best love" to me. It must be a mere orientalism,—& I do not like orientalisms. I have heard too many of them. . . .

Commended generally, on my arrival at home, for coming home in such good time. Too good time—if I am commended for it!— The last occasion in the world, on which I would practise works of supererogation.

Henrietta has been to the Commelines with Mrs. Martin, during my absence; & Bro, shooting partridges with Mr. Martin. We compared notes of happiness—& each of us contended for the prize. Surely *I* was happiest!—

Tuesday Sept 27th.

I wrote this morning to my dear Papa; that my letter might go with 2 brace & ½ of partridges. No letters in return. Composing a Greek song, for an air to the guitar. I rather like the *ideas*; but the *harmony* has been torn to pieces, by my looking first to the *musical* measure, & next to the poetical measure. "How *happy* could I be with either"!—and how unsuccessful with both. Reading besides. Mr. Boyd lent me Dr. Clarke's Sermon "What shall I do to be saved?" which I *began*. By the bye, I *thought* yesterday that I had let it fall out of the carriage. If I had, I would have taken Sappho's leap of forgetfulness. Perhaps I shd. have taken it, *before* the loss!— Singing on the guitar, in the evening.

Wednesday. Sept 28th.

. . . Hearing the boys—and now; it is agreed that we shall go to the Wyche!— Shall I go anywhere *below* the Wyche!— How happy I should be if I could! But no—I must not mention it; & if Bummy mentions it, she will be very good natured, & I— —very glad!—

Rain came on—& thunder & lightening besides,—so there is no going. I read some of Dionysius Tractatus de priscis scriptoribus. Not Dionysius's really, I suppose—& not very interesting.

Thursday Sept 29th.

No letter again. I have been reading, Iphigenia in Aulide, for the first time. The opening is very un-Euripidæan—which *I think* Porson observes in his Prælictio, but I forget his observations upon it. A cloudy sunny looking day—like my disposition. Bummy A & I set off in the wheelbarrow, to go somewhere—perhaps, to the Wyche; but the rain began at the Barton corner, & we were obliged to turn our backs on the hills. Found Mrs. Cliffe & Eliza & Mr. Allen Cliffe at home, when we arrived there. They did not stay long.

Friday Sept 30th.

Oh that party at the Bartons. "Ahi dolente *parti*— . . ta!" I must go to it, so I may as well make up my mind gracefully as ungracefully. The Peytons! The Biddulphs!!—

I wont go out of the house before six, at any rate. The drive there, & the talking there, will be exercise enough for one day—so let me get on with Iphigenia. . . .

The carriage went backwards & forwards with our party to the Bartons; therefore I of course made a point of going in the last carriagefull. Arabel & Sam & I, were lightened upon in the hollow way—which frightened me nearly as much as the sight of the tremendous assembly in the Barton Court drawing room, of Biddulphs, Brights, Cliffes, Peytons! I talked a little to two or three people, of whom little Fanny Peyton was by far the most agreable. I wish Berry had not gone to bed—or I wish I had gone there with her!— What a pity it is that some people shd. take more pains about covering their intellects than their shoulders!— Got home tired, & unanimous in every part of me, body mind & heart, that what is called "going out" should be called "the greatest bore in the world".

There was a letter from my dearest Papa today! & to me! He speaks of having heard of, not from, poor [Uncle] Sam, who describes himself in a letter to some Captain as being "low in body & mind". Somebody however, who has seen him, assures Papa that he is looking, tho' thin, better than cd. be expected. He *ought* to have written to Papa!— Papa, dear Papa, *seems* in good spirits, & writes most affectionately— May God bless him.

Saturday Oct. 1st.

Pheasant shooting of course,—& two brace & a half, & a hare, sent down to be packed up for London: & that is not *of course;* but very "good sport". I hope Bro will give me a brace for Mr. Boyd. By the bye, I had dreamt of going to see *him* today; but Mrs. Biddulph woke me, by asking Henrietta to dine with her,—& Henrietta will want the carriage.

After all Henrietta wants no such thing. She is to go in the other, with Bro & Sam—& Bummy A & I, I believe, are going out to drive. B proposed it herself. Perhaps we shall go to the Wyche; perhaps I shall go . . but I wont go to sleep again. Bummy wrote a note to Papa today, & she has been telling me its object—namely to enquire about Papa's plans & circumstances, in order to ascertain whether or not she may be free to return to the north & receive

Charlotte [Butler]. She says that if Papa's circumstances remain *as they were*, she will not on any account leave us, even to receive Charlotte. Dearest Bummy!— I told her that Charlotte has the first claim upon her—but I could not say it without tears in my eyes. I do not wish her to sacrifice any pleasure, much less so great a one, to our comfort—but I could not relinquish that comfort, the comfort of her society—, without pain.

What will Papa's answer be?—*My* hope of any change of circumstance, is very very faint indeed!— Bummy's seems to be strong!—

I have finished Dr. Clark's Discourse. It is very clever: but as all metaphysical discourses on scriptural subjects, must be,—seeking *only to* convince the human reason, it is unconvincing. At least this is true of one or two material parts, where even I have detected fallacies. Dr. Card's sermon on the Athanasian creed, is bound up in the same volume; & I have read it. How could Mr. Boyd praise it, as he has done!— "Impressive eloquence"! unimpressive verbosity!— "Convincing reasoning"! No reasoning at all! "An ardent zeal for truth"!— An excessive dogmatism in prejudice!— There is my commentary, on Mr. Boyd's!— I shall tell Mr. Boyd that the only passage which I like *very much*, is the one which speaks in *his* praise!— And that is the truth!—

Well: we have been to Malvern—& I have seen Mr. Boyd!— It was a most lovely evening. The air was too good for mere human beings to breathe!— We left our carriage at the Wyche, & walked along that lovely walk to the ash: and then Bummy said "Let us turn down this way", turning down *my way*. We walked & walked nearer & nearer Ruby Cottage, until I began to suspect *something*. Thro' the gate!— The something was developped! How pleased I was! Bummy told me that I might stay with Mr. Boyd, half an hour. How pleased I was!— Stayed for a few moments with Miss Bordman & Mrs. Boyd: & then up to Mr. Boyd! The room so dark, that I could scarcely see him: & I so unexpected, that I had to speak twice before he recognized me. He reproached me for coming for so short a time. "I wd. rather that you did not come at all than come so late; if this visit is to stand for a longer one". But he seemed satisfied when I promised to visit him again, long measure, on Monday. . . . [He] told me that he wished me to spend two or three days with him. I told him that it all depended on Papa's answer to Bummy's application, which answer might arrive on Tuesday or Wednesday. I am pleased at his inviting me; & wish—how I wish—that I could go to him!— But as a presentiment once said to me, *no more*! I soon said good bye, & went back to meet my party. Mrs. Boyd gave me Mr. Biscoe's letter, to read: to be sent back tomorrow. . . .

Sunday. Oct 2d.

I dont think Henrietta enjoyed herself or her party last night. What was the reason? She generally does enjoy everything of that kind.

I wrote a letter to Mrs. Boyd: a commentary on Mr. Biscoe's letter—& *advice*! Advice from *me*, who never know what is best to be done for myself!—who generally advise myself to walk into water or fire: *I advised* Mrs. Boyd not to write to Mr. Biscoe until she had ascertained the state of Annie's feelings respecting him: (*they* will not be *regarding* him—) & in the case of their being as I suspect . . un-touched,—to break off the business at once & altogether. Sent the letter, with a brace of pheasants for Mr. Boyd.

No Church at Colwall. Uninteresting sermon at Mr. Curzon's. He is going to lend me a book—William Rushton's *letters on particular redemption*—which is "to do me a great deal of good". I asked to lend it to Mr. Boyd. "Yes. I am going to write to Mr.— —" What was the name? "and I shd. like to have your & Mr. Boyd's annotations". "*My* annotations", I answered "wd. be valueless." So they wd.

I enquired Mr. Curzon's opinion of Miss Gibbons. He

enquired mine: And I said something of her *vanity* & selfishness, (tho' at the same time, I "liked her in several respects",—) which I have reproached myself ever since for saying. "Did Mr. Boyd observe it to you: or did *you* observe it?" "*I* observed it; & it does not render her Christian character attractive." Now what business had I to say anything of the kind? If I were a Roman catholic, I wd. whip myself for it. I dare say I am quite as *vain* as Miss Gibbons,—used to be at any rate,—& shd. still be, if I had had my own way. Miss Gibbons was very kind & feeling to me, in her manner at least: & I ought at least to have been *silent* before Mr. Curzon, whose good opinion she was anxious, I know, to obtain. Agreed with Mrs. Cliffe—I am to go to the wyche early tomorrow, & walk to Ruby Cottage; & she is to call for me *at four*. This will save me half a crown. Not that I grudge half a crown: but I am obliged to ask Bro for all my turnpike money—& Papa may not like the bill. *We* caught a squirrel; & *I* claimed it.

Monday Oct 3d.

Meant to have been off at seven. Off at a quarter past 8—& B & A my convoy. A lovely morning, which I hoped wd. turn into rain that nobody might be able to come for me. Found the majority at breakfast. The minority looked into the room in a few minutes, to ask "Is Miss Barrett here?" I shook hands with him. "I am going to walk up & down in front of the house for a little while". He walked there, a *very* little while. Went up to him, & he inspected, or rather *felt* my Greek Bible which I had brought with me—& I read the title pages, & preface—loud out. Then we talked about election; & "Oh wretched man than I am." On the latter point, he made me change my opinion. Certainly when you read the 6th. chapter [of Romans], & *then* the 7—the close of the 7th, appears to be a description of Paul in his unregenerate state, under the law. . . . Then, the Cliffe's came!! Very soon Eliza interrupted us. I said a few words to her, & sate down again, intending to remain in the room. But Mr. Boyd did not speak—wd. not speak. It was evident from his manner, that he wd. prefer my being out of the room. So I went—of course!— Went—of course!—

Mrs. Boyd & co dined, while I sate with Mrs. Cliffe. They were obliged to dine, on account of Annie, whom Mrs. Boyd is going to bring home. Mrs. Cliffe & I talked of Annie. B has been saying of her, what it is unpardonable to say. I defended her with vehemence, & tears in my eyes. No use in writing down here either attack or defence—but . . I wish she were married. Married, she soon will be, *I believe*: if there is faith in man—(which by the bye there isnt) for Mrs. Boyd means to *permit* Mr. Biscoe to take her to India—has written to him, *almost* to say so—& showed me the letter.

Called Eliza away from Mr. Boyd, & took leave of him—rather cooly. I could not help it. He said "are you obliged to go?" or "cant you stay?" or some thing of that kind. After all, I cannot doubt his preferring my society to Eliza's—but he does not value it as I value his.

He said to me today, "It is quite enough to satisfy me if you come here yourself, without your sending me any pheasants." Nevertheless I will send them, whenever I can get them. He intends to lend me Ignatius. Glad of it. I wish I had gone to Malvern today in my own carriage. For *then*, this rain wd. have excused my staying there, for a night at least. One thing has very much pleased me in one way—Mrs. Boyd consents to Annie's going to India. Now if she does go, she will go in March; & there will then be no obstacle to Mr. Boyd's staying at Malvern if we stay here, or going where we go—if we go from hence. At any rate the obstacles will be diminished in number.

May Annie be happy!— I am not . . & yet I *am* . . *I quite selfish.*

Tuesday Oct: 4.

Will there be a letter from Papa today? If there is . . what will it be—rainy or sunshiney?

I have been reading again the 6th. & 7th. of Romans. Mr. Boyd is certainly right.

We are going today to Mathon. I wd. rather stay at Hope End. And yet it is not kind to Eliza to think so; & after all I shd. like to see her drawing, before it is exhibited. One oclock—we shd. go now if we are to go at all.

How provoked I am. Henrietta has determined not to go, because Sam will want the horse at four—or rather (the only sufficient reason) because she dislikes it. She says that Eliza Cliffe is *my* friend. *My* friend!!! As if I ever did, or cd., or wd., apply that word so lightly!! I never applied it to any person but one; & that person is not Eliza Cliffe. I like her on many accounts; I am grateful to her on many accounts;—but she is not, & never cd. be my friend!—

No poney caught—because either H or I was careless. B says I: I say H—of course. Both of us, perhaps. So we did not arrive at Mrs. Cliffe's until nearly three, too late for the drive to Colonel West's. Glad of it. Eliza's drawing for the Worcester Exhibition, is perfectly beautiful.

Got home at 6, or past six; & had tea. From what Bummy said afterwards, we discovered that she had heard from Papa. No good, from her manner. My squirrel very well.

Wednesday. Oct. 5.

The bible meeting at Ledbury today. Sorry for it. It is our duty to go; and some allusion *may* be made to Papa's absence & the cause of it; & this, I cannot always bear.

No painful allusion, in a very uninteresting meeting: but Mr. Curzon startled me by asking me to go down to his house before I left Ledbury that he might have ten minutes conversation with me. What cd. he mean to say? Papa— Mr. Boyd, glanced across my mind! I am *so* used to hear what is distressing. I went with Mr. Curzon. He offered me his arm, & we walked very fast before everybody; & when we were safe & silent in his drawing room, he showed me both Miss Gibbons's letter & his own reply to it. She wishes to be baptized—& to come for that purpose to his house in ten or twelve days.

His object in speaking to me on the subject, which he did with every recommendation to secresy,—seems to be, that he is doubtful about her state—not from his own observations, but from Mr. Boyd's. I recanted my inconsiderate words of last Sunday—but I shd. be sorry if any recantation of mine, shd. seem to expose Mr. Boyd to any accusation of malice prepense in his charges against her. I am more interested about *him*, than about Miss Gibbons. Therefore I will write, I think, to Mr. Curzon, to explain my explanation.

A note from Mr. Boyd, to desire me to consult Cruden from [sic] him, on justification, & glorification. *A note* indeed! Down *one* page; & beginning "my dear Porsonia"!—I shall be convinced at last.

Shall we go to Malvern tomorrow. Henrietta says "Yes"; but she has agreed to dine at the Watts's, & there is sure to be a difficulty of some kind.

Began a letter to Mr. Curzon.

When will Mr. Boyd begin & finish a *letter* to me?—Not until he *changes*, *again*.

Thursday Oct 6th. 1831.

I finished my letter to Mr. Curzon today, & Henrietta took it to Ledbury where she went to dine with the Watts's. My letter speaks a part of my heart with regard to my dear friend—, & the whole of my heart with regard to myself. It is not an uncandid letter. If Miss Gibbons herself were to read it, she cd. scarcely, I think, be very severe on me.

Mrs. Cliffe here until after one o'clock—therefore no doing anything meo more—except talking nonsense—& except (the more agreable exception) arranging a plan for Malvern tomorrow. She is to be with us at ten; & Miss Peyton one of our "pleasaunt companie". They will be *my* "pleasaunt companie" only as far as Ruby Cottage!—

Bummy read the debates to Arabel & me [on Reform]—

after I had told a story, which Occyta did not seem to like as much as he generally does my stories, about the sea of honey & milk & wine—, & the prince who was born in the straights of Gibralter & was consequently half black & half white. That was "all out of my own head" as Occyta says! I have a great mind to write an opposition budget to mother goose's—Seriously, I may be goose enough to do it.

An answer from Mr. Curzon to my letter. His begins "my very dear friend". Lights make shades seem darker!—

There was a reform meeting at Ledbury today, to which all the boys down to Henry, went. Dearest Bro spoke, I hear, very well, & for ten minutes. How I shd. have liked to have *heard him!*— Mr. Curzon sent the Letters on particular redemption, with *his* letter.

Friday Oct 7th.

Well! It is a fine, windy day—& Mrs. Cliffe not come! She thinks I suppose all of the wind, & nothing of the fineness! Provoking!— A message is sent to Charlotte Peyton!— It may rain tomorrow! Provoking!— But she *may* come after all, for it is only just eleven.

Mrs. Cliffe came, & then the rain came. I put on my hat, but everybody else was reasonable enough to be prepared for a disappointment.

We did not go. Mrs. Cliffe stayed until three or four—longer than my patience did. Eliza at least will come tomorrow, in the case of sunshine.

I read on with Mr. Curzon's book.

The reform bill is sure to be thrown out of the House of Lords—, & then what will be the consequences? More fatal ones, than those of today's rain.

A great deal of music mending & binding, down stairs tonight, which occasioned a most sublime confusion. My head ached with it.

Saturday Oct: 8th.

A cloudy day again. Nobody *will* go, except me; & I *cant*

go. But I can & will go on Monday, that is, if I am well—et cætera!—

Mrs. Martin called here with Mrs. Hill; a lady who seems to have too many teeth, & quite enough ideas.

Rain again!— No going to Malvern.

Finished Mr. Curzon's book, which disappoints me by not exactly suiting my case. It suits Mr. Curzon's better—for it is directed against Fuller's Doctrine of indefinite redemption—i.e. the doctrine of atonement for *sin*, not *sinners*. The book appears to me to want compression & arrangement, & some other things besides. But I like much of it . . . .

No letters. Bro & Sam at Worcester.

Sunday Oct: 9th.

To church, & heard a bad sermon of Mr. Deane's for the *second time* . .

. . . The bill thrown out! majority 41!!! What will the people do!— What will the king do? What will Lord Grey do? Resign—or make the Lords resign. . . . I am *afraid* that there will be a change of ministry. . . . But on the other hand, what Tory administration *can* carry on the government against such an House of Commons? Well!—nous verrons.

I shd. have liked to have sent the news to Mr. Boyd as he desired, & as I intended to have done, if it had arrived on any day but Sunday. As it is, he shall hear everything tomorrow from *me*!—I *will* go to Malvern tomorrow. Arabel *wishes* & *ought* to go too: but her proposing such a thing will occasion an earthquake at least, down stairs. I hope, I hope, it may not do so; for my sake, as well as her's & Annie's!— Bro never wrote to Papa today!— I am fidgetted about it. Papa is sure to be uneasy & angry.

I believe, when I examine myself, that I am more than half sorry for Annie's return! When she was last at home, she made me feel *so* much pain!!— But I ought to forget *that*!— It is not remembering *that*, but fearing something similar to it; which makes me feel as "half sorry" as I do.

Arabel's going to Malvern proposed! Controversy on the

subject—& Bummy *contra*. It wont do! It is more prudent for A to give it up, particularly as in the case of her going, B wd. be left alone.

Monday. Oct 10th.

Arabel is very amiable & goodtempered. She gave up the point of going, earnest as she was about it, & not *sullenly*—for she wrote a note which I took to Annie. I did not leave home until 20 minutes past 8, intended to be 20 minutes past 7. Went by the Wyche, & found Mrs. Boyd at the exordium of breakfast. Annie was out—calling on Miss Steers. In a few minutes, I was allowed to go up stairs. Mr. Boyd & I talked about the Bill, until he appeared disinclined for reading. "The worst of it is, it disturbs one's mind". However we read afterwards a passage from the orations against Julian, & the one on Paschal Sunday.

I read a passage or two to him from Rushton's book; one in particular which I thought a satisfactory commentary on a difficult text in the 5th. of Romans "For as by one man's disobedience &c". Mr. Boyd said to me one or two things, which gave me pain—& not for *myself* individually. I cannot bear to hear him say anything which even *sounds* anti scriptural! The tears were in my eyes today: I could not help it— There never was a truer friendship than mine for him!— Do I not pray for his spiritual welfare! Lord Thou knowest!—And only Thou canst know whether his heart is right in thy sight!—

The opinion which he *tolerated* today, & gave me so much pain by tolerating, was Wesley's opinion; & that Wesley was a spiritual Christian, no Christian can doubt. And yet, I wish he had *not* tolerated it!—

Altogether, today I had not quite a happy visit. My doubts on the subject of his regard for me, rose more than once into a painful certainty. Others may be more *worthy* of his regard in all ways but *one*! *Not in that one*!!!—

He asked me if I had heard the result of Bummy's thoughts about going away—& if I wd. go to see him for a few days. He seemed to wish me to go. But the "*seeming*" might proceed from *a general spirit of benevolence—inclusive of me*. Oh how I hate that idea!! I submitted if it were not the best course to wait & see how matters were settled, without running the risks of displeasing Papa or acting unkindly to Bummy!—and he yielded, after observing that by delay, I ran the risk of the occurrence of circumstances which wd. prevent my ever visiting him at Malvern. He recommended to me the policy of *having attention paid to* Annie—lest in the case of our remaining at Hope End, she shd. make Mrs. B leave Malvern at the end of the twelve month. "I suppose—or I hope—that in that case you wd. still wish us to stay here"!—

Annie & Miss Boyd are two. From what I can understand & observe, there is some fault on both sides. One is provoking—& the other sensitive.

But I cant help blaming *Annie*!— As she was with me in the carriage,—for I took her in it, a little way,—I recommended a concileating manner to her! No! She wd. *not* conciliate!— She wd. *not* speak to Miss B any more!—

The carriage came at a quarter to 5. At 5 I went. Nota bene—never go the wyche road again!—I thought that I never should go the whole of it, last night! Such a hill!—

Annie *is* indifferent to poor Mr. Biscoe!!—

Mr. Boyd told me,—when I had told *him* about Arabel's intending to visit Annie this week,—that her coming wd. be an excuse for me to pay him another visit in a day or two!— I wish that "universal benevolence" were out of my head.— There was a letter today from Miss Gibbons to Mrs. Boyd. Her "very best love to me"—, & she wished very much "to hear from me". Now I do *not* like writing to her—& I do *not* like being unkind. What can I do!— . . . She will be at Mr. Curzon's on Thursday. By the bye Mrs. Boyd asked me, if she was going to be baptized, & if she had called on Mr. Curzon in her way thro' Ledbury. I answered evasively, "I believe she did *not* call"—

Got home in the dark. Guitaring in the evening.

Tuesday. Oct. 11th.

Gent has gone for the letters: what will be in them? If Papa writes, we shall all be scolded I know, for our silence. Bro's letter to him, shd. have gone on Friday instead of yesterday.

Today we are to dine at the Martins. A bore!—And yet Mrs. Martin lent me Dr. Channing's treatise "On the importance & means of a national Literature", & I ought to be grateful to her. I have been reading it this morning. It is a very admirable, & lucidly & energetically written production. The style is less graceful than powerful. Indeed it has so much strength, that the *muscles* are by necessity, rather too obvious & prominent. But its writer is obviously & prominently an extraordinary man—& if *he* were to dine at Colwall today, I wd. go to meet him, without sighing . . much!—

My love of solitude is growing with my growth. I am inclined to shun the acquaintance of those whom I do not like & love; on account of the *ennui*; & the acquaintance of those whom I might like & love,—on account of the *pain*! — Oh the pain attendant on liking & loving, may seem a little cloud,—but it blots from us all the light of the sun!!—

B H & I went to Colwall in B's carriage. The Commelines there—Miss C Miss L C & Mr. C Senior. Miss Commeline decides that half of me has vanished away in my thinness! Who can wonder at it? Mrs. Hill seems to me an amiable woman. She is said to have the talent of making friends. I do not envy her *that*. Has she the talent of keeping them?

Besides; the meaning which she attaches to the word *friend*, is probably not *my* meaning. Mr. Webb who sate next me at dinner, sang very well after dinner—with expression & spirit,—better than he talked. Mr. & Miss Peyton, Mr. Deane, H, & I have settled the English form of government for next year. It is to be a parthenocracy. For Universal suffrage will include our sex,—the married people will neutralize each others votes by voting pro & con; & then how can the young men be uninfluenced by the young ladies? Impossible!— "What a happy people, you will be," was my exclamation. Mr. D. asked me how Mr. Boyd was. Hearing his name in the midst of a crowd of people whom I cared nothing for, was like Robinson Crusoe's detection of a man's footprint in his desert!—

"He is as well as can be expected, considering the distress which he is now suffering in common with all good patriots".

"But he shd. be consoled by reflecting, that tho' the decision of the H of Lords has displeased *him*, it has pleased others".

"Not at all! That reflection increases his suffering. He has to bewail not only his own want of felicity, but the want of wisdom in his fellowcreatures". Mr. D. is a good-natured man.

Glad to get home!—

Wednesday Oct. 12.

Eliza Cliffe came to help Henrietta to bind music. I wd. not be *bound* to help *her*. An unsatisfactory day: my politeness drawing me one way & my studiousness another.

After consecrating about 12 hours to the binding business, H's music book is bound almost as well as if she had paid 6s for it. How much is time worth? Sixpence an hour?—

The rain came on, & arrested Eliza in her way home. If Mrs. Cliffe is angry, she deserves to be drowned!— Music in the evening. Guitar, at least, & singing,—which *ought* to have been music.

Thursday, Oct. 13.

Eliza went away soon after breakfast; & Bummy & Henrietta went away soon after her, to call at the Bartons. . . .

Mr. Curzon arrived at two; & he & I were tête à tête until five or near five, when H & B arrived. They have been to Colwall Green to invite Mr. & Mrs. Deane to dine here on Saturday; & to Colwall, where Mr. Martin has warned them off his premises by frigidity & rigidity. Bummy is clear on the point of his disliking *her*.

I am neither frigid nor rigid; it wd. be an improvement, were I a little of both; and Mr. Curzon may wish me to be *much* of both, rather than inconsiderate enough to forget his luncheon. How careless I was! And how hungry he must have been!—

Miss Gibbons is to be at his house tomorrow, & baptized on Monday! And on Sunday, I am permitted to divulge!—

A great deal of talking between Mr. C & me about election. I wish my mind were more settled on that subject.

Friday. Oct 14.

Mr. C stayed all night. Before breakfast this morning, I was writing a letter to my dear Papa, which *must* go today. At breakfast, Miss Peyton's poney arrived to enable Arabel to ride to Malvern. Very goodnatured in Miss Peyton!—Altho' Mrs. Griffith did not actually offer *me* a seat in her carriage, I might have had it: nay, I might have squezzed [sic] my little body into our wheelbarrow, if Bummy had not been alone & Mr. Curzon here!— As it was, I was obliged to stay behind!—

Mr. Curzon remained here until nearly three. He is an excellent Christian & most amiable man: but in conversation, he is . . heavy. There is no denying *that*! Besides I cd. not help thinking now & then, of Mr. Boyd!—

B & I went out to walk; & into the garden, for the first time since that loss which must be a loss for ever [EBB's mother]. I mean, Bummy's first time—not mine. *I* have been there very often. Dearest B's eyes had tears in them I am sure, tho' they were turned away from me!—

They came home at 5, or past 5. Sette was quite heroic about his teeth, as he is about everything; & Henry rather cowardly, as he is about everything. Arabel called at Ruby Cottage, while Miss Peyton & Henrietta went on to Miss Steers's. Very unkind of Henrietta not to call for one moment to see Annie after her four months' absence! But

I will *say* nothing. Arabel did not see Mr. Boyd. I wonder if he was disappointed at my not having gone. Henrietta says that he was *not*, & that I overrate his regard to me. No! I do not do *that*!— Mrs. Boyd has sent me a note by Arabel, to communicate Annie's return of love for Mr. Biscoe. "Oh! that prophaned word."!! . . .

Saturday. Oct 15th.

. . . By the way of distracting Georgie & myself from Homer, I let out my squirrel. He leapt up into the air, & climbed my bookcase, & performed so many tight rope maneuvres, that I was inclined to wish him to be tight again. Particularly in the evening, when Atalanta herself seemed to have no chance of catching him. Arabel & Bummy & Ann & I, were about an hour at it. At last, he wisely ran into his cage, when he cd. run no where else; & thus he was caught, as the anti-reformers will be. Mr. Deane & a goose for dinner. No *identity* hinted at!— He is a good natured man, & not without sense; & he has lent me the London Encyclopædia. I played on the guitar; but my voice had gone away with my breath, in the squirrel chase. He & Bro & H sang—or tried at it.

Sunday Oct 16.

At breakfast Arabel called upon me to divulge the secret. How angry Bummy was!—I "ought not to have received such a confidence!"— Now how could I help it? I am *not* to blame. I never solicited, but cd. not reject, much less cd. I abuse Mr. Curzon's confidence. I can only *regret* its being extended to me.

It has been on my mind from the first, that Miss Gibbons shd. have communicated her intention to her parents; shd. have acted firmly on it, but still have communicated it. Upon this point, however I was not consulted; &, as Mr. Curzon approves of the concealment, I shd. not have been justified in giving an opinion. He said to me today at the school, "Somebody sends her love to you"—& he announced the celebration of the ordinance of baptism at four tomorrow afternoon. May God bless & sanctify it to her soul. . . .

I had today a letter from my dear dear Papa—dearer to me than he ever was!—very kind & satisfactory, but silent on *the* subject. I am sure there is no hope!— Minny thinks the same; & she is more likely to be right than I am. Kenrick, she says, had a letter a fortnight ago, desiring him to purchase horses for ploughing, & announcing that everything wd. soon be finally settled! Well! however it may be settled, *God* will abide with *us*!—

All this makes me more anxious than usual to be with my dear friend Mr. Boyd as much as I can. Tomorrow my usual expedition is cancelled! But I am thinking that I may be well dedommagèe [compensated] by going back with Mrs. Boyd, sleeping at Ruby Cottage, & returning here on Tuesday. To come however to this happy conclusion, certain premises are necessary. Will she ask me? If she does not, I must stay on my own. If she does, my "yes" is ready, & how happy shall I be in saying it!— Bummy has scarcely spoken to me all day. How can I possibly help Miss Gibbons's being baptized?—

Tuesday Oct. 18.

Went to Malvern with Ann . . . Everybody in bed. Mrs. Boyd "motioned" me into her room, & there we discussed Mr. Biscoe, the probability of a letter arriving from him that day, & the possible nature of its contents. Mrs. B doubted his faith. I did not. An embassy from Annie took me up into her room, where I found herself & Miss Bordman in bed together. From thence I went in to Mr. Boyd who had breakfasted. I spent a happy day with him, hearing him repeat passages from the Prometheus, & conversing. Miss Hurd was in the house; for he had sent for her, supposing that everybody was going to Hope End & that he wd. be left alone. She came into his room only for a short time—& the paper was read to him only a little. Altogether I had nothing to complain of.

A letter from Mr. Biscoe! Mrs. Boyd *is* right. A cold letter! a resolved letter! He relinquishes for ever, Annie's love!— This—this is the love of Man! We were much afraid, even I was, of the effect of this letter upon her; but she bore it as calmly as I should bear my squirrel's running away. That such a conclusion should take place, is happiest for *both of them!*—

Well! I had wished Mr. Boyd good bye,—& had put on my hat, & was tying on my cloak, when Annie proposed my staying all night. I resisted— She insisted— And my heart let go its hold in a moment!— The temptation was too great!— Wrote a note to Bummy, & sent away the carriage. The plan is, to go home with Mrs. Boyd to-morrow; but in the case of her not going, I begged Bummy to drive for me to the Wyche.

. . . Mr. Boyd seemed pleased at my staying. He did not seem so much pleased just at first. He said, "Ah! *Ann* had to say only a word to induce you to remain." My answer was—"But if I had thought only of Ann, perhaps I wd. not have remained." And then I explained the broad line of difference between staying from home, *one* night, & many nights. Miss Steers came immediately after tea, & I was obliged to play a game at chess with Annie. Afterwards Mrs. Boyd dismissed me to Mr. Boyd. Sate with him until past eleven!—

Wednesday Oct 19th.

Annie & I slept together last night, & she described to me enough of the state of her mind while she was at Stanwell, for me to feel confirmed in my opinion about the happiness of certain chains being broken. She exacted my secresy towards Mrs. Boyd,—therefore I cd. console her only generally. I did not sleep well last night, & am not well this morning. Was in Mr. Boyd's room a little after nine. Nervous & out of spirits; so that during several hours of the day, I cd. scarcely keep my eyes clear from tears!— Read some of Gregory to Mr. Boyd. He was fancied to be cool in his manner to me; & there were other things which made me uncomfortable.

Miss Bordman gave him a Septuagint, which I think she received from her Father for the purpose. . . . I wish she had not done so. *I* had intended to do it & besides—

Perhaps it is wrong in me to feel as much annoyed as I really do. I am of an intolerably exclusive disposition; & yet I wish some other people were like me—

Mr. Boyd went out to walk twice today. That annoyed me too a little, tho' he did not stay long. Afterwards my spirits came back again while I was sitting with him;—& when it grew darker & darker, they were still more reinforced. "Do you think they will not come for you?" He seemed anxious that they shd. not!—

At last the darkness grew so palpable, that we had a candle & opened Gregory again—when, lo!—a note from Bummy dated from the Wyche! They were afraid of coming down to me; but I might either go to them, or they wd. come again for me tomorrow. "Tomorrow" Mr. Boyd urged eagerly, if not anxiously. "Tomorrow," said my inclinations. "Tomorrow" said my pen. Mr. Boyd & I had a happy evening again. A good deal of proing & contraing about whether I shd. wait until he went to bed before hearing Miss Boyd's story. She is like the Princess Scheherezade, but were she the Princess herself, I wd. not leave Mr. Boyd to go to her. So he yielded, and after all Her Royal Highness told no story, even after he *had* gone to bed.

Thursday Oct 20th.

Was in Mr. Boyd's room before nine. Heard him say over the passages in the Prometheus, & read Gregory. He told me that he had a great mind to buy a book mentioned in Bohn's catalogue, a very ancient edition of Gregory's orations, price £2—12s—6d—& that in that case he wd. ask me to make Papa get it for him. He might receive the book from me, & pay for it from his private purse,—& so escape a reproach of extravagance from Mrs. Boyd. I had made up my mind that if *I* procured it for him thro' Papa, he shd. never pay for it from his private or public purse. But he decided at last not to have it. It was an extravagant thing to do,—& besides, by taking the book, another copy of which he had, he wd. prevent some other person from having it. I smiled at this disinterested benevolence & resolved that the book *shd.* be his.

Writing out treasonable epigrams for Mr. Boyd, Mr. Curzon interrupted us!—But I was allowed to be present at the audience. A great deal of talking about the compatibility or incompatibility of intellectual & religious pleasures. Of course Mr. Boyd & I took the right side of the question. Dinner!— In the midst of it, the carriage came. I saw Mr. Boyd for a few minutes before I went away,—& then the good bye came. An effort was necessary to steady my voice & say it,—but the tears would crowd into my eyes in spite of every effort. He did not seem to care . . *much* about parting with me—

Henrietta & Arabel were my escort home. . . . Dear Bummy not at all angry at my having stayed. I had fancied her note cool, & Mr. Boyd had recommended me to put it into the fire & warm it,—but I dont think now that she meant to write cooly.

My spirits are rather depressed tonight!—*Rather!!*— . . .

Friday Oct 21.

I was cudgelling my brains last night, to find out how I could get money to buy that book for Mr. Boyd. At last I decided; & this morning executed my design. I wrote to Eliza who is at Worcester, & sent to her my editions of Bolingbroke's & Harris's works to be disposed of at Eatons's, desiring her to make him write immediately to Bohn for the Gregory. My books I wd. rather have not parted with but my heart & soul are fixed on this new purchase. I did not look *very* regrettingly on them, while Ann was packing them up!—Sent the sheet of epigrams to the Times newspaper. How happy I was yesterday, when my dear friend was dictating them,—& when *we* were consulting about & reforming some of them!— He told me to put *the bishops* into verse for him, as puzzling about them, made his head heavy.

Read!—& heard the boys read!—

Saturday. Oct. 22.

I have written a brief account of my visit my happy visit, my last visit—perhaps! to Malvern, because not having my Diary with me, I was obliged to trust my memory. I have been writing to Mr. Boyd this morning. My note to him may be *too* expressive of regard!! As his letters to me express actually *none*, I have often resolved to ice mine over also; but I dont know how it is—the frost scarcely begins, when a ray of sunshine melts it all away!— I wish I had told him of my having written for the Gregory. They hurried me so while I wrote, that I had no time to consider anything; & now there is no use in reconsidering anything! I addressed two lines to Mrs. Boyd in the envelope. I hope she wont think it is *too* little. My letter to Mr. Boyd began "my dearest friend". How will his begin to me? Lord Byron used to make "much ado about nothing" when . . . his friends addressed him as only "my dear Byron". Lord Byron was at school then,—& I am not at school!— Well! I cannot help it! The probability, after all, is that a certain person will write *no* kind of letter to me!—

I am reading Amadis of Gaul. The conceit of the old knight's garland half fresh & half withered, is a very pretty one—& may be put to use.

Sunday Oct. 23.

"Heigho the wind & the rain!" I wish they had come last Thursday instead of this morning!— No going to church. My squirrel has eaten three chesnuts out of my hand, & has tried to eat my hand besides. It did not bite much. I should grow very fond of it, if it wd. but grow fond of me, & if I cd. persuade it to become more odoriferous. We have brought a myrtle tree up into this room, for it to have leaping room upon. Arabel's proposition.

A long conversation down stairs this morning about our leaving Hope End. Bummy seems to have very very little hope . . *I have none.* Charlotte [Butler], if she comes to England at all, must come the last week of this month— And where is she to go? Dear Bummy is anxious & embarassed between the desire of receiving her, & the dislike of parting with us!—and no letter from Papa. There is one from Mrs. Boyd, who says, "Mr. B sends his kind love: he is going to send you two or three epigrams; but as he does not like to be the cause of your reading such things on Sunday, you may expect to receive them by Monday's post." So I suppose he *will* write with them,—or I shall be as burning hot as ever Amreeta cup made Kehama! *— Annie is not well—& Mrs. Boyd attributes her indisposition to distress of mind at Mr. Biscoe's secession. How distress of mind can be the consequence of the secession of a man whom she does not, did not, cannot love, I do not understand. That is one of the things which are "not dreamt of in my philosophy". Annie & Miss Boyd are to be sent here on the first fine day. Annie said something when I was at Malvern about bringing her nightcap some day, & sleeping here. I could not object; but there *will* be objectors. At any rate, if she comes with only Miss Boyd, she will not like Miss Boyd to return alone.

Bummy & I walked to the gate, because there was an interregnum in the rain. No preacher there!—

Monday Oct 24.

. . .My squirrel was found this morning, asleep under the cushion of my chair. Suppose I had sate down upon him!— He is growing more & more civilized, & has eaten out of my hand several times. I told Annie that she might have him, if she liked it. Now that he has become so tame, I hope she wont like it.

* Reference to Southey's poem *The Curse of Kehama.*

. . . Miss Boyd & Annie have arrived!— Perhaps Annie will propose staying. What shall I do?—

She has proposed it—she is going to stay. I drew Bummy into my room & told her how it was; & she was not argumentative about it. Henrietta was quite angry!!. I cannot help it. Annie has brought a letter for me from Mr. Boyd —beginning "dearest Porsonia"—

Miss Boyd & I walked round the park, & into the garden, until I, for one, was completely tired—& into every corner of the house besides. She took off her gloves, that she might feel with her hands, my staff of Marathon. I liked her all the better for that bubbling up of enthusiasm— After she had tired me, she said that my recompense should be in the manner of a Troubadour; & she let me lead her into the library where she told me a story yclepped "The mountain & the lovers," from the lais of Marie. Her voice & manner are unpleasing & ungraceful: but her language is so accurate & ready, that anyone with his eyes shut, wd. suspect a book of being before hers. She dined with us at two; & went away at five. Annie, I am to *take* to Ruby Cottage tomorrow morning. Hurrah!—

Guitar playing & book binding in the evening; the whole to conclude by Arabel & Annie sleeping together in the Turkish room.

Tuesday. Oct 25th.

Annie & Arabel & I were off at eleven. We were very nearly *off* in a less satisfactory manner; inasmuch as we discovered the insecurity of the iron rim round one of the wheels. Stopped at the Bartons, to save our lives. Miss Glasco superintended, very kindly. I like her. She called me her pet today, & "could not help treating me still as a child". I like her: but I am not sure that I could *love* her —even if I were to try!—which I dont mean to do.

Another interruption was a note from Mrs. Martin, received just as I was getting into the carriage, & saying that she wd. dine with us. So we must be back before six!—

Arrived at Malvern at nearly one—& soon went into Mr. Boyd's room. Miss Boyd was sitting with him, reading the paper,—& held up her hands in an interjectional manner on seeing me. "Who is that?" asked Mr. Boyd. "Whom do you think?" And then I spoke!— He seemed very very glad to see me, & was very very kind in his manner, & reproached me for not "making Ann come before". What did he mean by saying in his letter yesterday that he did not deserve my regard—that he was not sufficiently kind & attentive to me? There is only one way in which he *can* be unworthy of it—by its' not being reciprocal; & if I cd. get general benevolence out of my head, I wd. not believe in that species of unworthiness. With regard to his being inattentive & unkind to me, I wd. not hear his enemy say so; & why shd. I hear him?— If he wd. but write to me oftener & more at length!!— I did not comment upon his letter before him. I could not do that.

We read Gregory—a part of the funeral oration on his father: and we talked about what is called the times for the maturity & the decay of the intellectual faculties. I denied the whole hypothesis. As if man's mind were man's body, & had its three warnings!!— Sir Uvedale Price was as eloquent and imaginative at eighty—more so, in every probality [sic]—than he was at eighteen. And at sixty he first became an author.

It is very dangerous to hold such a doctrine: for to despond about the strength of one's mind, is to diminish its strength. Such a doctrine wd. do more actual harm at fifty, than the weight of ninety years cd. do, without it!—

Mr. Boyd confessed to me that he thought his translation of a part of the oration which we read today, translated at the age of 22, was well done. "He might say so to me"!!—

I do not infer from that little circumstance, but from very many, that his confidence in me is really the confidence of a friend. He evidently *thinks* loud out before me!—

I went out of the room for a few minutes while he went to dinner; but I was recalled before his dinner came to a conclusion. He wd. not mind dining before me!— And we talked until past 5. Then over the hill & far away!— I do hate saying good bye . . . to some people! . . .

Wednesday Oct. 26.

Well!—I had a very happy visit yesterday, & am happy today in thinking of it. How cd. I forget to say that Mr. Boyd told me "to . . . come again as soon as I could". Shall I not do it?—

Bummy proposes my driving to Eastnor tomorrow to see Lady Margaret. I will do it.

Thursday, Oct. 27th.

The wheel of the carriage is gone to Ledbury; therefore going to Eastnor is out of the question. A battle . . . about dining at Mrs. Martin's. She sent a note of invitation yesterday. I wish she wd. send no note of the kind to me. Bummy wont go,—but she wishes Henrietta & me to go. Now Henrietta always wishes to go everywhere,—so there is no veto from *her*. But I wish to go nowhere,—& it seems hard that my inclination should be forced whenever an opportunity is offered. I grew out of humour—& complained of it!— It was very wrong of me to be out of humour, particularly on such an unimportant occasion. I gave up at last—& wrote an assent to Mrs. Martin—, & then I made friends with dear Bummy. I cannot—I ought not . . to, bear, "displeasing her!—

After all, there need not have been such a fuss; for the rain settled the question finally. We cd. not go thro' it.

Dear Bummy is uncomfortable about Charlotte [Butler], who, if she does not come to England at the end of this month or at the beginning of november, will not be able to come at all. Dear kind Bummy has written to Papa to tell him so—but to say also that she will not leave us even to receive Charlotte, in the case of our being obliged to leave Hope End immediately. When will his answer come? — I feel, I feel, that not for *our* sakes, is dear Bummy so kind—but for the sake of one more beloved than the living can be!— That feeling makes me prize the kindness more. May God bless her for it!— Surely we ought to try to do everything most likely to please her. I was very wrong this morning. Sent a brace of pheasants to Mr. Boyd.

Friday Oct. 28th.

Drove with Henrietta to Eastnor. I think I would upon the whole have preferred going by myself; because I want to say to Lady Margaret what I shd. not like to say before a third person—for fear of *rejected addresses.* But Lady Margaret was not alone—& therefore no harm was done by my not being so.

A great deal *con* Miss Gibbons. Lady Margaret "*had* a regard for her". Ah! that *had*!— It was not meant for the affections!!— . . .

Lady Margaret said with a smiling face that she had been glad to hear of there being more probability of our not being lost to the neighbourhood—at least not so soon! The smile vanished when she heard my answer. I could say only, that I believed things remained as they were.

We got home at about four. A letter from Papa to Henrietta—& not *a word* in it!—How extraordinary! Poor Bummy does not know what to do. A parcel too from Ruby Cottage, conveyed to Ledbury by Mr. Curzon, & containing North's Plato, & a note from Mrs. Boyd—but with no message about the book. Mr. Boyd when I saw him last, wondered at my having only Foster's Selections from Plato, & at my not applying to Papa about procuring another edition of him. Now is it possible, that he means to *give* me this little book? I hope—I hope not!— It contains besides what I have read before, only the X book De legibus, & the 2d. of Alcibiades. I began to read De legibus.

Mrs. Boyd gives a bad account of Miss Bordman's father: a better one of Annie. I cant say that I am uneasy about

Annie. No letter from Alençon! Mr. Biscoe's evergreen love has withered—& like all earthly *eternal* things, is at an end. Is not that Annie's own fault?— Mrs. Boyd speaks of having heard . . . of one of the Cheltenham houses which were *desiderata* last May, *not* being taken. I suppose Mrs. Boyd is very anxious indeed, to make *me* so,—but she shall not succeed.

Saturday Oct. 29.

. . . Wrote to Mrs. Boyd,—& told her what I thought wd. have been the consequence, *had* she gone to "that desirable Cheltenham"—namely that by this time she wd. have deeply lamented it. I hope the consequence of my saying so, may not be a repetition of Annie's vote of censure! . . . How very unwell I have been today!— Told the stories of Sindbad the sailor & Baron Munchhausen, to the children this evening.

Sunday. Oct. 30.

We cannot persuade Bummy to write to Papa to urge his decision. After all, I believe that she is right. He is in possession of every circumstance relating to her embarassment, & is not likely to allow her to remain in it, if he is able to do otherwise. Poor dear dear Papa!—may God support him, & bless him!— I feel as if I loved him more than I ever did before!— . . .

Monday. Oct 31st

a mistake*

The *first of November*!—How & where will this month end to us? Shall we have moral joys as well as physical ones? Now I wd not be a prophet, & be able to answer my own questions for the world.

Tho' I said "no letter", yesterday, there was a letter from Mrs Boyd to me.

* This entry was originally dated 1 November, and the next eight entries were correspondingly misdated.

She speaks of St Lennard's, & of the advantage of our going there & her settling close to us! Well that wd make me very happy indeed!— I see how inclined she is to draw me again into a Malvern controversy—, but it wont do—I had enough of it last spring!— Henrietta went out to drive with Mrs. Martin: & all the boys ran with the hounds!—

Finished the 9th chapter De legibus. Plato's circles have made me giddy!— I cant make then out; but I must try at them again. I wish he were not quite so meta-meta-metaphysical!—

Tuesday. Nov. 1st.

Intended to be off to Malvern at seven. On being *awakened* at seven, "Ye Gods & *little fishes*" wd. have been an appropriate enough interjection—for the sky was full of clouds, & the clouds letting down rain "sans intermission"! — Ann & Arabel questioned or seemed to question the integrity of my brains, in still thinking of going to Malvern. . . I must go, if I can—so I will dress!— Dressed, breakfasted. It only sprinkled: & I set out!—sprinkled all the way to the wells, where it stopped—, & *I* soon stopped. Everybody in bed, except Mr. Boyd who had done breakfast, & to whom I went.— He seemed—oh he *was*—glad to see me! How could I ever doubt his regard for me! We read 158 lines from the 2d. oration against Julian. Very very very happy today!—

We were smoked out of Mr. Boyd's room two or three times, & were both of us, glad to get in again everytime! —Annie's fondness for me has quite returned! It stopped raining too—but began again before night . . . tho' the weather is rather steadier—of the two!!— She proposed a subscription for a scrap book,—& I was desired to take the paper home.

Dined at four. I was supplicated by Annie & Mrs. Boyd & everybody to stay. What was harder to resist, was Mr. Boyd's request on the same subject! But I did resist—to the eternal praise of my philosophy, be it spoken!—& came away after promising to sleep there another night. Dear Mr. Boyd asked me again & again: is it not wonderful that he shd. have asked *once* in vain?—But I thought it was better not to run the risk of making Bummy displeased— & so soon after my last aberration!— Went away at five— & got home in the dark. Nobody was angry. Bummy only said that I required more looking after than my squirrel, & that I ought to have a cage made for me!— What a happy day I have had today!— No letter from Papa. A note of invitation from Mrs. Peyton for Thursday, which was agreed to in my absence—*bore-ibile* dictu, again!— By the bye, I was determined that Mr. Boyd shd. know that the book which he wished for, did not remain in Mr. Bohn's shop when I *had it in my power* to buy it. I told him that *it was bought*. Therefore he must know about my having enquired—at least!— He asked no questions. That he might ask none, I put off my information till the last moment!—

Wednesday Nov 2d.

My cold is better, in spite of my wet drive yesterday. Reading Plato De Legibus—but read nothing very fine.

No letter. I hear that the fields;—all the fields, & grounds, are on the verge of being let, & that the *taker* & his wife are going to *live at the farm!!* May God bless my dear dear Papa! That is all my commentary. If resignation is *possible* to him, it shd. be *easy* to *us!*—

Went out in the cold & against my will!— Arabel & I have agreed to say nothing about the subscription plan— but to buy a scrap book for Annie!—the difficulty is only one—we have no money—which is a less difficulty than the subscription plan threatens. How cd. Annie be so inconsiderate. *I* am inconsiderate enough but I never *cd.* have *thought* of doing such a thing!—

Thursday Novr. 3d.

Going to the Peytons today!— Henrietta & I are north

& south about it. I would cry; if crying would keep me at home.—

They have arranged some plan about going in the close carriage, with carthorses. If we *are* to be upset, I hope it may be in going,—as by those means, the dinner may be averted. Six of us going!! . . .

Reading Plato. Some kind of philosophy certainly necessary.

Carthorses *wdnt* do; so we are to go in the wheelbarrow —two wheelbarrows full.

Went—nobody there except ourselves. My cough was the pleasantest part of the evening; & that was very bad & disagreeable. I am going to have a "prodigious" cold. Nem. con: . . .

They wanted me to sleep at the Bartons tonight. If I had known, what I knew afterwards,—that the people there mean to go to Malvern tomorrow, & thought of taking me with them, I wd. have dared it all!— *All* means the bed & the breakfast & the company. How ungrateful!—

Friday Novr. 4th.

My cold has increased, is increasing, & ought to be diminished. I could scarcely speak this morning.

No letter. I went to bed at nine, & read till half past ten —read Greek!— Finished Plato de legibus; that is his Xth. book. . . . I do not think that it can boast of many very fine things.

Saturday Nov 5th.

Reform meetings at Worcester & Hereford: Sam to the former, & Bro to the latter. I think too that my cough is reforming: but it is not "the whole bill" only a "bit by bit" reform.

I wrote my little poem called "the weakest thing"— with a view to Miss Bordman's album. She asked me to give her something, & the idea of this poem struck me. It is not "the weakest thing" I ever wrote,—but I dont know whether it is suited to an album.

Sky rocketting among the boys. We went to the window, & "laid our golden cushions down". Afterwards I was faint & hyster*icky*. Why, nobody can say.

Read two chapters from the 2d. Alcibiades.

Sam brings back the news of the cholera having appeared in Sunderland. May God shield our country, & dear friends —& dear selves!—

Sunday Nov 6th

Sam gave me at breakfast, a note from Mrs. Boyd, which he called for yesterday. Condolences about my cold! So Mr. Biscoe's last letter does not contain even the "affectation of feeling"! "Oh this—love! this love!" A cold thing at the warmest!— But Annie certainly must bear her part of the blame.

Bummy & Henrietta to church in the rain! Mr. Deane's farewell sermon. . . .

The Papers come—& the cholera actually in Sunderland —15 miles from Newcastle! I am glad, very glad that dear Bummy did not go there, & carry Charlotte there. Surely surely God orders all things wisely! Let not the pestilence come nigh us, oh God our shield— With such a shield we need not fear—& yet I am human & did fear in reading the paper today.

No letter from Papa. It is wonderful.

Bro & A & I wasted some yards of time today, in watching my squirrel who ate two or three chesnuts on my knee, & ran up Bro's shoulder. I intended to go to Malvern tomorrow—cold serving—but an invitation has come from Colwall, & our carriage must take B & H & Bro & Sam there, at half past four. What a bore!—Rhyme & Reason! But I am resigned to one misfortune, by escaping another. *I* am *not* to dine there!—Huzza!—

Read Hooker's Discourse on Justification. Admirable & amiable. It not only bears but *dares*, being read a hundred times. Read also 5 or 6 chapters of the Galatians,—& some of St Matthew's Gospel in Greek.

Monday 7th Novr

A fine day. How provoking, when I cant go to Malver...—Bro to Worcester.

Finished the 2d. Alcibiades, & liked it—

Tuesday Nov: 15.

I have not written a word in my diary for this week—& why? Because this day week I went to Malvern—& now I must go on in a diary-cal way.

On Tuesday, Gent drove me there, & after a long happy day, when at half past three he appeared with the carriage Mr. Boyd had begged me so much about staying, that I sent him home with a note instead of me. On Wednesday Henry brought the carriage for me,—& in spite of everybody's entreaties I had wished everybody goodbye, when he observed "Well!—it is sure to break down!—& Saunders says so too". And then I was informed of a breakage in the seat which wd. make my *sit*uation on it very precarious indeed. Therefore it was agreed that Henry shd. ride home the poney & leave the vehicle with Mr. Saunders. How happy I felt!—

I walked out with Mr. Boyd today, in front of the house!—

On Thursday, no poney was sent, & no carriage done! On Friday Sam arrived with a kind note from Bummy—but at the same time came a letter to Mrs. Boyd announcing the death of poor Miss Bordman's father, & I could not think of the joy of staying another day. Poor poor Miss Bordman!— I went in to the room where she lay on the sofa, the tears rolling down her cheeks. She threw her arms round my neck & kissed me, & I talked to her as well as I could, of the love of Him who afflicteth not willingly!—She bore it strongly in His strength!

I returned to Mr. Boyd, & walked out with him, & then we went on reading!

Read the letter from Papa which Sam had brought me,

& which I could not read at first, on account of being a good deal agitated by the bad news. Read it to Mr. Boyd. Bummy came to see me in Mrs. Cliffe's carriage. Very very kind of her!—

I am surprised at Miss Bordman's equanimity. She is amiable & has feeling, but not impassioned feeling!—

On Saturday, nothing came for me!— But Mr. Curzon most kindly, to see Miss Bordman.

On Sunday, there was a letter from Henrietta & Arabel; I was annoyed today by Mr. Boyd having Miss Boyd in his room so much longer than usual. For annoyed, read pained. I think I am never *annoyed simply!*— Miss Bordman's spirits quite astonish me!—Well! we should thank God for it!— Mr. Boyd asked me last night to propose going to the chapel today. It wd. be a kindness to Mrs. Boyd who seemed to have given up going to church or chapel, & who would sooner do it to please *me* than to please *him*!! Well! I hinted my wish as broadly as was civil! But she wd. not go—not even to please *me*!—And there was no appearance of reading the bible, or passing the sabbath according to the bible!— How much happier Mrs. Boyd & Annie wd. be, could they be enabled to draw nearer the only source of real happiness!—

On Monday I read to Mr. Boyd; & wrote a letter for him besides, to Mr. Barker. He seemed at a loss for something to say; & I suggested sending the political epigrams. "Oh yes" said Mr. Boyd—"they will fill up." "I suppose that is your motive for sending them to me!" "No! I do assure you! No, *indeed*! My motive for sending them to you, was the mere wish of amusing you a little. You have not much judgment in every thing". "I suppose in *nothing*—but in thinking that you are not cross!—" "You have not—certainly—, in *that*." We had been talking about the crossness which he persevered in attributing to himself. Mrs. Boyd attributed it to him—& *he* for his own part, was quite conscious that he had sometimes spoken crossly to *me*. Never in his life!—

He does not like Miss Bordman as much as he used to do.

He says that he does not like her *much. The reas*
she evidently does not value his society. Now if
valued it, the reason wd. have weighed the other
she might have been preferred to *me.* He does not
quick way of talking—"But if you had not *that,* y
be too fascinating— —& agreable"— Nonsense— We argued about his absence of mind. I think he has at least as much as I have!—

Mrs. Boyd came to tell me that the carriage was come! I had hoped, & Mr. Boyd's smile had *seemed* to hope, that the rain wd. have prevented its coming. I could not help shedding tears, as I said good bye!—

. . . We read a great deal of Gregory Nazianzen, during the course of my visit. I have marked the passages in my Gregory. He proposed to me to translate the two orations against Julian—& to translate the Prometheus into blank verse. I begged him to do it, instead of me; & there the entreaties dropped!—

On my arrival at home on Monday, Occyta came running down stairs to meet me *as if* he were delighted. Dearest little thing!— Afterwards he sate on my knee, & I told him stories.—

Mrs. Boyd proposed Annie's returning with me,—& I was obliged after a good deal of consideration & embarassment, to tell her *why* we were unwilling to have her with us. In my absence, off ran my squirrel. How provoking!—

Tuesday. 15 Nov.

By the newspapers, cholera seems to be retreating. No letter from Papa! I hear that he has been written to about withdrawing his cattle from the park which is taken together with the rest of the land, by Ward. I began a letter to Mr. Boyd, which I shall not be able to send, on account of the snow.

Wednesday Nov 16.

Off to Mrs. Cliffe's with Bummy & Arabel. Wd. rather

have stayed at home. At number one I shd. think, in the thermometer. Eliza showed us her preparations for lithography—& they gave us luncheon, & wanted us to stay all night—& gave me a History of a disputation of theirs about me in which Eliza had stated that I wd. not marry an angel from Heaven. Certainly if ever I were to make up my mind to marry, I wd. fancy my selection to be an angel, at the very least. But I never never will marry!—

I sent off a parcel to Mrs. Boyd this morning, containing books—a note from me to her—a note from Arabel to Annie—& a letter from me to Mr. Boyd. In it I said that I missed both him & the squirrel very much indeed,—tho' I was modest enough to believe in the possibility of its being best for both of them, that I shd. I wonder if he will answer my letter. I told him that he need not do so if he felt disinclined; & he does not care enough for me, to obviate the probability of his feeling disinclined. And yet I shall be certainly pained if he does not write. My letter was written rather in a playful than professing manner. I will write no more professing letters . . till the next time.—

Henrietta went away on Monday with Mrs. Martin & the Miss Biddulphs, to pay a visit to Mrs. Jones. She is now at Ledbury where she will sleep tonight. Bro went with her; . . .

A reading evening down stairs!—Bummy over the Quarterly, & I over Camoens, & Moliére!—

Thursday Novr. 17.

Reading Camoens last night, suggested what I have been writing this morning—"Catarina to Camoens". I do not dislike it. A letter from Papa, speaking of his return!—

Henrietta returned, & delighted with her visit. But she always is delighted with anything like a visit—except where the Boyds are either active or passive. She brought—what delighted me in no degree—an invitation from the Biddulphs to Bummy & me for next Tuesday, to dine & sleep there. Botherissimè—I dare say Bummy will go.

Friday Nov. 18.

No!—Bummy wont—she followed me up stai
breakfast to say so. I was determined not to oppose a wish of hers—& luckily no wish of her's ran counter to mine. Henrietta quite angry with me, because Bummy wdnt go. It was all my fault—*my* fault!!!! and I *ought to be ashamed of myself!*— A note of invitation from Mrs Martin addressed to us all four, about dining & sleeping at Colwall. Now if we all four had been judged necessary to go, I wd. have gone par necessitè. But what wd. have been the use of my going with Bummy when I hated it superlatively & Henrietta liked it superlatively. Henrietta out of humour with me. To Mr. Boyd's I can go at any time—to Mrs. Martin's never!— Comparing for a moment Mr. Boyd & Mrs. Martin!! I never cultivate the acquaintance of any one who can be of use to me!— Translate *that* by— —any one who has a large establishment, & gives gay parties.

I wish Henrietta would estimate people more by their minds than she actually does—, & that she were not so fond of visiting for visiting's sake. At any rate, as I do not attempt to oppress her with my influence on that or any other subject, I have a right to be myself unoppressed by her's. I told Bummy that if *she* wished me to go to Colwall, I wd. go. Bummy evidently did not care about it.

Reading Iphigenia in Aulis. I will go thro' it now.

Telling stories to Occyta & Sette, in the evening. Cinderella & Blue Beard!—

Saturday. Nov. 19.

Getting on with Iphigenia . . I am very much interested in it—particularly in the scene between Iphigenia & her father. How much simple affectionate nature there is in her character! The opposition between her's, & Clytemnestra's stately dignity, is skilfully conceived.

Miss Glasco & Miss Peyton called—& Miss G talked to me about [Thomas] Moore. His friend Mr. Corry could not find out what article in the Edinburgh was his; & Moore figures himself in consequence, on being masqueraded. I wonder if I shall pull off the mask, or leave it on.

Bummy & Henrietta are not come & not coming home today. Henrietta called for a few minutes to say so. She must be quite happy between the Miss Biddulphs & Mrs. Martin— How *un*happy could *I* be with either? not that I mean to under-estimate Mrs. Martin, who deserves better of me & everybody. A letter from *Mrs. Boyd.* She reports that Mr. Boyd has a "pretty message" to send to me, but that she cant tell him of her being in the act of writing Therefore he had no means of sending it. I certainly think that he *might* have written himself. But never mind!—

Bro "cut Miss Wall dead" at Worcester today. Sorry for it!—

Sunday. Nov. 20.

. . . The Cliffes came to dinner. Not so Bummy & Henrietta, who are not coming home again today. As I understood that they, Biddulphs & all, were to be at the gate this evening, I hesitated about going, *for fear* of an invitation. It was wrong to hesitate. I went, & then a little plot of Bummy's was blown up. She had excused herself & me from dining at the Biddulphs on Tuesday, because I *had a swelled face!*— Behold me at the gate with cheeks as thin as usual!—

I have had a pain in my face for the last two or three days—but the swelling is among things invisible.

Mr. Curzon hinted at my taking him either to or fro' Malvern in our carriage,—tomorrow,—& Arabel & I promised the fro', & settled to set off early tomorrow morning. How pleased we were. And now comes an embarrassment!—Bummy has desired Bro to take the carriage to Colwall tomorrow morng, for them to come away in— What in the world shall I do!—

Monday Novr. 21st.

Arabel & I got over the "triste embarrass" by writing to

Bummy, & begging her to "*walk*" home. Agreed
we set off at about eight. Found Annie half dressed
Boyd quite undressed. Nearly ten before I was a
into Mr. Boyd's room. He spoke to me very kindly—& we read the exordium & peroration of Gregory's 2d. oration on the paschal.

Mr. Curzon talked for about one half hour to Mr. Boyd while I was in the room. He & we did not go away until five. Dark all the way. Talked about Mr. Boyd whom Mr. Curzon "cant understand," & about our Hope End business which *I* cant understand. Let down Mr. C at our gate. Rather a happy day. For the *very* happy ones . . Eheu fugaces!—

Tuesday. Nov 22d.

So I hear Bummy was very angry at Arabel's going with me yesterday. What she said before the boys about Annie, was enough to make *me* so, & did. It is *not* kind.

Saturday. Nov. 26.

Wrote to Mrs. Boyd to beg her to write & let me know whether I should be acceptable to her party on Monday—to write to Eastnor. Lady Margaret asked me to stay with her two or three days; but I wont stay a day later than Monday morng. And late enough,—by the presiding Goddess of Ennui. Ann & I set off in the wheelbarrow. Dinner & tea & supper very solemn. The Dowager Lady Somers, & Miss Baker constituting the *omnes.*

Sunday. Nov 27.

Heard Mr. Higgins twice at church, & once in the Eastnor dining room. Dont like him—or rather, cant tolerate him! . . . Lord Somers cd. not help admiring the manner in which my hair was dressed—!! at dinner today—just like Vandyke's pictures—*or* Sir Peter Lelys. Mem. to repeat that compliment wherever my long locks make themselves unpopular. . . .

How stupid we are!—And how wise I am! to have brought my desk, & left my key!—

Monday. Nov. 28.

Read when I was in bed last night, Marmontel's Sheperdess of the Alps. Very pretty; but the heroine never never shd. have married again. Well! that cant be helped now. Talked to Miss Baker, about . . love!—She told me some passages in her life, which *might* have been left dark passages, without injury to her or me—or at least, lit by only a *sky light*!—after all she is a sensible woman.—

Nota bene—her prophecy, that Lord Somers will marry again. If he does, he should marry some great great great great do do do do granddaughter of Stentor, or the courtship will never get on with his deafness. Nota bene—my prophecy, that he will vote *for* reform, tho' he thinks *against* it.[1] Glad to get away from Eastnor. A letter from Papa to me. An expression in it about "the happy results" of our long separation, seemed to me *at first*, to glance at a particular subject. Other people consider it a general expression & so it may be. What can the report be to which Mrs. Boyd alludes? I am not very uneasy. . . .

Evening past away in a more lively manner than my two last evenings did. Miss Glasco is going to exhibit her puppet show, & has engaged Bro & Henrietta as performers in it. Wont do with Papa.

Tuesday Nov. 29.

Today Miss Boyd & Miss Bordman leave Malvern. Had a letter from Mrs. Boyd which I ought to have had last Sunday; & then I might have gone to say good bye on Monday. But it is as well . . I cant bear saying good bye. — And I shall see more of Mr. Boyd, who always must & will stand first in the canvass, by going on Wednesday. Mrs. Boyd says that she has invited Miss H M [Henrietta Mushet].!!— I annoyed. I wont go to Ruby Cottage as long as *she* is there—shant be wanted & *wont* be wanted. Sent

two little poems & a letter to the editor of the N M
Bulwer, I think his name is. If he does not pay me
contributions, what in the world am I to do with
debts?—

Papa is coming this week. Dear dear Papa!— . . .

Wednesday Nov 30.

Off to Malvern, by favour of Mr. Lane's driving, at eight in the morning. Slipped gently into the house, & presently into the kitchen, to find out whether Mr. Boyd had had his breakfast. Jane just going to take it up to him. So I ventured to precede it.

He seemed pleased to see me, & I had a happy day with him. He "*assured* me" that Miss H M's coming was by no means *his* wish—but Mrs. Boyd's & Annie's. The annoyance is wearing off—& perhaps I may go to Ruby Cottage while she is there—after all. We read passages from Gregory's apologetick,—comparing his marks with mine, in different copies,—& came to the conclusion, that our tastes certainly do agree!! And so they do.

I began to write my Caterina in Annie's album. Got home at a little after five—& too lazy to write further particulars.

Saturday Dec 3d.

A letter from Mr. Boyd—a very short one—but kind & in his own manner. Pleased to receive it. If he cared *very* much about pleasing me, he wd. write *very* much oftener. Mrs. Cliffe & Eliza called, & spirited away Henrietta & Arabel to sleep at Mathon!— Suppose Papa were to come home in the meantime!

Sunday. Decr. 4th.

A few lines from Papa in a fish. We are not to write,—& he is to come home "early in the week." Arabel went back to Mathon, with the intention of riding with Eliza & Mrs. Cliffe to Malvern next day. If little Billy cd. be ridden &

driven at once, I wd. be driven to Malvern to-morrow. As it was, I was in an agitation about going, & at last by Bummy's inspiration, called up my impudence & wrote a note to Mrs. C, begging her to drive me there.

Monday. Dec 5th.

Sent my note, had an affirmative answer, & walked down to the gate with Bummy to meet the carriage. The worst of it was, that Mrs. C & Eliza made another proposition to meet mine, namely that they wd. sleep here—because otherwise they might have been benighted in going round & round on my account. Agreed to, of course: but, thinks I to myself, if Papa were to arrive on Tuesday Morning & find them here!—

Well! but I had a pleasant three hour visit at my dear friend's house. I was in his room before he was; & when he heard my voice, he smiled as if in pleased surprise. He wished that I could have come in our own carriage, & have stayed later!— We talked a good deal—yet not a word about——what I dont want to hear. I wonder whether some people are penetrating.

Tuesday Dec 6th.

We spirited away Mrs. C & Eliza & Mr. Allen C who made one of our party by an *un*happy accident,—for fear Papa shd. come. But he did not—& not a letter!—

Wednesday Dec 7th.

No letter—no Papa.

Thursday Dec 8th.

A letter to me: and papa is to be with us tomorrow. My dear dear Papa! His coming is a thing feared & wished for! For what feelings must, & what circumstances may, attend it.

Phillips's sacred literature which I had sent for to Eastnor, by Mr. Boyd's request, arrived. Now, thinks I to myself if I cd. get to Malvern after dinner today, how pleasant it wd. be. By these means I could deliver the book immediately & have an interview with my dear friend before Papa's arrival. Je propose. Ran down stairs to Bummy, & had the game in my own hands. She wd. go with me. Very kind of her. She & Arabel & I set off accordingly at past two;—& what with the rain, & what with the fog, which imitated rain most successfully in the distance, I cd. scarcely get Bummy on. Contrived it however . . I was set down at Ruby Cottage, & they, after offering to take Annie with them, drove on to Gt Malvern. Annie was at Miss Steers's!—

Mr. Boyd certainly pleased to see me. I read what he wanted to hear out of Phillips—& something from the apologetick besides. A happy visit of nearly an hour & a half. He gave me Wesleys treatise on Predestination. On our way home over the hills Bro & Sam frightened us with their gallopade in the dark. My hands & feet went to sleep meo more.

Friday Dec 9th.

Our beloved Papa arrived . . . between 11 & 12. Tho' the thoughts of seeing him made me sick & trembling hours before, yet when I saw his dear face, my fear of distressing him outgrew other fears. I did not faint; or cry . . much. Henrietta & Arabel cried too! Our dear dear Papa.

He is apparently well, & in good spirits. He talked to us all day, in his animated agreable manner; & I could almost believe him to be happy.

Only once his eyes wandered to the window. There were those horrible cows of Capt. Johnson's in the park. His countenance changed; & his eyes were turned away.

Saturday. Decr. 10th.

Wrote to Mr. Boyd a long letter, to give him an account of the tongues[1] & politics. I told him not to answer it, unless he felt inclined to do so—*will* he feel inclined?

Bummy has been speaking to Papa. She will not tell me exactly what was said—but two things are clear—that we shall go—& that we shall *not* go immediately.

Sunday Dec 11th.

Read Wesley's treatise. It is clear & powerful; but not by any means satisfactory to me everywhere. Papa & we walked down to the gate, to hear— —nobody. The Bristol students were minus: on account of the rain perhaps.

Monday Dec 12.

Rain by buckets. Finished the Iphigenia in Tauris—not worth re-reading!—and began the Hippolytus.

Tuesday Decr. 13th.

Reading Greek—Hippolytus. A letter from Fanny to Bummy, about engaging Miss Steers. [as governess]

Wednesday, Decr. 14th.

Bummy wrote a note of propositions to Miss Steers: and Arabel sent Annie's newly painted basket by the same conveyance.

I wish for Fanny's sake, that Miss Steers may consent to her proposal; & for Annie's sake, that it may be rejected.

A note from Miss Steers, who says neither yea nor nay, —but desires to see Bummy tomorrow. Hurrah!—I hope B may go.

Reading the Hippolytus.

Friday Decr. 16th

Bummy wdnt go at first—settled that she wdnt: and I ran up stairs in an *in*-disposition. Presently up into my room came Bummy. She wd. go. I had been walking up & down, in my dungeon building mood, half resolving not to go with her on Monday for fear of— —?—My resolution is not to be tried. We went. The rain & mist did all they cd. to drive us back, when we had travelled half way; but they

View taken from the other side of the Alpine Bridge, 25 June 1831, from a pencil sketch by Henrietta Barrett

From the schoolroom window, 1831, from a pencil sketch by Henrietta Barrett

missed their object. I argued so logically & entreated so persuasively that we went en avant!— Bummy was supererogatorily civil to Mrs. Trant, & wd. call on her. Half an hour's boring. And then on to Miss Steers where Bummy wished me to go in & hear the preliminaries. Went in. Miss S disinclined for Ireland. On *Annie's* account I am glad: on no other. She would be an excellent governess. She unites a very active & cultivated mind, to agreable ladylike manners, & many accomplishments. Arabel drove me to Ruby Cottage, & returned to Bummy after a few minutes warming. Mr. Boyd pleased to see me. A *very* happy two hours visit! I read to myself some extracts from his translations & letters against Exley, in the Methodist magazine; and begged him to let me take the book home. Granted— tho' I *am* so careless! He does not like the idea of our going to the isle of Wight; *because he* does not like the idea of crossing the sea. "Unless you wish to go there yourself, do try & prevent such a plan." "I assure you I do not wish to go there. I wd. rather go anywhere where *you* wd. go!—" He certainly means to be with us wherever we go!—

Got home thro' wind & rain & darkness. Papa not angry. . . .

Saturday. Dec 17th.

Arabel told me last night that Miss H M was expected at R C at three. We did not leave it until four. What an escape!

A letter or rather note waiting at home for me, from Mrs. Boyd,—conveying a message from Mr. Boyd. His love, & he hoped that I wd. soon be able to go & see him. He *said* much the same thing to me yesterday. Could I not spend a whole day with him as usual, & soon? I suppose he must really wish it.

Monday. Dec. 19th.

Annie is to go to Mathon to day. Mrs. Cliffe's carriage is the medium; & I have been dreaming that Mrs. Cliffe's goodnature might *mediate* for me, & suggest calling for me at our gate at least. All a dream. The waking was not agreable. But I read myself into a good humour. Hippolytus is not one of Euripides's best plays, tho' it is very superior to the Ipheginia in Tauris.

Tuesday. Dec 20th.

The Cliffes & Annie came. Annie says that Miss Mushet is a phrenologist, as well as being wonderful in other things. I am indisposed towards Miss Mushet. Not that I am "jealous" as Annie suggested, of her knowledge of Greek. If her knowledge were double what it is, I shd. not be jealous of that; & if it were none at all, I should feel equally *indisposèe*— I shall not like going to R C while she is there—I wonder how long she will stay.

Wednesday. Dec 21st.

What did I do today. Greek of course. But I was idle, as I have been lately, about my diary; & kept no account. We drove to Eastnor.

Thursday. Dec 22d.

A note from Eliza enforcing a proposition which she made to Bro yesterday, about their (Annie & all) sleeping here, on the night of the puppet show. I wrote an assent. A note enclosed from Mrs. Boyd. In it she says that Miss Mushet is plainer than she was, but "just as amiable as ever". If she was & is amiable, how did Mr. Boyd's coolness towards her, arise? and why should it not be thawed away now? I shall *not* like going to R C— But I said that before.

Finished the Hippolytus,—& began the Supplices of Æschylus. I read a part of it before; but I have left off now my *partial* habits of reading.

My dear Papa in good spirits.

Friday Dec 23d.

No memorabilia—Attributable in part to my idleness. I

wrote to Mrs. Boyd, & did not say a word about going to R C.; but sent my note there by Henry. She wd. not keep Henry—She will write tomorrow. My reason for sending him, was that Mr. Boyd might have the Methodist Magazine which he wished to have in a week! A week today since I saw him!—

Saturday Dec 24th.

It was determined last night, by Papa & the rest of the senators, that the boys shd. have a holiday today, Christmas eve. A relief to me. Miss Glasco is to exhibit her puppet show next Friday, & she wants my prologue. I hate that kind of composition—am not in a humour for it—but I suppose she must have what she wants.

A note from Mrs. Boyd. I am "very naughty but very kind" for sending the turkey. Mr. Boyd she "dares say," "will write to me next time". Never! when he can help it. He is "quite reconciled to H M notwithstanding all his fears".

I knew it wd. be so. If he does write to me, his writing will be no proof of his having thought of me,—but only of his having received a turkey! Low spirited this evening. Wrote to Mrs. Boyd three times—before I cd. write what pleased me. I said at last "I have thought that Mr. B wd. like Miss H M as much as ever; so you see your information was anticipated". Not a word about his writing to me, or my going there. If I were to go there, & to perceive that he wd. have preferred my having stayed away,—Oh I cannot get over the reluctance.

Sunday Dec. 25th.

My letter went—

We went to church; & as B H & I took the sacrament there, we went to chapel also before we returned home. A nothing-particular preacher at the latter place. No letter! Christmas day—& I am out of spirits.

Monday. Dec. 26th.

A continuation of the Christmas holidays. A pain in my face & head kept me awake all last night,—& I am not at all well this morng. A note from Miss Glasco. She want so know what her rascally poet is doing about the prologue. Promised to let her have it tomorrow. And yet how *can* I write when I am so unwell?

The Cliffes & Mrs. Best & Annie called. They wont sleep here on Sunday,—*because* Mrs. C does not esteem my note as being sufficiently pressing; and thinks that I was quite in earnest in recommending her to sleep at the Horse & Jockey [public house in Colwall] instead of here!!!!— Maddox came. . . .

Wednesday. Dec 28th.

Finished the prologue. Read it to Bummy & Papa—& both of *them* pleased. Sent it off by Bro to Miss G—& both of *them* pleased. *I* am pleased besides: and am a great deal better.

A note from Mrs. Boyd, to tell me of Annie & Eliza & Mr. A Cliffe having been at R C, & of all she has heard about my horribly rude note to Mrs. Cliffe!! Wrote a few lines to Mrs. B, offering a bed to Jane for Friday night—& one line of astonishment at Mrs. C's obtuseness. Sent it by Maddox whom we took to the Ledbury Turnpike. . . . *Us* means H A & me. Dear Stormy's birthday. [his 17th]

Thursday Dec 29.

Gent took Bummy's *final* to Miss Steers today; & a note full of addenda to my note yesterday, to Mrs. Boyd. He has come back. As she was not at home, there is of course, no answer. And no letter for me by the post!! It is clear that Mr. Boyd did not, & does not, intend to write to me, notwithstanding what Mrs. Boyd said. Is it kind?— Perhaps it is *better*. I am not sure whether I ought or ought not to go to R C without waiting much longer for an intimation from him on the subject. After all, I can only be *pained*; & to that I am accustomed. So perhaps I had better go. If I do not, my staying away may be made an excuse for his quarrelling with me,—& to *that* I am *not* accustomed. I cd. *not* bear *that* kind of pain. I wonder what book Miss H M is reading with him. There is no use in wondering—

H & A have ridden to Mathon, to combat Mrs. Cliffes *estravaganzas*. Do I wish them all to sleep here tomorrow —really *wish* it?— I wish dear Annie to do as *she* wishes; & I wish Mrs. Boyd not to be displeased with me or any of us. But I am not, I believe, in a humour for a crowd of people. May I escape the Barton crowd tomorrow! Ora pro nobis—

I knew from the beginning, how it wd. be about Miss H M. Well! The last time I was at R C, I was very happy. The last time!—

H & A come back. Mrs. C intractable!— A brought a note for me from Mrs Boyd. Mr. Boyd sends me a *message*! of thanks for the turkey, and expresses himself "sorry at my not having come over, yet, *as*" (What force there is in some words!) "he wishes the two rival Queens to meet". And so I am to go to R C to be shown *off* & *with* Miss H M!!— The coolness of Mr. Boyd's expressions, & the indifference he shows about writing to me, went to my heart; & when I was in the room by myself, I could not help shedding actual tears. He did not deserve one of them—and yet they *were shed*!—

Wrote a note to Mrs. B, in which I told her the real reason of my not having been to R C before. "I remembered that Mr. Boyd might have reading to do with Miss Mushet at the time of my arrival; & that such an interruption wd. be neither pleasant for him nor me. Certainly not for *me*"— . . .

My spirits were so depressed this evening, that it was an effort to me to talk even as little as I usually do. Write myself down an ass!—

Friday Dec 30.

Sent my note to Mrs. Boyd. What will be thought of it?—

Not, I hope that I was out of humour when I wrote it. I am more, much more angry with myself than with Mr. Boyd. *He* has professed too much—& *I* have expected too much. We are both in fault: but my fault is the worst, because it has been persevered in, longest—& against clear evidences. I said in my note that I wd. try to go to Malvern tomorrow, for an hour; but that if I did not go, I was not to be expected next week, on account of the boys who have had their christmas holidays & shd. have no others immediately. I almost hope that I may not go.

Eheu!—Papa has sent me word that I must not stay at home tonight!—

Curling hair & dressing to meet a crowd of people whom I know nothing of, & care for less than I know. Off at half past six: And saw Ionson Bluebeard & my prologue enacted at eight. The puppets are admirable; very very ingenious —& put to shame many whom they counterfeit. Bro spoke my prologue, & spoke it very well indeed. Applauded; & Miss Glasco presented me afterwards with a wreath of bay! If Mr. Biddulph had been there, he was to have placed it on my head, with an oration to boot. An escape!—

Fifty people we were, in all; or perhaps rather more. The outside of Mrs. Watsons head, larger a very great deal, than the inside. Does she *plume* herself upon that? Annie kind in her manner to me. I think I feel kindness more & more susceptibly. Eliza sate next me some time; & I told her some of my thoughts about my want of etiquette, & Mrs. C's want of judgment. *She* told *me* that Mr. Boyd had wondered before her, at my not having been to visit him as usual. I have determined to go tomorrow.

Got home at half past one: & Occyta pretended not to be sleepy.

Saturday. Decr. 31st.

I have been to R C. The fog made Bummy protest at first against my going; & then the rain made me resign myself to its effects. But the rain cleared away,—& the clearing away of the fog seemed to be the *future in rus*: so Arabel & I set off to the Wyche. She drove of course,—& we left the carriage, & the poney *rugged* close to the turnpike. I nervous & fidgetty about R C. Down the rocky path—Arabel's short way—not mine!! Went into the house! Nobody in the dining room, or drawing room! Into Mr. Boyd's room! A made me go! Mr. B & Miss M reading together. She is five feet ten & plain; with an agreable voice,—but rather an independance & unshrinkingness of manners. Very unaffected tho', & sensible. She did not seem to think of leaving the room. Mr. B said that he was sorry to hear of my having been unwell—& that he had not expected me today on account of the rain!— Mrs. Boyd came in,—& A & I went out with her. Had luncheon & talked as lingeringly as I cd. I did not like the idea of going back to Miss M. Presently she came down, & then I went up. Mrs. Boyd had proposed my going up, before.

He began to talk to me about my letter. There were two things in it. About the prologue; it cd. not require his revision,—but reading it, wd. *not* have been troublesome to him. And then, about my going to see him. "There was plenty of time for him to read with Miss Mushet— Did I forget that she was staying in the house &c?" I answered, I recollected when *I* was staying there that he did not like Miss Cliffe or anybody to interrupt him. "Did I really conceive the cases to be parallel? Miss Cliffe & I! If I thought that he cd. compare me with any other person, he cd. only say that he was *sorry for* it." And yet his manner was not the manner I liked. And when he asked me to go soon & early as usual—to go next week—or if I cd. not do that, early in the following week, his manner was not the manner I liked.

[The remainder of this day's entry is cross-written.]

Does he not evidently wish me to go then, for *my* sake, —not *his*? My spirits were gone!— A & I were at home at 20 minutes to five. Miss M walked with us to the Wyche, much to my annoyance.

The last day of the old year!— What will next year see? A great deal of sorrow perhaps,—& perhaps my grave.— Oh Thou in whose hands are the forces of life & death,—& whose will is wisdom & love—Thy will be done.

[This entry concludes the first portion of the Diary. The second half is written in a separate book (see Preface).]

Jany 1st 1832 Hope End.

Sunday. I suppose I must go on here with my diary,—as I cant get another book.

This is the first day of a new year; and I am not in the humour for being wished a happy one. Into thy hands oh God of all consolation, into thy merciful hands which chastise not willingly I commit the remains of my earthly happiness; and Thou mayest will that from these few barley loaves & small fishes, twelve basketfuls may be gathered.

My heart sinks within me—but not when I think of Thee!— Lord gracious & merciful, teach me to think of thee more often, & with more love—

No church. Examination day on the heath;* & almost everybody, except Papa & Bummy & me, went there. *We* down to the gate. A good sermon from Mr. Curzon's *vice*. In the evening Papa read to us Mr. MacGhee's letter to Dr. Whately Archbishop of Dublin, on the subject of Irish education. An admirable letter. *I* abused Dr. W. as I always have & will do. He wrote against evangelical religion, & clinched his arguments by a translation of Plutarch's treatise on superstition. An intimation that Plutarch knew more of christianity than he did?—

Monday Jany 2.

. . . Packed up Mr. Boyd's Gregory (Gregory's poems) & Mess[rs]. Pilkington & Beverley on the unknown tongues, which I put within Mr. Boyd's parcel, for Miss H M. I hope she (yet not exactly *she*) may think me attentive in doing

* i.e., of Wesleyan Methodist candidates.

so. I cant bear anyone to think me . . what I am!— Last night I read some of my diary to Arabel in bed! My diary is not meant to be read by any person except myself: but *she* deserves to be let behind the scenes. Mine are very ill painted.

⟨. . 4 . .⟩

Friday. Jany 6

I fancied lastnight that I heard Papa whisper to Occyta a proposal about taking or sending him & everybody to Worcester. All fancy!—

Where was Fancy bred
In the heart or in the head?—

Not in the *head* I think, on this occasion. Mdme de Sevigné says that the thoughts early in a morning, are couleur de rose. Mine were so much the contrary, before I got up this morning, that they made me cry—

Wrote to Mrs. Boyd. It is better to do so. Told her how jet black my spirits were. Desired *to be remembered* to Miss Mushet. My best regards are kept for better occasions. Finished the Choephori, & began the Eumenides. Read more than 500 lines of Greek, & was more tired by them than by the 800 the other day, because I met with more difficulties. Enervated & inclined to go to sleep.

This is the twelfth day. How many happy twelfth days I have spent!— If it is fine tomorrow, I must make a proposition about R C. But it wont be fine. *Fogissimo* all today!— . . .

Saturday. Jany. 7th.

I have been to R C. Bummy & Henrietta almost disinclined me from thinking of it; but at last I put on all my brass, & went into the dining room to ask Papa for some silver. No objection from *him*! Henry drove, & Sette & I were driven. Got to R C at about half past twelve, or a little before: & talked to Mrs. Boyd *as long as I could* in the dining room— . . . Miss H M came into the room, & after a minute or two, I went up into Mr. Boyd's. He showed me his three new books, his Dion Chrysostom, & Gregory, & Heliodorus: and I read one or two short passages out of each. He told me that he had written to ask me to spend a day or two with him! *Would* I do such a thing? No indeed— There was a passage in Gregory's funeral oration on his father, of which he cd. not make out the meaning. I was made to try at it. It did not appear to me quite incomprehensible,—but then, I am not infallible. At a quarter past three I went away. Not a happy day: I wd. not mind sharing or yielding my laurels, if I had any, with or to anybody: but in the regard of those whom I regard, I must be aut Cæsar aut nihi, [Either Cæsar or nothing].

⟨. . ½ . .⟩

Dearest Occyta playing with me all the evening. I do love him. . . .

Sunday Jany. 8th

. . . ⟨. . ½ . .⟩

After dinner, Arabel told me about something which Bummy had heard from Mrs. Best & seemed pleased at repeating, respecting the Boyds going away next May. Altho' we shall probably be gone before then, the very idea of their going possibly before we do, made me feel quite unhappy.

Papa & I talked about predestination this evening. The first time I have ventured on the subject these two years— I mean with *him*.

Dreamt about Adolphe & Endymion, & a lady who was by turns Emily & Amalthæa, & of her murdering Endymion whose soul was infused into Adolphe. Papa reproached her. But she held up her beautiful face, & said, "I am yet very fair". "Clay Walls" said Papa!—

A funny dream!—

Monday, Jany. 9th

Papa has made today another holiday. Out of spirits this

morning—& feeling disinclined to read Æschylus or do anything in the way of Greek. Prayed for help from God: and He in answer to prayer, has often made me happy when all other resources seemed shut against me. Surely I shd. trust Him.

Wrote my poem on the cholera. I think I like it, & shall send it to the Times tomorrow. I wonder if, tomorrow, I shall hear from or about Mr. Boyd, or about *us*. I wish I were more comfortable.

Tuesday Jany. 10th.

Sent away my poem to the Times, this morning.

Out of spirits all the morning, & unwell & thinking about the post, the Malvern post & the London post. *Will* Papa hear anything

⟨. . 4 . .⟩

[*Thursday, January 12.*] wonder if I shall have a pleasant —a happy visit. Better not to hope it— . . .

I sent a note today, to ask little Curzon to come here tomorrow, & dine, & sleep. The boys are in a phrenzy with me for it; & Sette came up to ask me if the report were *really true*. Poor little fellows! I am sorry I have asked him for tomorrow, as it is Sam's birthday [his twentieth] & their holiday: but what can a body do more than make an apology?—

Arabel wishes to go with me to Malvern. I wish she may be able; but there is sure to be a "factious opposition."

She is to go!—Hurrah!—

Friday. Jany. 13.

Arabel & I off at half past eight or before. A clear cold morning. It is clear that it was cold!— We drove along the upper road by Steers's Hotel. Splendid view; but I doubt whether the poney approved of it as much as we did.

Nobody down stairs at R C: & Mrs. Boyd sent down to desire me not to go in to Mr. Boyd's room until she had seen me—so there I sate, & had to write out my poem about Camoens in Annie's album, & have breakfast the second, before Mr. Boyd sent for me. Went up stairs. He would not have *taken the liberty*!! of sending for me if he had not soon expected his barber!!

⟨. . 10 . .⟩

[*Thursday, January 19.*] see my mouth—(Quære were there gass lights round my mouth?—) & she [Miss Mushet] told Mr. Boyd, it was painful to look at it. It indicated intense feeling, & deep suffering!— A great deal of feeling is expressed also in Arabel's countenance. Mr. Boyd's head is "very intellectual".

He asked me to "come again soon." So I will, if I can!— Got home before five. Bro at the Onslows, Arabel & Sam at the Peytons,—B H & I at dinner at Hope End. B thought me quite mad for going this morning.

No letter from London.

Read some of the Eumenides, but cd. not finish it. That enchanting little beast Occyta wd. not let me go up stairs in time.

Friday. Jany 20

Finished the Eumenides. . . . So Arabel is not coming home. A bore. I don't know what in the world to do without her,—& the most provoking part of the business is, that I dare say she wd. at least as soon be here as there. Daisy & Sette to the Bartons, for pigeon shooting. The most cowardly mean-spirited, *no*-spirited amusement possible. If it had been a tiger hunt!—

Henry dined there, & rode back by himself at twelve o clock at night. Minny in a flustration, which was a frustration. Nonsense.

No letter from Papa!—

I have now read thro', regularly thro', every play of Æschylus. He is a wonderful writer; & no one ever thought like him, or expressed his thoughts like him, from the beginning of the creation until this 1832—

By the bye, Papa's not writing is almost as wonderful, as Æschylus.

Read two Olympic odes,—& one, not a short one.

Saturday. Jany 21.

. . . Bro & Arabel came home. *Very* glad of it. B & H walked to the Bartons for A. I walked by myself, & reveried.

No letter from Papa!—

It is doubtful whether or not the cholera is in London: If it is, & if Papa remains there, I shall be miserable. My misery depends on two *ifs*, & one might keep me from it. Sent my prologue & a few lines to Annie; & my books & a few lines to Eliza Cliffe— . . .

Sunday. Jany. 22d.

Will there be a letter today?—

There was one for Henrietta, but nothing in it satisfactory,—except that Papa cannot leave London before Tuesday, which seems to indicate that on Tuesday, he may be able to leave it. He is delighted with my verses on the cholera, & considers them "beautiful, most beautiful." He has . . . given them to the Editor of the Pulpit in which they will soon appear.

Now as Papa wont be at home until Wednesday at any rate, I certainly might go to Malvern tomorrow, sleep there, & return on Tuesday. Henrietta & Arabel see no "just cause or impediment"—but Bummy can see thro' a post where poor Mr. Boyd is concerned.

Monday. Jany. 23d.

. . . Finished Baxter's Saints Rest. Quite exquisite!—After finishing it, nothing ought to distress or disappoint me. I will read it again before I die,—that is, if I do not die before the expiration of "the years of man",—which in all probability, I shall do. I am "not (I think) built for posterity"—as Mr. Martin says of Colwall.

Now I write down my palinodia. Dear Bummy has been

here to speak of my going to Malvern, & has *proposed* my staying until Wednesday!! Hurrah!—I am going. She & A will convoy me to the wyche.

They did,—& walked down with me & my bundle. Mrs. Boyd at dinner. My companions stayed only a few minutes; & then I dined, & then I went in to Mr. Boyd. I really believe he was pleased. A smile lasted on his face for several minutes!—& he told me not to go into the drawing room for the snuffers which we wanted, for fear they shd. keep me there. It wd. be better to ring the bell.

We went on with Gregory's oration on Christmas day; & after tea went on with the going on. Half past eleven before we went to bed!—

Tuesday. Jany 24th.

In Mr. Boyd's room before breakfast, & reading. Read until twelve; & then he proposed walking out. It was a surprise to me when he asked me to walk *with* him,—and a pleasure! Up & down the garden for half an hour!—

⟨. . . .⟩

He spaeks of her, [Miss H. Mushet] not in a very cordial manner. He speaks of her being uncandid in argument: and "she wd. rather never see a book again than never see a dog. There's mind for you!"—and she irritated him & made his head heavy on Sunday evening!— Perhaps he spoke as he did, only because he was temporarily irritated:

⟨. . .⟩

She has a sensible unaffected manner as I said before, & she appears to be particularly goodnatured & obliging; but she is *not* an interesting person to me.

Wednesday. Jany. 25th.

I lay awake last night listening to the rain, & hoping that it wd. rain on. But it did not!—a fine morning.

. . . Finished the oration. It is very fine & Mr. Boyd has determined on translating it. I begged him to do so. Miss H M will be his secretary. I protested against his sending it to the Methodists' Magazine, few of whose readers could estimate a line of it.

He wished *me to* translate it while he was translating it, & at the end make what "is odious." I wd. not do such a thing for all the seas & deserts thrown in!— Besides, (I know him,) the very act of seeming to compete with him, tho' suggested by himself, wd. diminish his regard for me. And really there is none to spare.

Mr. Boyd asked me to visit him again next week— That I cant do!—except by a morning visit.

I see plainly that Mrs. Boyd & Annie have determined on leaving Malvern next May!—

Annie asked me at breakfast where I had advised Mr. Boyd to settle?— What a question!— I cd. not help the tears coming into my eyes.

All well at home. Sam with H[enry] T[rant] somewhere!— I wish they had not come for me until tomorrow.

Thursday. Jany. 26th.

Wrote a very kind letter to Mr. Boyd, expressive of my regard for him, & the happiness I had in being with him.

Began to read over again Gregory's oration,—even to translate it: not with the intention of showing my translation to Mr. Boyd or any body else, not with the wish of competing with him; but that by translating the whole I might have a clearer idea of parts, & might save him the trouble of thinking on some points which appeared to both of us, obscure. I shall not even tell him of my having translated it. Mr. Curzon came at 3 & stayed till 10— Kind of him.

Friday. Jany. 27th.

Going on with my translation which I have just finished. I have written as hard & fast as I cd. write,—& therefore had no time for sentencerounding & polishing. In two days more I cd. accomplish that: & then my version wd. not be a very bad one—*tho' I says it as should'nt*. Mr. Boyd meant to be a fortnight about it. I shd. be four days. Write me down a dray horse. . . .

Saturday Jany. 28th.

Finished my translation quite, & sent off my letter to Mr. Boyd. . . . A letter from Malvern came which deranged me altogether. The greater part of it, was from Mrs. Boyd & kind enough—but there were a few lines from Mr. Boyd. He asks me to spend two days with him next week—

And he does not mean to translate the oration. It is too much labour!— He *has* translated the passage at the close of the oration on the son, which I admire so much, & which he wishes me to "come & see".

⟨. . 4 . .⟩

[*Thursday, February 2.*] . . . [Mr. Boyd] asked me to visit him again next Thursday or Friday or Saturday, to finish my criticisms. But I am not to mention at home his reason for wishing to see me then: for fear he might be under rated by a misapprehension of it. That is a feeling which I do not understand. Sir Uvedale Price had no personal regard for me, & yet he used to speak openly of sending me his mss 26 miles, to be criticised previous to their publication!—

Mr. B had thought of writing to ask me to pass two more days with him in the capacity of his secretary; as Miss H M found the fatigue too much for her. I told Mr. Boyd immediately that in the case of my coming, being a convenience to him, I was ready to come. He answered in a quick way—"Oh it was only in case of Miss H M being unwell!—She is quite well now"— I said nothing.

He speaks of Miss H M as if he did not like her. He says that she takes no interest in what he is writing, is of an uncandid mind, & very different from what she was formerly.

Miss Heard has told him that I am the most engaging person she ever knew, & that she quite adores me!— I

Hope End, the view from the deer park and the view from the lower pond, from two water-colours in Philip Ballard's sketch-book

[illegible]. Sweet Occyta playing with me all the evening. I do love him.

Began a note to Mr. Boyd tonight. [illegible]

Sunday. Jany. 8th.

Finished & sent my note to Mr. Boyd. I thanked him for his invitation, & spoke of his letter being "a black swan" & spoke of Mr. Wallace & Mr. Darcy, & the epigram on Lady M C. [illegible]

After dinner, Arabel told me about something which Bummy had heard from Mrs. Best, & seemed pleased at repeating, respecting the Boyds going away next May. Altho' we shall probably be gone before then, the very idea of their going possibly before we do, made me feel quite unhappy. [illegible]

Papa & I talked about predestination this evening. The first time I have ventured on the subject these two years, I mean with him.

Dreamt about Adolphe & Endymion, & a lady who was by turns Emily & Amalthea, & of her murdering Endymion whose soul was infused into Adolphe. Papa reproached her. But she held up her beautiful face, & said, "I am yet very [fa]ir". "Clay walls" said Papa! — a funny dream.

Facsimile of the Entry of 8 January 1832

heard this a little bitterly. People like me better at first than they do afterwards. I wish they wd. not like me at all. I dont mean to imply that Miss H.'s language was not exaggerated.

Took courage & told Mr. B of my translation of the Prometheus. He seemed pleased, & surprised at my having done so much, & so unparaphrastically. I asked him inconsiderately, if he wd. read it, if he wd. read some part of it!— His answer did not please me: and yet he did not say "I will not"—

⟨. . 4 . .⟩

Friday Feb 3d.

Bro returned [from a visit to the Commelines.] before breakfast: & our dearest Papa before twelve. I thought his face was grave when he kissed me—but fatigue & a bad cold may have been the reasons of his gravity—

⟨. . ½ . .⟩

persuaded him to go to bed; & he slept for three hours. In the evening he was quite cheerful. While he was asleep, I went on with my Prometheus.

Saturday Feb 4th

Mrs. Martin called & saw Papa & all of us. Papa talked in a fast feverish manner, as if he were determined to be considered "himself". He told Bummy that he wd. be happy to see James [Graham-Clarke]!— But James wont come, I am certain!—

B A I (Henrietta riding punch) drove as far as Barnets. A lovely day!— Busy with my Prometheus. I have finished the 370th. line. Reading what I have written to Bro who approves very much indeed. If I publish it, I will also publish a preliminary essay which might be made very critical & interesting.

Sunday. Feb 5th.

Everybody gone to church save me. . . .

Mr. Curzon preached beautifully.

Not in a humour for writing in a diary.

Monday Feb 6th

Hard at work at the Prometheus. Finished the translation of 130 lines. Who cd. write in a diary after that?— Tired; & walked up & down, to make my self more physically so than mentally. Papa at the Ledbury Committee,—& presented every member of it with a bible.

Tuesday Feb 7th.

Translated a hundred lines of Æschylus. Up & at work both today & yesterday before breakfast.

A letter from Malvern. A few lines from Mr. Boyd, begging me to go to him on Thursday. I did not think he wd. write, & am rather pleased. Rather!—

Wednesday Feb 8th.

Up before breakfast, at work— Finished another hundred, in spite of Mrs. Trant & Mr. Curzon. The latter dined here, & I must go down now & drink tea with him. Going to Malvern tomorrow!—

Thursday. Feb. 9th.

Bummy & Arabel went in the carriage to Malvern with me: & H & Stormy were outriders. We went after breakfast, at eleven o'clock. Mrs. Trant carried my party to Gt Malvern in a fly, & I pursued my course to R C in my wheelbarrow.

Mrs. B Annie & Miss H M in the dining room. I soon went up to Mr. Boyd. . . .

He immediately talked of going out to walk with Miss H M— But I ought not to blame him. He assured me again & again that if he had not had a heaviness in his head he wd. not have thought of it—that he *preferred* staying with me. I urged him to go. After all he did not!— He found that I cd. make my criticisms as I was reading,—&

therefore he wd. stay to hear them: & they lasted until half past three. . . . We had Gregory out, & it was pronounced to be certainly right in defiance of the Latin version which was in my critical teeth.

Before I went away, I asked if Mrs. B had mentioned going away in May. Not lately. "But why shd. you be anxious for us to stay when you think there is no chance of staying yourself altogether at Hope End?" Because the period of our staying is uncertain.

Left Mr. Boyd at four. He asked me to go again next week to examine some observations of Billius on the oration which he has translated— By the way it is really a beautiful translation.

Friday Feb 10th.

Writing—but not in my diary.

Saturday Feb 11th.

Intended to have finished the Prometheus today. Not possible.

Sunday Feb 12

At church; & found the Cliffes there— They had luncheon here; & upon Papa's invitation agreed to dine here on Wednesday. They sleep here besides. I hope Annie wont hear of it, & be on the Trojan horse i.e. a very high one.

Monday Feb 13

Writing hard.

Tuesday Feb 14

Oh ye Athenians how hard do I work to obtain your praise. The Prometheus not finished after all.

Wednesday Feb 15

I have finished my translation. 1075 lines of Æschylus translated in a fortnight. And I think I am satisfied—

tolerably satisfied. But the original is too magnificent for translation.

Mrs. Cliffe & Eliza came. Nota bene Mr. Davis's coming too. It was odd & cool. Nothing in this world can be at the same time, odd & *cold.* I dont admire Mr. Davis as much as either Mrs. Cliffe or Eliza does. He does not suit *me.* He is talkative & forward & pedantic & self complacent. He does not suit *me.* Slept here,—& kept us up previously in an awful suspence, until nearly two— Too bad!— Intensely stupid evening. Eliza was at Malvern on Tuesday. Miss H M is to stay until April & take Annie with her.

Thursday Feb 16

After Mrs. C & E had gone away, I wrote to Miss Bordman. I asked her to dissuade Mrs. B from leaving Malvern. Will she try, or not?— I wrote a long & kind letter. Then I began to copy out my Prometheus. I must endeavour to finish by tomorrow, as I must positively go to R C next day.

[*Saturday, February 18.*] . . . After tea, he (Papa) suggested my writing to Mr. Barker & enquiring whether Valpy wd. publish my work in the Classical Library. Wont do it without consulting Mr. Boyd. Wrote to him tonight, a short letter—

Monday Feb 19th [sic, for 20]

A letter from Mr. Boyd! How it surprised me. He does not like the Valpy plan.[1] *If* the translation is good enough to be creditable to me, it shd. be published separately; besides he has made a confusion between the Family & Classical library!— His letter is cool enough. I answered it by a note of explanation on Valpy's work; by rating very humbly my translation—& by telling him how little inclined I feel to publishing, & how I have wished that I had never done so. The real truth!— If I never had, I never shd. have been exposed to the pain which has been & is oppressing me.

Tuesday Feb 20th. [sic, for 21]
Bro & Sam to Mrs. Trants.
I could not write today.

Wednesday. Feb 21st. [sic, for 22]
Another letter from Mr. Boyd. . . . He enclosed a letter from [Mrs] Smith. . . . Mr. Boyd's letter was written by Miss H M,—& cool enough still. I wonder he shd. have thought it worth while to write it at all. He "cannot see" why I should regret having ever published. I wish *I* could not. He does not "disapprove of Valpy." He is translating the exordium of Gregs. 2 Paschal oration. I read it with him last november. He desires me to send him the beginning of my translation, & 30 or 40 lines of one of the choral odes. What is his motive? Not, I am afraid, a wish of seeing my work. Perhaps he perceives that my manner of writing is not what it was. I sent the extracts, & wrote in my "new style",—begging him not to read what I sent.
Would I not a thousand & a thousand times *rather* have *his* work attended to than mine?—
Mr. & Mrs Curzon came. A discussion about Mr. B in the evening. Mr. C evidently does not think well of his religious state. I was writing some of my preface this morng.

Thursday Feb 22d. [sic, for 23]
The Curzons did not go away until nearly three. Mrs. C is certainly improved. Mr. Curzon is what he always was—a follower of Christ in spirit & conduct—kind & feeling.

⟨. . 4 . .⟩

Saturday Feb 24. [sic, for 25]
What did I do today?— Not write in my diary. Bro Stormy Henry & Sette to Worcester. 5 tugs & Sette's tooth,—& he did not cry!

Sunday. Feb 25th. [sic, for 26]
Confined in the house all day with one of my violent

colds. Did not even go down to chapel. . . . No letter. Yes! —there was one from Eliza Cliffe, speaking of Annie's album, & the present which I mean to give Mr. Boyd on his birthday. I have determined upon Scholefield's Æschylus, —& shall write to Eliza to say so.

Monday Feb 26th. [sic, for 27]

Wrote to Eliza,—but cd. not send my letter. Wrote also two or three lines to Mrs. Boyd, to enclose Mr. Hockin's catalogue for Mr. Boyd,—& to say that we hoped Annie might receive her scrapbook this week.

In the evening I wrote out *A thought on thoughts* by Bummy's desire, for Papa to read. He read & liked it extremely, & asked me to give the copy right to him.

Tuesday. Feb 27th [sic, for 28]

Finished the preface to my Prometheus,—& delivered it to Papa in the evening. I read it or rather spelt it aloud,—& in my opinion, [he] did not *very much* . . . like it,—tho' I am assured otherwise by other observers.

⟨. . 2½ . .⟩

Saturday. March 3d.

Preliminaries of a sore throat,—but tamarinds cured me. Miss Baker came at half past two, & spent an hour with me. She objects to such books as Corinne & Mathilde, because they lead the mind to expect more in life than can be met in life. Well!—allow that they do!— The expectation brings more happiness than any reality,—as realities go,—cd. do. Romance of spirit is a far rarer fault than worldliness of spirit. I wish I knew a few people who had been "spoilt" by reading Corinne. I know nobody. . . .

Miss Baker has a melancholy opinion of the West Indies. It wd. be agreable to know that Papa's estates are not burnt up[1]—& still more agreable to know where we are going! Fear as well as Hope . . deferred, maketh the heart sick.

Sunday. March 4th.

Dearest Henrietta's birthday [her 23rd]. May God bless & preserve her & make her happy!— Did I write down in my diary last Tuesday that Bummy wrote to Miss Battie to ask Mr. Battie to enquire of Hatchard [the publisher of Piccadilly] whether he wd. read my ms of Prometheus, & consent to publish it together with about 30 original poems, in the case of his aproving it? I think—indeed I see—that I did not. An answer may arrive today. Nay or yea? Nay!— in my opinion; tho' B says differently. . . .

Monday March 5

Dear H's birthday kept; & I took advantage of the holiday by going to Malvern with Arabel . . . Annie was lying on the sofa in the drawing room [of Ruby Cottage] with a pain in her face,—& Mrs. Boyd with symptoms of a cough. As soon as I cd. get into Mr. Boyd's room, I went there. He made me read his preface & some additional translations.

He had had my extracts read to him. After some verbal criticisms, he observed with regard to the blank verses that some of the lines were beautiful, some poor: a circumstance for which he did not so much blame me, as Æschylus. It could not be otherwise in any literal translation of the Prometheus. With regard to the lyrical portion of the extracts, they seemed to him "rather poor", considering they were my writing—but then "the short time you were in writing them"!— . . . "Has anything [been] fixed about your going away?" No indeed!—nothing!—

He lent me Blomfield's Æschylus, at my request.

Tuesday. March 6th.

My birthday [her 26th]!— My thoughts will go to the past—the past—to the ever ever beloved!— My happy days went away with her!— If I were to count up every happy hour since, how few they wd. be!— But there is no use in all this! The tears which I am shedding at this moment are as vain,— — —as if they were smiles!— In another year, where shall I be,—& what shall I have suffered?— A great deal I dare say—and my heart appears to be giving way even now.

Wednesday. March 7th.

A letter from London to Bummy from the Batties. A note from Mr. Battie informs her that Hatchard is ready to publish my book; but not a word about the copyright. He seems to have misunderstood her,—or else Mr. H will have nothing to do with it. B & I have determined on writing to explain. I have written a very explanatory note to Mr. H, & she has enclosed it to Mr. B. I know perfectly well, that H will turn his back on me!— Well! I dont much mind.

Friday March 9th.

The Cliffes came,—& Eliza brought the Album for Annie. It is a beautiful green one. I hope she may think the first epithet. Scholefield for Mr. Boyd's birthday is to come soon.

Getting on with notes.

Saturday March 10th.

Notes again. Out walking. I dont feel quite well,—& no wonder—for my spirits are quite worn threadbare.

Sunday March 11th.

I was not at church,—& B H & A only half way there. A letter from Mr. Boyd brief enough, but to ask me to ask Papa to allow me to go to R C on Monday & stay until Thursday; for the sake of writing his digamma essay for him. Miss H M has an inflammation in one of her eyes!— Now I wish very very much to go; but am very very much afraid of asking.

I asked Papa in the evening. He will not allow it. He says that I am turning into a shadow, & looking worse & worse, —& that he will not be a party to giving me any fatigue.

I assured him that writing for Mr. Boyd cd. not fatigue me so much as what I do every day at home. He told me that if I liked to hold a pistol to my head—ainsi soit il—but that he wd. not have anything to do with it.

I dont exactly know why. Only it would have been a pleasure to me to have gone there, . . *knowing* that I was not in the way.

Monday. March 12.

Wrote a letter to Mr. Boyd— . . I never will be too kind again to anybody, in the way of writing or speaking. Told him what Papa said!— Told him that I was far far more disappointed than he cd. be; for that Miss H M's eyes wd. probably soon be well, & that when he wd. have "a more agreable & satisfactory, tho' not a more willing & anxious secretary, than I could be". After I had sent away the letter, I regretted that expression. I think he will take some notice of it. Out of spirits all day.

Tuesday: March 13th.

Not daring to say a word about going to Malvern, & yet wishing to go. At last I sent Henry down to Papa at eleven, to ask if Papa had any objection to my going. None!! A went with me. Arrived there at half past one, & met Annie at the door. Into the drawing room,—& after a proper pause, into Mr. Boyd's room. He had written to me!—and my last letters to him were lying on the table. So was the commencement of his essay on the digamma, which Miss H M, whose eyes were convalescent, had been writing for him that day. Miss Hurd was to be sent for the next day, *to proceed.* I read the essay—so far,—and liked it very much. He asked me why I had not sent my extracts from Prometheus, to him? I told him that I wd. really prefer his giving an undivided attention to his own work. He told me that. . . in fact he thought it better for me not to send them for a few days: until he had finished his essay. Ainsi soit il—. Not a word was said about my observation in my yesterday's letter: therefore it was certainly an accurate one. And yet Mr. Boyd's manner to me, was kind today: like his own old manner. He gave me a lecture about the poney being thin. I will take care that it shall have more corn.

Before I went away, I asked him, if anything was settled about their going. Nothing about the *place*. He told me that *he thought they wd.* go.

⟨.. 1$\frac{1}{3}$ ..⟩

Sunday March 18.

Did not go to church: but B H & A did—besides all the boys except Bro—poor Bro—who is rather rheumatic. I read Bunyan & the Greek testament, instead. Rain came, & Mrs. Cliffe did not. Rain off,—and we off to the school. Mr. Curzon preached beautifully. Afterwards he asked me when I was going to Malvern. I answered, "some time this week": and he desired me to herald him on Thursday.

⟨.. $\frac{1}{3}$ ..⟩ . . .

Wednesday March 21st.

Mr. Boyd gave me Nonnus's paraphrase of St John's Gospel—*lent* it to me—yesterday; that I might hunt for hiatus[e]s for him. I was reading some of it today, which is the day of the general fast.[1] Whenever he says exactly what is in Scripture, he does not say it as well as Scripture says it: and whenever he introduces more than is scriptural, he does it ill. *Jesus wept* is "*done into*" Jesus shed "unaccustomed tears from eyes unused to weep". . . . The whole of the passage, that exquisite narration, respecting the woman taken in adultery, is omitted.

I was quite exhausted with fasting today. My head was dizzy, & my limbs languid, & my mind incapable of applying itself to any subject. This was not I believe altogether as it shd. be. I wont fast again without being more sure of Scriptural premises than I can feel just now. At church.

Thursday March 22d

Not reading Nonnus,—but correcting my *press* instead. My translation does not please me altogether. No letter from Hatchard, again!—

Friday March 23d.

My dear friend's birthday (HSB's 51st). May God bless him. I said so when I prayed.

Sent my Scholefield, with this line from the Chœphoræ written on the first leaf—

ειθ᾽ ειχε φωνην ἐυφρον᾽ αγγελου δικην.

(if only like a messenger it had a kindly voice)

That *did*. Wrote a note besides,—

⟨. . 2 . .⟩ . . .

Tuesday March 27th.

Went to Malvern with B & A. So much pro & conning about *who* should go, that we were not off until past eleven. Provoking. Left B at Mrs. Trant's,—& A drove me on. Into the dining room at R C, where I waited half an hour at the very least, before Mr. Boyd let me go into his room. Scholefield was lying before him, covered with white paper. He said a great deal about it—, after he had said a little about my coming so late. He *is* certainly pleased with my present to him, binding & all. I looked at different readings in it for him,—& read to him nearly two whole odes from the Supplices. . . . He said today that it was one of the unpleasant circumstances attending his blindness, that he was forced to have recourse to the services of those whom he did not like! "Now when Miss Mushet is kind enough to offer to read anything for me, I cannot help taking advantage of her doing so: and I dont like Miss Mushet." I observed, "I thought you did like her very much." "I did for the first four or five days—but not since,—not since I have discovered what kind of mind she has".

Nothing more, he says, is settled,—since I was last at

R C. What will be settled at *last*?— I hear from Arabel, that Mrs. Boyd *may* go to Frome on Monday. I am sure that is, to make enquiries about houses,—tho' Arabel says it is not.

Annie & Miss H M talk of coming here on Thursday,—on Annie's way to Mathon where she will sleep. She *ought* to be asked to sleep here—and yet I am not anxious about it certainly.

〈. . 2 . .〉

[*Thursday March 29*] . . . Henrietta says that she [Miss H. Mushet] does not like Mr. Boyd very much!!! She told Henrietta how very extraordinary he is,—& how nervous —& how he encourages his nervousness by giving up to it!!— She spoke highly of Mrs. Boyd for whom she professed to entertain the "greatest regard:" tho' she blamed her for being too *submissive* to Mr. Boyd!!!!!! It is settled now. I do *not* like Miss H Mushet. Before I knew all this, she asked me to show her my room,—& I showed it. Here she told me that Mr. Boyd rejected all associations, & considered everything abstractedly. Not true.

Mrs. B brought a note for me from Mr. Boyd. Cool enough—but he wishes me to write my name in Scholefield,—& to send him some more extracts from my translation. He likes the last better. Prometheus's speech is reported, "extremely good." This morning, I wrote two or three lines, about hiatuses,—& sent them to him by Mrs. Boyd. After they were gone, I walked out with Bummy. Felt tired,—& was very unwell afterwards. How weak & thin I am growing.

Friday March 30th. 1832.

Better today. Wrote out some lyrical extracts for Mr. Boyd,—& sent them to him.

Finished the Andromache. I have now read every play of Æschylus Sophocles & Euripides. I must go quite thro' with Pindar next.

A letter from Mr. Battye to Bummy. Hatchard wont buy the copyright—tho he *will* publish—that is, if I please—which I dont.

Saturday. March 31st.

Dearest (Uncle) Sam's birthday [his 45th]. God bless him! — Henrietta & Arabel went out to ride with Eliza Cliffe, thro' Cradley woods, & I dont know where. H has made an engagement with E to ride there again on the 28th of next July. Will that engagement be kept?— . . . While H & A were away, I was very very unwell. Fainting & hysterics—but they went off at last. Maddox came.

Sunday April 1st.

The 1st of April!— How time does pass away,—& joy with it!—But the beginning of next month will be more painful to me—perhaps it will—than the beginning of this. *They* went to church,—but I did not. I do not feel at all well, tho' better than I felt yesterday. Reading St John's Gospel,—& Nonnus's paraphrase upon it. I do *not* like Nonnus.

Went down in the carriage to hear Mr. Curzon. He preached a good sermon; & Miss Glasco had the advantage of it. He is to come here on Wednesday.

Tuesday. April 3d.

To Malvern with Henrietta & Maddox. Met Mr. Boyd walking with Miss H M, a little past the turnpike. Not very far from the place where I met him first. How much has been felt & unfelt since then! He did not ask me to get out of the carriage & walk with him, or I would have done so; but he turned back immediately, & was at R C nearly as soon as we were. We called for one moment at Mrs. Trant's; & she was out. H drove Maddox on nearly to the Great M turnpike, & I was left at R C. Mrs. Boyd talked to me, but about nothing interesting, either to me or her. . . . Annie will at last marry some one whom she cannot love, & who cannot make her happy. In to Mr. Boyd's room. He asked me if we had not met today where we met first. His Scholefield was lying before him,—& he made me read some passages for him in the Agamemnon, & the first chorus of the Supplices, nearly from the beginning to the end. He did not, from some reason, ask me to write my name in it. He has either forgotten it, or changed his mind.

I told him of my having now read every play of Euripides; & he seemed very much surprised, & called me "a funny girl", & observed, that very few men had done as much.

A return to the subject of Annie's invention respecting Mr. Boyd's "*wish* of leaving Malvern." It appears that he has mentioned it to her, & that she denies having even named his name!— The result of which denial, is, that he doubts the veracity of the other party: suggesting that B & A may have made up the story from an amiable motive as far as I am concerned—to diminish my regret in the case of Mr. Boyd's going,—by diminishing my regard for him now!— He made me promise to propose a *confrontation* to Arabel. I promised: but I am annoyed at his having made a fuss about such nonsense; & told him so. When I was going away, he asked me to forgive him; & observed that he had something to forgive *me*, on account of my having believed the possibility of his being guilty of any conduct so "base & deceitful." I told him that I never accused him of a *long* process of dessimulation,—but supposed on the contrary that he had lately changed his mind on the point in question.

He said, it wd. be only kind in Papa if he wd. consent to my spending a few days with him. There is no use in proposing such a thing.

. . . In consequence of Mrs. Trant having gone to Eastnor, Henrietta was by herself & walked all over the hills in the same company. Miss H M told Mr. Boyd that she was very pretty; & that in the case of Miss H M having been a man, she wd. have fallen in love with her. She *is* certainly —very pretty. Got home in good time. I thought as I drove away from the door where Miss H M & Annie were standing . . "Shall I ever see Annie standing at that door again"? Why did the thought come to me?— I half promised to go to Malvern again next Saturday,—but Miss Mushet will be there. I dont like to meet strangers. And besides, Mrs. Trant is to be here—which I dont like either.

Wednesday April 4.

I read yesterday in Mr. Joseph Clarke's Sacred Literature, that Nonnus is an author whom few can read, & fewer admire. So that my opinion is nothing outrageous. I do *not* feel well; & look like a ghost. Mrs. Martin called, & thought so too!—

Henrietta & Arabel are both of opinion that B is trying this morning to speak to Papa. They are right. She has spoken. She has been here to tell me that she is going to Kinnersley tomorrow to stay away until Tuesday!!! only Tuesday!! & wishes me to go with her. Now *that* I hate—& I have made over the pleasure, such as it may be, to Henrietta!— B tells me of having proposed to Papa, her going on Friday,—& of his objecting on account of his being unwilling for her to pass thro' Ledbury on the day of the church missionary meeting without attending it. Something is certainly the matter,—or B wd. not go to Kinnersley for so very short a time,—or so suddenly as not even to let them know of her intention. Either *we* are going,—or Papa is going to London. Oh I hope—I do hope *he* is not going away from us again.

After dinner, B & I lay down on the bed in her room; & talked. I said something about the probability of Papa's going away, & her answer was—"I shd. not be surprised— I think, Ba, you are anxious to leave this place altogether." I acknowledged I was—considering everything. Mr. Curzon came today with his little boy, & is to sleep here. While he was coming, B H A & I were sitting on the grassy green hill above the rock, basking in the lovely sun.

He was agreable this evening.

Thursday, April 5.

Dear B & H off at 20 minutes to twelve. They mean to spend one day with Miss Price, & to return here on Tuesday certainly. Mr. Curzon left us between two & three. Not at all well, is the description of *me* today. In the evening I lost a game at chess to Papa.

Friday, April 6.

How extraordinary it is, that Papa shd. take no part in the Church missionary society today. But I am glad of it; for last year, what a scene there was in consequence of his doing otherwise. I believe he has sent his subscription. His not going, & Bummy's going, make me feel confident that something is coming. Bummy told me with tears—"nothing shall induce me to remain away from you longer than Tuesday". Dear dear Bummy.

They have been dragging the pond—Sam & Stormy in the water. I have been reading Pindar's 9th Olympiad, & must go back to it. Pindar's *subjects* are of little interest to my mind. Arabel has written to Annie, observing upon her want of memory in the late affair. That is *certainly* the mildest construction; & is *perhaps*, the true one.

Saturday April 7th.

What did I do today? Not write in my diary.

Monday April 9.

Finished not only the whole of Synesius's poems, but four odes of Gregory, contained in the same little volume. And yet I really read nothing superficially. There is a great deal in Synesius which is very fine. He stands on a much higher step than Gregory does, as a poet; tho' occasional diffuseness is the fault of each. I like the 7th. hymn extremely. A slip of paper in the first leaf, tells me that in Mr. Boyd's opinion the 1st. 5th. & 6th. are perhaps the finest, next to the 9th. I wd. lay a very strong emphasis on *perhaps*. The 9th is, I agree with him, decidedly the finest.

A & I walked out on the terrace opposite the drawing room windows. Oh I do wish, fervently wish, that something were settled. I cd. be happy—at least, happier, if it were.

My eyes ached tonight with reading today.

⟨.. 2 ..⟩

Wednesday April 11.

Dearest Occyta's birthday [his 8th] . . .

⟨.. 3 ..⟩

Monday April 16.

Rain! and no going to Malvern. I am very sorry. But we might have gone on the clearing-up, if Mrs. Cliffe had not been afraid of trusting her horse on the heavy roads. So Eliza explained in a note, which prorogued our journey until Wednesday. I am not half inclined to go on Wednesday. Began to write to Mr. Boyd about Synesius—but I wont send my letter until tomorrow. Mrs. Hanford & Miss Martin called here.

I wish I could get at some Greek books which I cant get at!—the Alexandrian writers for instance, & Plato whole—& Athenæus—& Aristophanes.

Tuesday April 17th.

I always think on Tuesday—"there may be some letter, some decisive letter to Papa". But none comes—nothing comes!—

. . . I scarcely slept all last night. What shall I do tonight? Read the two last Olympic odes today,—except a few lines of the last but one. The very last, to the Graces, is most harmonious & beautiful. I recollect Mr. Boyd's repeating it to me at Great Malvern in 1830, when I was paying him a long & happy visit. *νυν δ' ολωλε*!!— [now perished] Not the ode—which is deathless.

Bro fishing at Mathon,—and now at 8 oclock, he has not returned. We dine almost every day, at seven or near seven. What can Papa be doing, in the small portion of ground in which he can do anything, so long & late? Oh I do wish—what is vain.

Wednesday. April 18.

Mrs. Cliffe & Eliza took Arabel & me to Malvern; & it began to rain before we arrived at our gate, & rained all the way. Annie met us at the door of Ruby Cottage. . . . Went into the dining room. I felt so depressed, that I should have been merciful, in letting myself cry. But I would not permit *that*. Soon into Mr. Boyd's room. He received me kindly, & asked if I had heard any more harm of him. I said, no. And then he told me of Mrs. Boyd having repeated to him an "extraordinary" expression which she had made use of, in her letter to Arabel—that he had only one objection to quitting Malvern; namely his dislike of travelling!! [H S B] said to Mrs. Boyd—"That was a very extraordinary observation for you to make. Miss Barrett will suppose that I have no objection to leaving her!" Mrs. Boyd's answer was, "Ba knows she is going away herself". I observed she seems to have doubts of it sometimes. "Then," replied Mrs. Boyd, "she is very foolish." Besides, he said, Mrs. Boyd's expression was incorrect in every way. "I have an objection to leaving Malvern on account of my health, which has been better here than any where else." . . . [Miss Mushet] came in & sate working a provokingly long time, while Mr. Boyd & I disputed about Calvinism, & the claims of metaphysical & physical science. He told me afterwards that I was very cunning; that I did not argue so well when he & I were together, as when other persons were present—that he never heard me so powerful in argument as today. I could not forbear smiling. That was *not* a compliment. He asked me if I observed any similarity between Synesius & Pindar. Surely not.

He let me stay in the room while he dined; but by *my* request. We did not go away until five. They all came to the door, & I proposed going to the Wyche tomorrow or next day, & running down to see them.

. . . Pouring all the way home. Mrs. Cliffe afraid to face Papa, put Arabel & me out of her carriage,—below the first gate,—& home we had to wade in mud & thin shoes. They were in the middle of dinner!!! B came out, to ask me to go to bed! We went up stairs to dress & have dinner in my room,—& were not scolded after all. . . .

Thursday April 19th.

Wrote to Mr. Boyd about the parallel passage in Synesius & Anacreon,—& nearly went thro' the whole of the first & Second pythian odes. The first is very very fine,—& there are splendid things too in the second. B spoke rather not very harshly today; & I could not help crying for nearly an hour afterwards. My spirits are quite beaten down on all sides. How shall I go thro' next month?— . . .

I went out by myself, thro' the garden to the hill above it, where I walked up & down, & thought of one who liked to walk there.

Nothing has happened.

Friday April 20.

Good Friday.

How time is going. Made this list of days & cried over it afterwards. B H & A to church. No—A did not go—, as I found out afterwards. Read 8 Greek chapters from St Luke's gospel. A letter from Annie . . . [who] asks if Arabel thinks that Mr. Barrett wd. like them to live near us— In Mrs. B's opinion "he wd. not."

Arabel wrote to Annie immediatedly, & she means to send it before breakfast tomorrow, that Annie may have it before she goes. Arabel wd. not say much. She did maintain the point of Papa's inclination, and the probability of his being very sorry, if they were to leave Malvern while our plans were unsettled. She said besides, I dont know what Ba will do if you dont settle near us.

The Peytons have invited me to go in the Car to Malvern on Monday, when they promise to set me down at R C.

Saturday April 21.

I am *not* well . . .

Read the 2d. Pythian—& walked out a little. In the evening Papa read us Mr. Curzon's prospectus of the Echo, the new periodical he wishes to edit & print in Ledbury. It wont answer. His letter to Papa, engages Papa's "dear daughter" as a poetical contributer. . . .

Sunday, April 22.

All at church except me. I am not at all well, tho' better since the morning. B made me promise to sit down stairs while they were absent, on account of my room being voted close. The closeness of my room, never never injured me. Mrs. C. & Eliza came,—& we walked down to the gate. I fancied that the lady who sate near Arabel was Miss Mushet. No!—after service Mr. Curzon gave a note to her from Annie. So they are gone.

Monday April 23.

Walked down to the gate with B H & A to meet the Peytons' carriage. The sky looked lowering & B portended a rainy day. Never mind!—we got off. The rain came on as portended; & they left me in a cataract at R C. Mrs. Boyd sate with me for a moment in the drawing room & then I was dismissed to Mr. Boyd, with a pen & ink. He wanted me to make a memorandum of the additional number of Greek lines he has learnt, & also to write my name in Scholefield—to put "To" before Hugh Stuart Boyd, & "from his friend E B Barrett" afterwards. I wrote "from his attached friend". He has learnt 8000 Greek lines, except

80,—& this 80 he wishes for my aid to acquire. I shall like it!— I heard him repeat a good part of Gregory's ode to his soul. Indeed, he learnt some more of it, while I was with him.

Afterwards we doubted how to select the 80 lines. . . . He has nearly decided on some of the geographical descriptions in the Prometheus,—& we are to begin upon them next time. With regard to my Prometheus, he told me how much he shd. like to hear it read—that Mrs. Boyd said she had no time—but that even if she had time, he knew perfectly well, she wd. not like to do it. She wd. not read a page of his own translation. She has no taste for anything of that kind—

If she has no taste, she might have kindness. But I answered truly that I never expected him to read the whole, & was much obliged by the degree of trouble he had already given himself. Mrs. Boyd is certainly an extraordinary woman, to be Mrs. Boyd.

. . . A great deal said about my not having invited Annie this winter—& Mrs. (Cliffe) opposed. So Mrs. (Cliffe) has had the ostentation & want of delicacy & want of truth to have maintained not only at R C but to Miss Steers that *in consequence* of *certain reports*, she had invited Annie to Mathon & taken her to Worcester. It is not true!!!— . . . but there is no use in writing. The world is the world. I cannot make it Heaven. . . .

Mr. Boyd pressed me earnestly to go to see him for two or three days— "There is no harm in asking!— Do ask your Papa." I was obliged to say "I will think of it": tho' thinking is vain!

Went away in the pouring rain. Left

〈. . 18 . .〉

HEREFORDSHIRE,
ON THE BORDERS OF WORCESTERSHIRE.

IMPORTANT FREEHOLD & COPYHOLD ESTATE,
A desirable Property for Residence and Investment,

CAPITAL MANSION, WITH OFFICES,

Pleasure Grounds, extensive Garden and Grapery, Farm Buildings, upon a superior principle,

AND UPWARDS OF

FOUR HUNDRED AND SEVENTY-TWO ACRES

OF EXCELLENT MEADOW, PASTURE, ARABLE, & WOOD LAND, & HOP GARDEN.

Particulars and Conditions of Sale,
OF THE VERY IMPORTANT

FREEHOLD ESTATE,
With a small Part Copyhold,

CALLED

HOPE END,
SITUATE

In the Parishes of Ledbury, Colwall, and Coddington, in the County of Hereford,

On the Borders of Worcestershire,

About Two Miles from Ledbury, commanding the Romantic Scenery of the Malvern and adjacent Hills, with Views from various parts of the Property, highly interesting, and of great extent.

THE HOPE END MANSION
IS ADAPTED FOR THE ACCOMMODATION OF

A NOBLEMAN, OR FAMILY OF THE FIRST DISTINCTION,

Is Pleasantly seated in its own Grounds, having an extensive Lawn in front,

WITH A FINE SHEET OF WATER, FED BY SPRINGS, CASCADE, &c.

And well Stocked with Fish,

AND IS APPROACHED BY AN EXTENSIVE CARRIAGE DRIVE, LEADING THROUGH THE GROUNDS, WHICH ARE LAID OUT IN A PARK-LIKE STYLE, AND WITH ACKNOWLEDGED TASTE.

The Residence is Erected in the Eastern Style of Architecture,

AND MAY JUSTLY BE ESTEEMED

A CHEF-D'ŒUVRE, UNRIVALLED IN THIS KINGDOM.

The Domestic Offices

Are well arranged, and amply supplied with excellent Water;

COMPRISING

COMMODIOUS STABLING & COACH HOUSES, and various other OUT-OFFICES:

THE BEAUTIFUL PLEASURE GROUNDS,

Intersected by extensive Gravelled Walks, include a SHRUBBERY, ornamented with magnificent Timber Trees, thriving Evergreens, Parterres of Flowers, &c.

AN ALCOVE; PRODUCTIVE WALLED GARDEN, CLOTHED WITH CHOICE FRUIT TREES,

And containing a Grapery, &c.

ATTACHED TO THE PROPERTY THERE IS

A WELL-CONSTRUCTED FARM YARD,

With Bailiff's House, and substantial Agricultural Buildings, planned in a superior style,

AND THE WHOLE ESTATE COMPRISING

SUNDRY COTTAGES, WITH GARDENS,

CONTAINS UPWARDS OF

FOUR HUNDRED AND SEVENTY-TWO ACRES

OF

Excellent Grass and Meadow, Arable, and Wood Land, Hop Garden, and Plantation,

In a fine thriving State, the Soil of a very excellent Quality, producing fine Grain, Hay, &c.

AND FORMS A MOST ELIGIBLE PROPERTY FOR RESIDENCE AND INVESTMENT,

In an excellent Neighbourhood, the Country abounding with Game, and enjoying the Beauties of the Eastnor Woods, with its Fertile Scenery.

HOPE END has been justly considered to vie with EASTNOR CASTLE,

AND MAY BE PRONOUNCED THE CHIEF ORNAMENT OF THE SURROUNDING COUNTRY:

To be Sold by Auction,

By Order of the Mortgagees under a Power of Sale,

BY MR. REID,
Son-in-Law and Successor to the late

MR. JOHN ROBINS,
OF WARWICK HOUSE, REGENT STREET,

AT GARRAWAY'S COFFEE HOUSE, 'CHANGE ALLEY, CORNHILL,

On THURSDAY, 25th of AUGUST, 1831, at Twelve o'Clock.

The Estate is distant from Malvern about Four Miles, and the Canal from Ledbury to Gloucester affords every facility for the Conveyance of Produce to that City and the neighbouring Towns; and this will be considerably extended by the intended Continuation of the Canal to Hereford. There are Coaches daily to and from the Metropolis.

The Mansion to be viewed by Tickets. Particulars may be had of James Holbrook, Esq. Solicitor (who will grant Tickets), and at the Feathers Inn, *Ledbury*; Swan, *Ross*; City Hotel, *Hereford*; the Foley Arms, and Belle Vue, *Great Malvern*; of Mr. Bentley, and at the Star and Hop Pole Inns, *Worcester*; Plough, *Cheltenham*; Angel, *Oxford*; and in London, of Messrs. Freshfield, New Bank Buildings; at Garraway's; and of Mr. Reid, No. 170, Regent Street, where a Plan of the Estate may be seen, and Tickets for viewing may be had.

NOTES

4 June 1831

(1) A very derogatory remark. The shoe polish firm of Robert Warren advertised by means of commercial jingles. Charles Dickens worked as a boy in their 'blacking factory'. The line ending each verse referred to in the Diary entry for 9 June ran: 'And *he*—he was a King.'

(2) Held at the Feathers Hotel in Ledbury, kept by Luke Taylor, to celebrate the return to Parliament of Mr Hoskins, a supporter of the Reform Bill. The *Hereford Journal* 8 June 1831, reported that '95 gentlemen sat down to a splendid dinner . . . the healths of the Chairman, Colonel Money, Captain Johnstone . . . E. Barrett jun. Esq. . . . called forth able and eloquent addresses from these gentlemen.'

5 June

(1) Otherwise Sir William Thornhill in Goldsmith's 'The Vicar of Wakefield': ' . . . I should have mentioned the very impolite behaviour of Mr. Burchell, who, during the discourse, sate with his face turned to the fire, and at the conclusion of every sentence would cry out *fudge*, an expression which displeased us all, and in some measure damped the rising spirit of the conversation.'

9 June

(1) EBB and Mr Boyd used Blomfield's edition (see *Who,s Who*) and also Richard Porson's, Scholefield's and that of Schutz. Sometimes referred to as the Seven Chiefs.

11 June

(1) The deliberate misquotation from the psalm and the underlinings were evidently a play on the names of the two family estates: Uncle Sam's Cinnamon Hill in Jamaica and Hope End.

17 June

(1) (Oliver Goldsmith), 'An Elegy on that Glory of her Sex Mrs. Mary Blaize,'

> Her love was sought, I do aver,
> By twenty beaus and more;
> The king himself has follow'd her—
> *When she has walked before.*

23 June

(1) In debating the customary Address to the King after the opening of Parliament on 21 June the issue of Reform was a major topic, and

some acrimonious personal exchanges passed between certain of their Lordships. A report of the debate occupied thirteen columns in *The Times*, 22 June 1831.

1 July

(1) The sale was announced in *Berrow's Worcester Journal*, 23 June 1831. The notice also appeared in the *Hereford Journal*, 29 June 1831. The crops comprised 160 acres of grass, 26 acres of wheat, 12 acres of peas and 4 acres of beans.

3 July

(1) 'Voice and nothing else.' (Plutarch: 'A man plucked a nightingale and finding almost no meat, said "It's all voice ye are, and nought else" '.) This was the Rev. E. Elliott, who normally preached in Gloucester, and was filling in for Mr Curzon.

4 July

(1) A typical scholarly joke of Mr Boyd's. This is a punning allusion to the celebrated feud in 1697–9 between Richard Bentley and Charles Boyle (later Earl of Cork and Orrery), regarding the authenticity of the *Epistles of Phalaris*.

11 July

(1) EBB evidently believed that the loss of her mother was heralded during the summer of 1828 by the death-watch beetle.

13 July

(1) This menagerie, in which lions and tigers paced in small, exotically painted cages and frightened the horses in the street by their roaring, was removed from the Exeter 'Change in 1828 prior to demolition during the widening of the Strand in 1830.

16 July

(1) Joanna Baillie (1762–1851) poetess and dramatist. Walter Scott called her 'the highest genius of our country'. Author of *Plays on the Passions*. Her literary salon at Hampstead attracted a number of distinguished writers. Mr Spowers also lived at Hampstead.

30 July

(1) The Socinians, following the doctrine of Lelio and Fausto Sozzini set forth in the Confession of Rakow (1605), held that Christ was not the Son of God, but a prophet of God's word. It had been proposed at a Bible Society Meeting in London on 4 May that non-believers in the Holy Trinity should be excluded from membership. After a long and tumultuous discussion it was put to the vote and not carried. EBB's attitude is consistent with her lifelong belief. In a letter from Florence to Mrs David Ogilvie in 1852 she wrote 'I can't

help thinking that all these church walls English, Scottish, Roman, equally must all be swept away, before Christ can be seen standing in their midst.'

4 August

(1) See *EBB/HSB*, p.40. EBB was upset when Mr Boyd sent for the Terence he had used at school, which he had given her in 1829.

8 August

(1) Derived from Daniel O'Connell (1775–1847), M.P. for Dublin, who favoured 'repeal of the Union' and energetically agitated for the Irish Catholics. A controversial political figure disliked by Mr Moulton-Barrett and a hero to EBB's brother Stormie, and also to the Martins.

21 August

(1) As Annie was staying at Stanwell, the seat of Sir John Gibbons, the inference is that Lady Gibbons was attempting to nip in the bud any romantic attachment between Annie and one of the unmarried Gibbons boys; either Richard (then 24) or Joseph (18).

1 Sept

(1) *The Times*, 30 August 1831, announced the arrival at Falmouth on 26 August, of the packet *Cygnet* with mails; she had sailed from Jamaica on 21 July.

8 Sept

(1) In contrast to the sunny coronation of George IV on 19 July 1821, that of William IV was so wet that an eye-witness wrote 'On us let it be pleased to pour—long may it *reign*.'

19 Sept

(1) Fortunatus possessed an inexhaustible purse and a wishing cap: both he and his sons were eventually ruined by these magic gifts. Although EBB had inherited £4,000 from her grandmother the previous December she evidently handled no money herself, and was constantly worrying about the lack of it.

(2) The Grand Duchess Helena (1807–73), daughter of Prince Paul of Württemberg and sister-in-law of Czar Nicholas I of Russia, made an excursion from Cheltenham to Malvern Wells on 29 August, with a numerous suite. In spite of EBB's disapproval, the story, whatever it was, must have amused her, even though she dared not commit it to paper.

24 Sept

(1) Bion of Smyrna (*fl.*c. 100 B.C.), best known for his *Lament for Adonis*, which EBB translated and published in her *Poems* (London, 1850), I, 191–8.

28 Nov

(1) Both prophecies were correct. Lord Somers married his cousin Jane Waddington, a widow. And in the House of Lords, he voted for Reform.

10 Dec

(1) A reference to the extraordinary scenes that had taken place at Regent's Square Church in October. Four thousand people (among them Mr Barrett) crowded in to hear the Rev. Edward Irving preach. He exhorted the Holy Spirit to speak through 'the mouth of his servants', and there was an uproar when several members of the congregation were inspired and spoke and shouted in 'unknown tongues'. It became quite a fashion and sparked off a storm of theological argument. EBB writes amusingly of this to HSB (10 December 1831).

19 Feb 1832

(1) Despite this, the translation was published by Valpy. (*Prometheus Bound, Translated from the Greek of Aeschylus. And Miscellaneous Poems*, London, 1833).

3 Mar

(1) *The Times* 20 February 1832, reported a partial insurrection of the slaves in Jamaica, principally in the parishes of St James's, Portland and Trelawney (the Barretts had land in St James's and Trelawney, although their principal estate was in the parish of Cambridge): 'Shortly after the 20th of December the slaves on several estates refused to go to their work, and large bodies of them met together and set fire to many plantation buildings. On the 30th of December martial law was proclaimed . . .'. The Barrett estates escaped damage.

21 Mar

(1) *The Times* 21 March 1832, carried a Form of Prayer 'To be used in all Churches and Chapels . . . on Wednesday, the twenty-first day of March, 1832, being the day appointed by Proclamation for a General Fast and humiliation before Almighty God, . . . For obtaining pardon of our sins, and averting the heavy judgments which our manifold provocations have most justly deserved; and particularly for beseeching God to remove from us that grievous disease with which several places in this kingdom are at this time visited.'

INDEX